HOSPITAL POLITICS IN
SEVENTEENTH-CENTURY FRANCE

The History of Medicine in Context

Series Editors: Andrew Cunningham and Ole Peter Grell

Department of History and Philosophy of Science
University of Cambridge

Department of History
The Open University

Titles in this series include:

Health Care and Poor Relief in 18th and 19th Century Southern Europe
Edited by Ole Peter Grell, Andrew Cunningham and Bernd Roeck

Hospital Care and the British Standing Army, 1660–1714
Eric Gruber von Arni

The Making of Addiction
The 'Use and Abuse' of Opium in Nineteenth-Century Britain
Louise Foxcroft

Melancholy and the Care of the Soul
Religion, Moral Philosophy and Madness in Early Modern England
Jeremy Schmidt

Health, Sickness, Medicine and the Friars in the
Thirteenth and Fourteenth Centuries
Angela Montford

Hospital Politics in
Seventeenth-Century France
The Crown, Urban Elites and the Poor

TIM McHUGH

LONDON AND NEW YORK

First published 2007 by Ashgate Publishing

2 Park Square, Milton Park, Abingdon, Oxon OX14 4RN
711 Third Avenue, New York, NY 10017, USA

Routledge is an imprint of the Taylor & Francis Group, an informa business

First issued in paperback 2017

British Library Cataloguing in Publication Data
McHugh, Tim
    Hospital Politics in Seventeenth-Century France : The Crown, Urban Elites and the
    Poor. – (The History of Medicine in Context)
    1. Hospitals – France – History – 17th century. 2. Public welfare – France – History –
    17th century. 3. Medical policy – France – History - 17th century. 4. Sociology, Urban
    – France – History - 17th century. 5. France – Social conditions – 17th century.
    I. Title.
    362.1'1'0944'09032

Library of Congress Cataloging-in-Publication Data
McHugh, Tim.
    Hospital Politics in Seventeenth-Century France: The Crown, Urban Elites, and the Poor
    / by Tim McHugh.
       p.   cm. – (The History of Medicine in Context)
    Includes bibliographical references and index.
    1. Social medicine – France – History – 17th century. 2. Medical care – Political aspects
    – France – History – 17th century. 3. Health care reform – France – History –
    17th century. I. Title.
    [DNLM: 1. Hospital Administration – history – France. 2. Hospitals – history – France.
    3. Social Welfare – history – France. 4. Health Care Reform – history – France.
    5. Health Policy – history – France. 6. History, 17th Century – France.
    WX 11 GF7 M478h 2007]
    RA418.3.F8M34 2007
    362.1'042–dc22
    2006030023

ISBN 978-0-7546-5762-0 (hbk)
ISBN 978-1-138-27600-0 (pbk)

Contents

Contents

Acknowledgements

I would like to thank the Senate of Victoria College in the University of Toronto, the British Institute in Paris, the Committee of Vice-Chancellors and Principals of the Universities of the United Kingdom, the Huguenot Church in London and the Province of Ontario for their financial support without which this work would not have been possible.

I am eternally grateful to my PhD supervisor, Roger Mettam, for the profound influence his understanding of French history has had on me and his promptness in vetting and returning earlier drafts of the thesis. I could have hoped for no finer person for guidance. I would like to thank Julian Dent who first stimulated my interest in the history of early modern France. My thanks are also due to those who benefited me with their wisdom and knowledge of the subject: Colin Jones, Julian Swann, Peter Campbell and Mark Bryant who all offered advice at critical times.

The archivists of the Archives de l'Assistance Publique Hôpitaux de Paris deserve a great deal of credit for pointing out valuable sources on the history of the two Paris hospitals included in the study. I would like to thank those at the Archives départmentales de l'Hérault and du Gard who likewise provided me with assistance.

Last but not least I would like to thank my beloved wife Melissa, and my son Thelonious, who offered me endless support during the research and writing of this monograph. I would like to give thanks to my mother who helped me in many ways. Finally, I would like to express gratitude to my parents-in-law the Aitkens for their financial support.

Abbreviations

AAP HG	Archives de l'Assistance Publique, Hôpitaux de Paris, fonds Hôpital Général.
AAP HD	Archives de l'Assistance Publique, Hôpitaux de Paris, fonds Hôtel Dieu.
ADCA	Archives départmentales des Côtes-d'Armor.
ADF	Archives départmentales du Finistère.
ADG HD	Archives départmentales du Gard, fonds Hôpital de Nîmes (Hôtel Dieu).
ADG HG	Archives départmentales du Gard, fonds Hôpital Général de Nîmes.
ADG	Archives départmentales du Gard.
ADH HG	Archives départmentales de l'Hérault, fonds Hôpital Général de Montpellier.
ADH HD	Archives départmentales de l'Hérault, fonds Hôtel Dieu de Montpellier.
ADIV	Archives départmentales de l'Ille-et-Vilaine.
ADM	Archives départmentales du Morbihan.
AN	Archives nationales.

Introduction

Since the 1980s Western governments have increasingly sought to retrench their social welfare spending. In much of the English-speaking world, politicians have placed emphasis on solving the problem of poverty by withdrawing the amounts of assistance available to the poor and underprivileged in an effort to force the unemployed back to work (and, additionally, to trim governmental budgets). Politicians have justified the retrenchment of services by arguing that the individual is responsible for their own condition. They have argued that the national welfare systems that developed during the twentieth century have made the underprivileged dependant on handouts and have sought to wean them off such dependency through a shift from welfare to 'workfare'.

The focus on the reform of the modern social welfare system in politics since the 1980s has increased the importance of studying past attempts at poor relief. The contention of some politicians that the care of the poor was undertaken historically through charitable means alone has been used in attempts to discredit modern state-run welfare systems. During the early modern period new elite groups – judges and lawyers, bourgeois investors and financiers – in French towns and cities came to overshadow those merchants and tradesmen represented by medieval forms of urban governance. Social position for these urban elites depended more on a combination of office-holding and wealth rather than rank in a guild. By the seventeenth century these new patricians were assuming more of the functions of urban government. Many French towns and cities undertook reforms of their systems of social welfare. The elites used new forms of poor relief and charitable medicine to assert their social leadership in their cities and towns. The reform of poor relief and health care shifted assistance for both the able-bodied and the sick poor from outdoors relief to within institutions following the merger of religious, economic and social theories on how to eliminate poverty in the late sixteenth and early seventeenth centuries. Poor relief and health care were not absorbed by the central government as part of its natural evolution during the seventeenth century. These systems, while not managed by the state but by local authorities, had long been the tradition in France, and the urban elites recognized their responsibility to care for the poor of their communities. The assumption of more power over welfare by the central government in later centuries was a direct result of pressure put on it by the social elites who coalesced during the early modern period to form urban patriciates.

Poverty in early modern France has been the subject of a great deal of study in recent decades. The interest taken by historians in the plight of the poor has been renewed since the 1960s as a natural progression in the development of the field of social history. Since the publication of the work of statist historians at the turn of the twentieth century, numerous studies have been made on the subject of charity and the poor in the seventeenth and eighteenth centuries. The focus of these studies has been placed largely on three aspects: uncovering the poor as individuals, the charitable imperative which characterized most attempts at assistance and the role of the state in co-ordinating relief throughout the kingdom. The modern historiography of the subject began with investigations into the origins of the involvement of the state in public assistance. Published in the early twentieth century, the works of Léon Lallemand and Christian Paultre are the most representative of this statist approach to the history of charity. Paultre argued that the crown during the reign of Henri IV undertook a comprehensive campaign to repress the beggary and vagrancy which had become a crisis for early modern France.[1] Although he discussed the role which individuals from the elites of the kingdom played, he attributed the leadership of such new endeavours to the central government.[2] He argued that the crown feared the disorder caused by the new 'professional' poor and therefore undertook to increase the authority of the absolute monarchy over poor relief throughout the country.

Léon Lallemand concurred with Paultre, arguing that the crown took the initiative away from the Catholic Church in organizing the form of social assistance during the early modern period.[3] He viewed the period from the fourteenth to the sixteenth century as one marked by the growth of the number of poor in the kingdom and the consequent threat caused by this increase to the social order. He observed that all European monarchs attempted to curtail the problem of beggars through legislation during the sixteenth and seventeenth centuries, arguing that the French government increased the strength of its mechanisms of policing the poor by creating the Hôpital Général of Paris in 1656.[4] He believed that central government policy towards the poor was strengthened further through the means of the Edict of 1662 which commanded the creation of a network of hôpitaux généraux throughout the kingdom.[5] The theses of both Paultre and Lallemand, because they relied heavily on the analysis of the texts of royal edicts, overstated the role which the crown played in the provisioning of poor relief while ignoring evidence from charitable institutions themselves which would support an argument that local elites played a greater part.

Conscious that these earlier historians ignored the religious aspects of early modern charity and poor relief, the work of Jean-Pierre Gutton has attempted to reintegrate religion into this history. He has argued that early modern social welfare was marked by a traditional Christian charity which was given new vigour by the works of the Counter-Reformation. This religious outlook existed concurrent with an absolutist approach of social control which developed to force marginal groups to conform to the standards of the elites.[6] Gutton, concentrating his studies on the city and hinterland of Lyon, argued that during the late Middle Ages certain categories of the able-bodied poor began to be perceived as potential social dangers. Sixteenth- and seventeenth-century institutions were developed in order to reduce this threat to the hierarchy. He cited the economic theories proposed by mercantilist authors as being major influences on the development of hospitals of confinement during

---

1   Paultre, 1906.
2   Ibid., p. 141.
3   Lallemand, 1909–12.
4   Ibid., tom. 4, pp. 255–9.
5   Ibid., tom. 4, pp. 261–72.
6   See, for instance, Gutton, 1970 and Gutton, 1973.

the seventeenth century. In earlier periods the poor had been seen as figures of compassion and objects of pity, but during the seventeenth century they became pariahs deserving of being separated from the rest of society.[7] Influenced by the theories of Lallemand and Paultre, Gutton argued a Marxist position that the final three centuries of the ancien régime were a long evolution whereby the crown took control over the hospitals of the kingdom, social welfare and health matters.[8] He maintained that the failure of the central government to develop fully a nationwide system of hôpitaux généraux in the period between 1656 and 1680 was the administrative weakness of the ministry. He contended that although Colbert was the minister responsible for the economy of the kingdom, he did not have authority to impose the desired social welfare policy over the whole country because: 'les quatre secretaires d'Etat sont comme quatre ministres de l'Interieur puisqu'ils se partagent l'administration des provinces.'[9] This geographical division of administrative duties among the Secrétaires d'Etat prevented any national system from being implemented by the government. Although Gutton correctly cited the role which both religious and economic theories played in the background to the creation of new charitable institutions in the seventeenth century, he attempted to make his evidence conform to his theory of the development of the modern welfare state. Like earlier historians, he overestimated the goals of the crown by declaring that the central government hoped to manage welfare in the kingdom in order to stamp out troublesome social problems.

Jean Imbert has written primarily on hospitals in France during both the Middle Ages and the early modern period. He has argued that during the period between 1500 and 1789 the central government assumed legal authority over all forms of charitable institutions.[10] Following a Marxist model of history as well, he theorized that the development of the modern medical hospital began during the early modern era. He argued that during the early modern period the state began the reform of existing charitable institutions and promoted the creation of new types of hospitals. In his theory, the reform of poor relief systems was due to a conjunction of the growth of power of the absolutist state, the disappearance of leprosy as a major danger to the people of the kingdom and the increase in the numbers of the destitute caused by economic change and dislocation due to war. He argued that the state was able, because of the relative weakness of the church during the late fifteenth and sixteenth centuries, to secularize many medieval hospitals and wrest legal authority over the distribution of charitable assistance and the repression of the criminal poor through royal legislation.[11] Although Imbert qualified his argument to concede that the sixteenth-century monarchy could not claim authority over issues of social welfare throughout the kingdom, he overstated the goals of Louis XIV's government:

---

7   Gutton, 1970, pp. 289–95.

8   J. Gutton, 'Aux origines d'un ministère de l'Assistance et de la Santé dans la France de l'Ancien Régime', in Harouel, 1989.

9   Ibid., pp. 290–91.

10   Imbert, 1993.

11   Ibid., p. 21.

Political unity made a decisive progress and the king extended his power to oversee the protection of his subjects, including the most poor among them … but in the sixteenth century the power of the crown was not well enough established to impose itself over all and it was only with the initiative of Louis XIV that a theoretically uniform hospital legislation saw the light of day.[12]

He concluded that the inability of even a strong monarch like Louis XIV to impose a national system of social welfare was due to the financial weakness of the state. He claimed that, although the foundation of the Hôpital Général of Paris was the start of a campaign by the central government to rid the country of vagrancy, the inability of the state to pay for new hospitals meant it had to rely on local elites to provide financing, and therefore its sovereignty over these institutions was diminished. Despite such a problem, Imbert stated that the attempt was a qualified success for the crown, noting the large number of such hôpitaux généraux established in the kingdom by the time of the Revolution.[13] Imbert compelled his evidence to fit his attempt to trace the development of the modern hospital during the course of the ancien régime. For example, he cited the Edict of 1662, which authorized cities and towns of the kingdom to create hôpitaux généraux as the cornerstone of the royal social welfare policy. Imbert conceded that the edict had been issued in order to prevent the Hôpital Général of Paris from going bankrupt, but he argued that the crown was acting in its own self-interest in order to prevent the failure of its project, rather than from the request of the Parisian elites who managed the hospital.

Emanuel Chill concurred with statist and Marxist arguments that during the development of absolutism during the fifteenth, sixteenth and seventeenth centuries the lower classes of western Europe suffered greater hardship and insecurity than ever before.[14] He argued that the undertaking of the repression of vagabondage through legislation during the sixteenth century had failed, creating the need for a new government programme to control the poor. The new system of hospitals of confinement developed by the crown in the seventeenth century, he contended, was the result of a convergence of social problems, absolutist tendencies and religious attitudes. In effect, his theory differed little from that of the above historians, except that it cited the main inspiration behind the new institutions was the French Counter-Reformation.[15] He believed that the crown, influenced by the new Catholic religiosity present in the decades after 1600, sponsored the confinement of the able-bodied poor in secure locations where they could be properly trained to reject their faults which had been the cause of their poverty. The motivation behind seventeenth-century poor relief was the desire to cure the poor, and not to cure the causes of poverty.[16] Chill also relied heavily on published royal edicts for many of his sources, which has given him an unbalanced picture of the involvement of the central government in the foundation, management and financing of charitable institutions.

---

12 Ibid., p. 10.
  13 Ibid., p. 87. Imbert cites the number of such hospitals at 177, a figure which is taken from the equally statist Jeorger, see Jeorger, 1977, pp. 1025–51.
  14 Chill, 1962, pp. 400–24.
  15 Ibid., p. 400.
  16 Ibid., p. 423.

Recent British and American historians have preferred to undertake studies of local charitable relief systems rather than broad studies of the state of social assistance in the kingdom as a whole. Cissie Fairchilds, in her history of poor relief in Aix-en-Provence, has characterized the seventeenth century as a period of transition of the forms and motivations of public assistance.[17] Her work focused on the forms of relief offered to the poor of the city and the sacrifices made by members of the local elites to ensure the proper operation of charitable institutions. She argued a Marxist theory that medieval notions of religiously inspired private almsgiving were forsaken in the first half of the century, but that the idea of the responsibility of the state for the national welfare of its citizens had not yet been fully developed:

> Although the emerging absolutist state increasingly viewed the poor as economic problems and as threats to public order, and therefore had made pretensions toward regulating public assistance, the state was not yet powerful enough to do this effectively.[18]

While she argued that the crown left much of the administration and financing of charitable institutions to locals, Fairchilds viewed the growth of the legal power of the absolutist monarchy during the seventeenth century as a necessary part of the natural progression to overall governmental control of social welfare and health care. In part, the reason for her belief that the crown desired to assume authority over the local issue of welfare was her confusion that the members of all levels of government – such as those in the city consulate and the judges of the Parlement – were part of a broad concept of the state.

Kathryn Norberg criticized French historians for not examining areas of history beyond the political when studying the changes made to forms of poor relief during the early modern period.[19] In her study of charitable assistance in Grenoble, she concentrated on the role played by French culture, in particular by counter-reformation Catholicism, in shaping poor relief in the kingdom. She believed that the shift away form outdoor relief to institutionalized assistance came, not from the growth of the state, but from the Catholic renewal which emanated from both the church hierarchy and the elites of French society.[20] Norberg rightly emphasized the part played by female members of the local elites in the care of the poor, but she overstated the role of central government figures in the foundation of new social welfare institutions.[21] Norberg, like Fairchilds, unfortunately examined the history of seventeenth-century poor relief in the city as a precursor to the development of new attitudes about charity and assistance during the mid eighteenth century.

Since the 1980s Colin Jones has done important research on the history of medicine and poor relief in France. He has argued convincingly that the revival of the 'charitable imperative' in France after the Reformation unlocked great potential for urban hospitals and their services. Nuns from the new nursing orders colonized hospitals during the seventeenth century, bringing medical knowledge based on

---

17 Fairchilds, 1976.
18 Ibid., p. x.
19 Norberg, 1985.
20 Ibid., p. 61.
21 Ibid., pp. 16–19.

academic medicine to the greater part of the French population for the first time.[22] He has, however, attributed much of the initiative behind the reform of poor relief and hospitals during the seventeenth century to the state. He asserts that the crown first turned to local officials to improve the quality of social welfare during the sixteenth century. Dismayed by the localities' inability to reduce the number of beggars in the kingdom, the crown turned to the newly invigorated bishops for help during the seventeenth century. The government's initial efforts at securing compliance with its desires were unsuccessful, but by the 1670s its agents in the provinces were becoming better at compelling local elites to follow its lead.[23]

The common denominator among all of these historians was to accept at face value the claims of the government of the French state about the nature and extent of its power. Roger Mettam has demonstrated that much of the pretension to absolute power on the part of the crown, especially during the reign of Louis XIV in the decades after the Frondes, did not reflect the actual strength of the government, but was made to convince powerful elites to co-operate with the monarchy.[24] He has also shown that one of the most successful policy cornerstones of Louis XIV, especially during the early part of his personal rule, was the return to a traditional form of monarchy. The role of the central government was to undertake foreign relations and the defence of the kingdom. The relationship between provincial and local elites and the crown was more complex than the narrowly defined centralized autocracy often cited by statist and Marxist historians. While royal ministers did not wish to push the direct authority of the central government into areas traditionally managed by provincial and municipal institutions, they were concerned that such institutions carried out their tasks efficiently.[25] This situation was particularly true of an issue such as poor relief when the refusal to conform to custom could disturb royal agents in the course of their normal duties and put undue stress on resources which the crown could normally tax to sustain its own finances.

This study has been undertaken to reassess the relationship between the central government and the local elites responsible for the deliverance of assistance to both the sick and able-bodied poor. Recent revisions about the nature of government and power in the ancien régime have created the need to re-examine the history of charity and poor relief. What were the responsibilities of both the crown and local elites in the provision of care? Did the crown in the seventeenth century wish to increase its power over local issues, in particular over institutions that dispensed charitable health care and poor relief? To what extent did urban elites view crown edicts about social welfare as absolute commands? Did localities accept their duty to care for their own poor? Did they do their best to provide services for their communities?

This book will be divided into three main components. The first part, consisting of Chapters 1 and 2, will examine theories about charity and poor relief and the state's edicts on hospitals. Chapter 1 will focus on the ideas developed in the sixteenth and early seventeenth centuries regarding the proper form relief should take and

---

22   Jones, 1989, pp. 162–205.
23   Jones, 1989, pp. 215–39.
24   Mettam, 1988, p. 257.
25   Ibid.

the motivation behind such action. The ideas of humanists and mercantilist authors will be assessed for their impact on the thought and practice of the elites during the seventeenth century, especially their development of the theory of *enfermement*, or the confinement of the poor. The ideas of the Catholic Reformation will be explored, examining the process by which the performance of charitable works became one of the main aspects of leading a Catholic life in the seventeenth century. The chapter will conclude with a brief study of the Compagnie du Saint-Sacrement which was influenced by the ideas of both secular mercantilist economists and the theologians of the Catholic Reformation and helped to disseminate these ideas to the urban elites of the kingdom. Chapter 2 will explore the relationship between the reform of poor relief and the central government. The chapter begins with an examination of development of the crown's role in poor relief during the later medieval period. The monarch formally established his position as arbiter between localities in the matter of poor relief during the Black Death in 1350. By the sixteenth century the crown issued edicts claiming final judicial authority over hospitals (removing this right from the bishops and in opposition to decisions made by the Catholic Church during the Council of Trent). Here, too, the crown did not develop this position further, using it mostly as a way to placate Protestant fears that charitable institutions would be used to convert the vulnerable. During the seventeenth century, the crown governed along traditional lines, acting as a patron to important institutions and groups (such as the Paris hospitals and the Jesuit missionaries Chaurand and Guévarre in the 1670s), but only in order to show its general approval, not to provide any material support. The crown sought to assist local authorities in upholding their duties to care for the poor of their localities in order to prevent the movement around the country of large numbers of the poor seeking relief. This commitment on the part of the crown to ensure that each locality lived up to its obligations resulted in the Edict of 1662, which was an effort to protect the newly founded Paris Hôpital Général by calling on other towns in the kingdom to live up to their responsibilities. The chapter argues that during the seventeenth century the crown did take an active interest in the revenues of defunct hospitals, establishing commissions to secure their finances and to utilize them to provide pensions to retired military officers through the Order of Notre-Dame de Mont Carmel until the death of Louvois. The chapter ends with the argument that the pressure put on the crown by local elites and aristocratic reformers caused the central government to reassess its role from the end of Louis XIV's reign onwards. The crown discovered the usefulness of being seen to be more active in pursuing the goals of *enfermement*, but this involvement was very limited before the reign of Louis XV and the Great Confinement of 1724.

The second part of the book, consisting of Chapters 3 and 4, will examine the relationship between the central government and the urban elites of Paris in the provisioning of poor relief. Chapter 3 will view the history of the Hôtel Dieu of Paris, the city hospital dedicated the care of the sick poor. It will attempt to disprove the belief, based on the writings of late-eighteenth-century critics, that the hospital was a badly managed institution designed to warehouse the ill and dying. The chapter will examine the functions, the administration and the finances to show that the civic elites of Paris took great pride in managing what they considered the best hospital of its kind in the kingdom.

Chapter 4 will explore the history of the Hôpital Général of Paris. It will examine the role played by the civic elites in the origins of the hospital. It will focus on the care which they took to administer and finance the institution in order to show how they supported the idea of confinement. The chapter will also discuss the relationship between the hospital administration and the central government, arguing that royal edicts which dealt with matters of poor relief throughout the kingdom had been requested by the powerful elites of the capital who managed the institution.

The third section will compare the systems of poor relief in the capital with those of the smaller provincial cities of Montpellier and Nîmes. Chapter 5 will examine the two main institutions of public assistance in Montpellier: the Hôtel Dieu and Hôpital Général. It will focus on the administrative change made to the board of directors of the former caused by new power relationships in the city. The reasons for the foundation of the latter will be examined in order to show the initiative taken by the civic elites in organising the new form of poor relief.

Chapter 6 will concentrate on the history of Nîmes, and will examine the problems faced by a city whose population was divided between large Catholic and Protestant communities. It will focus on the role played by religious tensions in the form which assistance took. The ability of local elites of both faiths to tolerate the charitable endeavours of each other will be demonstrated by the history of the Protestant hospital founded during the period under study. The role played by the alliance forged between the Intendant and the urban elites in the creation of the city Hôpital Général after the Revocation of the Edict of Nantes will be evaluated.

This work argues that charitable health care and poor relief continued to be local issues in the seventeenth century, as they had been traditionally. For too long seventeenth-century France has been regarded as a roughly formed welfare state in its infancy. Historians have believed that the central government was prevented from developing a fully realized policy towards poor relief by structural problems in both the administration and finances of the kingdom. In fact, there was no significant change in the position of the crown regarding poor relief. The medieval kings of France had issued decrees to ensure that localities cared for the poor long before the supposed centralized repression of the absolutist government of Louis XIV. The idea of the Sun King as the forefather of the French welfare state no longer rings true given new research on the goals and limitations of the seventeenth-century state. The central government did not seek to take control of social welfare; rather it emphasized the traditional responsibility of localities to care for their own poor. When the crown did involve itself in matters of poor relief, it was usually to assist, through royal legislation, local elites in their duties. This monograph will attempt to reintegrate the social aspirations of urban elites into the history of French poor relief, arguing that the reform of hospitals was undertaken by local elites according to local circumstances and for a mixture of Catholic Reform, economic and social motivations. These elites used new forms of poor relief and charitable medicine to assert their social position and control over their cities and towns. The reform of poor relief and health care shifted assistance for both the able-bodied and the sick poor from outdoors relief to within institutions following the merger of religious, economic and social theories on how to eliminate poverty in the late sixteenth and early seventeenth centuries. Thus there was continuity in local responsibility for poor relief at the same time as there was change in the form poor relief took. The urban elites of the kingdom understood their duty to provide assistance to the destitute of their communities, and most did so to the best of their abilities. Reforms of poor relief were local and shaped by local experiences, not as part of the crown's drive toward centralization and standardization. In the kingdom as a whole, welfare reform during the seventeenth century was spasmodic not systematic. Where the reform of poor relief and health care was seen to be necessary, local elites founded institutions of confinement and improved hospital services for the sick poor (as far as local conditions allowed). But where such reforms were not perceived as needed, or not affordable, local elites ignored central government edicts to build new institutions.

Chapter One

Theories of Charity and Poor Relief

During the seventeenth century hospitals came to be perceived as the best means of providing assistance in French cities. Whether it was caring for the sick poor in hôtels dieu or confining the able-bodied in hôpitaux généraux, a shift from outdoor poor relief to institutional assistance occurred in many of the kingdom's urban centres. Ideas about poverty and the poor first formulated in the sixteenth century were further developed and groups of activists sought to implement them. An orthodoxy had developed by the sixteenth century that there were two types of poor. Firstly, there were the deserving poor, or those who had some sort of obvious hindrance to earning their living, for example the crippled, the infirm, the elderly and the very young. Secondly, there were the undeserving, believed to be those wilfully idle individuals who lived a life of fraudulence and criminality, spreaders of disease, vice and disorder. In France an orthodoxy amongst theorists coalesced in the early decades of the seventeenth century that poverty was the result of the faults of the individual. Theorists argued that poverty was a problem that could be cured through the method of confinement that monitored the progress of the poor to cure their faults and to become productive and moral individuals.

This chapter will examine several of the strands of thought which helped to develop the attitudes of the kingdom about charity and the poor themselves. The first section will investigate the writings of sixteenth-century and early seventeenth-century humanist and mercantilist economists, demonstrating that many of the forms that poor relief took over the course of the seventeenth century derived from these sources.[1] The second section will view religious ideas through the Catholic revival of the early seventeenth century represented by the works of François de Sales to the continuance of devout activism during the conflicts within the Church during the reign of Louis XIV. The third section will examine the advocacy of a paternalist attitude toward the poor by noble writers. The last section will examine the ideas and efforts of the Compagnie du Saint-Sacrement which combined the three strands of economic, religious and social theories in its attempt to reform Catholicism in France during the middle decades of the century. The spread of Catholic Reform ideas among the elites of France during the early seventeenth century, such as those of François de Sales and Vincent de Paul, added a renewed charitable obligation of individuals to humanist ideas on the economy, such as those of Laffemas and Montchrétien. Humanists had argued that society could recover much of the lost

---

1   The terms mercantilist and mercantilism will be used in this and future chapters, despite the fact that they were coined by eighteenth-century critics, as a convenience to denote the works of a group of sixteenth-century and seventeenth-century economic theorists (including men such as Barthélemy de Laffemas and Antoine de Montchrétien).

potential of the poor through training the healthy to acquire good work habits or providing health care to cure the sick. At the same time, ambitious patrician families sought to emulate the paternalism of the old nobility by caring for the poor urban population. These three trends merged within the ranks of the Compagnie du Saint-Sacrement which promoted the idea of confining the poor in public institutions, the theory of *enfermement*, where those assisted could be retrained.

Mercantilist views on poor relief

The poor had existed in medieval French towns, but they were believed to be an inescapable fact of life. Many viewed poverty itself as a sanctified state of existence. From the middle of the fourteenth century, however, the fear of the plague profoundly affected the way in which the poor were seen. During the later medieval period, the distributors of charitable relief began more often to separate those whom they considered the true poor from the false.[2] The sick poor, the infirm and categories of the able-bodied such as the elderly and the very young were deemed unable to care for themselves. Those without a visible hindrance to employment were undeserving. Reason dictated that most able-bodied adults who did not have a legitimate source of income must therefore survive from illicit begging and criminal revenues. The elites of the kingdom made an association between the poor as carriers of disease and an image of them as undesirables spreading heresy, criminal behaviour and social disorder. The theories about poverty and poor relief which were to become orthodox in the seventeenth century were a development of medieval ideas.[3]

During the sixteenth century, humanist authors were profoundly influenced by classical precedents when they considered the problems posed by poverty. In particular, political theorists were concerned about the ways in which the ideal republic should deal with the matter.[4] Henry Corneille Agrippa, writing in the early sixteenth century, was greatly influenced by the late medieval picture of vagrants as carriers of the plague in his argument that the truly poor must be assisted:

> It is in the interest of the republic, as it is also required by religion, to take care of the poor and the sick so that none are induced by their condition of poverty to sin and to steal, and that wandering beggars do not infect towns and there throughout the kingdom with the calamitous contagion of pestilence, and that they may not fall dead from hunger or that they may dishonour and abuse humanity.[5]

He concluded that it was for these reasons that men had established charitable hospitals in many of the towns and cities of the kingdom. He stressed the need to

---

2   Geremek, 1987, p. 169.

3   Ibid., pp. 167–9.

4   It should be noted that the term republic (*republique*) used by these authors was utilized in its Latin *res publica* definition, referring to the idea of government in general. In the sixteenth century it could be used to describe both a monarchy like France and an oligarchy such as Venice.

5   Agrippa, 1630, p. 295. This and all further translations are the author's own unless otherwise noted.

be sympathetic towards the deserving poor while at the same time being vigilant against the lazy and idle: 'All these authorities (both biblical and classical texts) teach us that we must not hate poverty itself rather that for us to detest vagrancy and criminality.'[6] Agrippa placed his emphasis on the argument that vagrancy was a state of being opposed to the laws of nature: 'because begging in public and wandering idly from town to town have been matter prohibited throughout antiquity among all people and nations'.[7] He added an element of criminality to his impression of vagabonds and the false poor. He stressed that they were undeserving of Christian aid because their immoral and fraudulent imitation of sickness and infirmity cheated the truly deserving of assistance.[8]

Such humanist authors reinforced the traditions of providing local care for the poor and a paternalist approach to assistance. Jean Bodin, noting the civil strife in the kingdom in 1576, argued that social disorder was caused by the discrepancy between the rich and poor. He concluded that differences of this sort were the root causes of instability in history:

> Of all the causes of seditions and revolutions in republics there is none greater than when a small number of subjects possess excessive wealth when compared to the extreme poverty of the majority. History is full of such examples where we can see that those who have claimed many other reasons for their malcontent against the state have inevitably grasped the first chance that presented itself to strip the rich of their goods.[9]

Bodin argued in favour of paternalism in order to maintain public order in the kingdom. He cited the example of the ancients to demonstrate his belief that seigneurs ought to behave as fathers to those under their power: 'the master ought to behave with moderation towards his slaves ... the ancients called the head of the household the father of the family, not the lord of the manor.'[10] The rich owed their position to the labour of those under them. In return, the poor were deserving of help when it was needed. Bodin believed that the problems of sixteenth-century France were caused, in part, by the abdication of the duties of the rich towards the poor. He was convinced that the poor were the greatest victims of usury, being forced to borrow from moneylenders in order to survive. The interest on money borrowed to subsist in bad years forced the poor to languish in poverty through good years. This continual poverty, he felt, led to a resentment of the rich, who profited from the misery of the majority of the population, and led inevitably to social problems:

> Because when one has more wealth than another, and he seems to be richer in material goods, he also desires to be higher than others in honour, in delights, in worldly pleasures, in his manner of living and in his outward appearances: he also wishes to be revered by the very poor who he despises. And because of this, the public and the poor themselves on their part develop an envy and ferocious desire to appear as the rich man does, or even

---

6   Ibid., p. 296.
7   Ibid., p. 295.
8   Ibid., p. 297.
9   Bodin, 1576, p. 543.
10   Ibid., p. 33.

more worthy then him, but for all that they remain overwhelmed by hunger, poverty and misery.[11]

Bodin emphasized that there was a need for a certain degree of equity among the subjects of the kingdom.[12]

While Bodin was sympathetic to the plight of the truly poor, he concurred with Agrippa about the need to curb the idleness of vagabonds. Although he believed that it was opposed to the spirit of Christianity to chase the poor from towns and cities, he argued that it was more merciful to use the poor as forced labour in order that they might provide those who gave assistance some profit from their work:

> I am told that by receiving as indentured servants the infinite number of vagabonds and the usurers who prey on them will be diminished. This sort of poor, after having consumed everything, wants only to repay their creditors with falsehoods. We might chase away such vagabonds and idlers who devour towns and suck like wasps the honey from the bees. We might also banish those men who are proven to be thieves and bandits. Hunger and the bad treatment offered to the poor bring such popular disorders to our towns. It is necessary to feed the poor and not to kill them. For it is to kill them if we refuse them nourishment or if we chase them from the towns, just as Saint Ambrose said. As for usurers, I reply that the law of God has taken their case into account. Debtors will serve their creditors for seven years, the number set by the law of the XII tables practiced in the West Indies and in the greater part of Africa, after which time their debts will be satisfied.[13]

He argued that the best course was to establish municipal workhouses in order to provide aid for those unable to work and to teach the able-bodied unemployed a skill.[14]

As for incorrigibles, Bodin advocated forcing them back to work by means of indentured servitude or by conscripting them into the army and sending them to war outside the kingdom.[15]

The theories of Agrippa and Bodin influenced greatly the works of late sixteenth- and early seventeenth-century economists. Three main concerns marked the works of these authors: maximizing the amount of precious metals in the kingdom, expanding the internal economy and increasing the revenue derived from external trade. The attention such writers paid to the poor came from the second of these issues. These theorists viewed the poor simply as an unproductive source of labour. Ideas about how to force the poor into work proliferated at this time. Barthélemy de Laffemas saluted the efforts of Catherine de Médicis in establishing the manufacture of silk in the kingdom to provide employment for the poor.[16] He viewed the encouragement of industry in the kingdom as the best method to halt the flow of cash away from France. New manufactures would prevent raw materials from being exported in order to be transformed and then reimported into the kingdom as luxury goods. By increasing

---

11   Ibid., p. 544.
12   Ibid.
13   Ibid., p. 48.
14   Ibid.
15   Ibid., p. 587.
16   Laffemas, 1602.

the number of industries in France, he believed, the kingdom would be rid of the problem of idleness, leaving only the incorrigible poor. His son, Isaac, argued that it was necessary to establish a system of *bureaux publiques* which would observe and police the poor to force the most stubborn vagabonds into a productive life.[17]

Barthélemy de Laffemas advocated a form of confinement for the poor to retrain the able-bodied, arguing for the creation of work villages near each city where incorrigibles could be divided by sex and observed at work to prevent them from slipping back into idleness and immorality.[18] His system of confinement would be accompanied by reform of the tax system of the kingdom in an effort to simplify indirect taxes, therefore reducing poverty by lowering the cost of living.[19]

Antoine de Montchrétien echoed the arguments of Laffemas in his *Traicté de l'oeconomie politique* published in 1615. Better known as a dramatist before this work appeared, he was influenced by the economic ideas of Jean Bodin and Barthélemy de Laffemas and by examples of practices he had personally witnessed in the Netherlands. He argued that the wealth of France was due to a happy coincidence of geography which gave it a good climate for agriculture and abundant natural resources. This advantage, however, produced both the greatest benefit and problem facing the country: the size of its population. The inability of the kingdom to utilize its labour pool to its fullest extent forced some workers to emigrate, while others remained unemployed and were forced to beg in order to survive.[20]

Montchrétien believed that unemployment was a morally corrupting force in society, advising Marie de Médicis, to whom the book was dedicated, that 'men reduced to doing nothing are soon induced to doing evil.'[21] He agreed with Bodin that poverty was the greatest threat to the social order in France:

> Because the bad treatment of the poor very often leads to popular disorders in the towns and then such disorders are spread to the countryside by the contagion of poverty which is transmitted both far and wide. There is no better method to treat these evils all at once than to provide work for the poor.[22]

Montchrétien concurred with Laffemas that establishing manufactures of luxury products would help to remove those wishing to work from the danger of a lifetime of poverty. The unemployed could find work and at the same time the kingdom's tax base would be increased.[23] He encouraged the foundation of institutions of confinement, similar to those which he had observed in the Netherlands, that taught the children of the poor to become productive subjects.[24] To complement these work

---

17 Laffemas, 1606, pp. 100–104.
18 Cole, 1931, pp. 81–2.
19 Ibid., p. 82.
20 Montchrétien, 1889, pp. 25–6.
21 Ibid., p. 65.
22 Ibid., pp. 105–106.
23 Ibid., pp. 79–80.
24 Ibid., pp. 103–105.

schools for children, he encouraged towns to establish workhouses to imprison able-bodied adults in order to force them to put aside their innate idleness.[25]

While Montchrétien had dedicated his book to the Regent, he did not propose that the central government do more than provide legislation designed to encourage each village, town and city of the kingdom to assume the responsibility of its own poor. This argument, influenced by ideas of natural law, fitted with the localist outlook held by most men in France:

> It is right, it is indeed natural that each must improve and manage his own lands; each region must feed and employ its own people ... In all the towns of this kingdom, I see only Lyon where this principle seems to be in effect. For there it is not permitted for shopkeepers or the owners of manufactories to employ anyone from outside the city in the place of those natives who ask for assistance ... It seems very reasonable that each town should have something in particular as well as some reserve for its own children so that it can do well by them.[26]

Montchrétien concurred with the tradition of the kingdom that poor relief was the responsibility of the locality, not the crown.

These mercantilist economic ideas, derived primarily from traditional concepts of poverty and social welfare, formed the foundation of the orthodoxy on which the majority of ideas of poor relief during the seventeenth century were based. Such ideas influenced the actions taken by the elites of the kingdom – whether the consuls of cities like Nîmes, the Présidents of the Parlement of Paris or crown ministers – to ensure social order in the kingdom.

Catholic Reform theories of charity

The Catholic revival following the Reformation began in the middle decades of the sixteenth century, but the instability of the French state after 1560 hindered the implementations of the Council of Trent's reforms. But at the beginning of the seventeenth century, the Catholic Church in France entered a period of increased activism following the end of the Wars of Religion and the internal peace between Catholics and Protestants marked by the Edict of Nantes in 1598.[27] In part, the new religious optimism which inspired many French Catholics was the result of the teachings of François de Sales. He was born to a noble Savoyard family in 1567. Following an education at the Jesuit Collège de Clermont and at the University of Paris, he began missionary work in the Protestant province of Chablais in Savoy in which he had some small success in his attempts at converting the locals, but his greatest importance was as a theorist and author.[28]

François de Sales argued that too many Catholics avoided leading a life of devotion due to its difficulty and perceived unpleasantness. Many, he maintained,

---

25   Ibid.
26   Ibid., pp. 113–14.
27   Delumeau, 1971; Lebrun, 1980; and Taveneaux, 1980 are all good introductions to the history of the Catholic Church in seventeenth-century France.
28   Kleinman, 1962, pp. 39–45, 64–80.

wrongly believed that individuals could only live in a truly religious manner if cloistered. In the *Introduction à la vie dévote*, first published in 1608, he insisted to the contrary that a devout life could be led by those participating in the secular world:

> The world sees that the devout serve, pray and suffer injuries, give to the poor, limit their ambition, choke and stifle their passions, deprive themselves from sensual pleasures, and do these and other sorts of deeds which by themselves and by their very substance and quality are strict and rigorous. But the world does not see the warm interior devotion which makes all of these duties agreeable, sweet and easy.[29]

He believed that true devotion could be practised in all walks of life, differing with the circumstances of the individual. He stressed that the path of devotion must be undertaken sensibly: an artisan who spent all of each day at prayers would not be living according to his station in life.[30]

François de Sales qualified the traditional belief in the sanctity of the poor in order to allow his wealthy devout audience to figure among them:

> Very happy are those who are *poor in spirit* because the kingdom of Heaven is for them. And thus, those who are rich in spirit are unhappy because the misery of Hell is reserved for them ... He who is poor in spirit has no riches in his heart nor does his heart reside within worldly goods.[31]

He explained these definitions by arguing that it was different to possess wealth and to be corrupted by it:

> There is a difference between having poison and being poisoned. Apothecaries possess almost every sort of poison in order to treat many diverse illnesses, but they themselves are not poisoned by these poisons because they do not have the poisons in their bodies but rather in the shops they keep. Thus, you may have wealth without being poisoned by it, that's to say if you had wealth in your house or in your purse but not in your heart. To be a rich man in this world and a poor man in spiritual terms is the greatest fortune for the Christian because he has by this the comforts of wealth in this world and the merit of poverty for the next.[32]

He argued that the rich could be 'poor in spirit' as long as they used their wealth for the charitable purposes for which God had given it. This argument reassured many of his readers that a devout life could be followed without entering a cloistered community or putting aside one's personal wealth.

The charity which François de Sales sanctioned was not simply the granting of alms to beggars on the streets. He wished to portray a truly Christian way of living as being accessible to anyone, but it was not his intention to overstate the ease with which the individual could earn salvation. He encouraged the devout to undertake an active and participatory form of charity:

---

29 de Sales, 1641, pp. 6–7.
30 Ibid., p. 10.
31 Ibid., pp. 224–5.
32 Ibid., pp. 225–6.

For if you love the poor put yourself among them often, take pleasure in seeing them in your house and go to visit them in theirs. Speak freely to them, be well at ease when they approach you in church, in the road and elsewhere. Speak to them as one of them, talk with them as you would with a comrade, but be a rich man when it comes to giving, share your wealth with them like the most generous.[33]

While many of the ideas which François de Sales proposed were original, his presentation suited the hierarchical nature of ancien régime France. It was the popularity of his message that the rich could lead a devout life, coupled with his advocacy of a charitable activism, which made him such an important figure in the history of charity and poor relief. His books of piety continued to be reprinted throughout the seventeenth century, influencing many religious and secular thinkers throughout the period. Vincent de Paul founded the Congregation of the Mission in 1625 and the Daughters of Charity in 1633 to further the cause of this new activism.[34] Later in the century, both Louis Bourdaloue, a Jesuit, and Pierre Nicole, a Jansenist, could cite the ideas of François de Sales in their works.

Charity and the Jesuit–Jansenist conflict.

The enthusiasm of the devout for Catholic Reform activism during the early seventeenth century continued throughout the second half of the century despite the divisions within the church that developed during the middle decades. The Catholic Church in France during the reign of Louis XIV was full of internal conflicts. Jesuits and Jansenists were divided over the individual's motivations that lay behind charity; however, both sides encouraged giving, and, in doing so, continued the emphasis on the individual's religious obligation toward the poor well into the eighteenth century.

Jesuit ideas about the proper observance of the charitable obligation of the individual were those which many, both in the hierarchy of the church and the central government, wished to promote as orthodoxy during the reign of Louis XIV. The influence of the Society of Jesus was reflected in its monopolization of the position of the confessor of the king between 1649 and 1715. The ideas which influenced the Jesuit position towards charity were formulated in the late sixteenth century by the Spaniard Luis de Molina. His main theme, contrary to Augustinian tradition, was that the love and mercy of God were unlimited. He argued that it was inconceivable that God would leave most of humanity devoid of any possibility of salvation. It was equally unimaginable to him that God would abandon those who sought earnestly to find him. Nobody was precluded from heaven; to gain access a man had to have faith, do his Christian duty and truly repent his sins. Molinists did not claim that rich men could buy their way into heaven without real contrition.

Molina developed the concept of *grâce suffisante*. Man possessed the power to believe in the true God, however imperfect his faith might be. An individual could love and serve him with the assistance of the church and the sacraments. There

---

33 Ibid., p. 232.
34 See Pujo, 2003.

was no insurmountable obstacle to achieving personal salvation in the nature of the individual because God gave man the ability to choose freely between salvation and damnation. The Jesuits argued against the Augustinian concept that man could neither refuse grace nor avoid damnation if it was predestined for him. They followed a humanist tradition that viewed this emphasis on the inability of man to act out of anything but self-interest as removing the merit accrued by choosing the right path.

Molinist theology put its emphasis on the power of good works to aid the quest of the individual for salvation in order to define official Catholic thought in contrast to Protestantism. Catholics were reminded that only by performing good works in person could they help their quest to lead a pious life:

> Have you ever visited a hospital or a prison that your heart was not raised to God beforehand? What thoughts occupied your mind there and what meditations did you bring away with you? Thus when your piety begins to fade, it is there without fail that you shall reignite it. When your faith begins to weaken and to languish, it is there for certain that you will awaken and strengthen it.[35]

During the reign of Louis XIV, the Jesuit preacher Bourdaloue promoted Molinist thought on efficacious grace, believing that charitable works offered a way to assist one's salvation in the next world while alleviating the plight of the poor in this one:

> Just as in the word of God I have explained for you, this exhortation will be useful equally to both you and the poor alike. The poor by profiting during this transient and mortal life and you by profiting in a more sure and immortal life. Charity will cleanse the body of the poor and it will cleanse your soul: the poor will take some sustenance from it in this world and it will make you win an infinite glory in eternity.[36]

He assured Catholics that their attention to their Christian duty would be taken into account in their final judgement.

The Jesuits believed that man had the power, through his free will and God's help, to turn the possibility of salvation offered to him via sufficient grace into reality. Man through his actions, they argued, could win a measure of God's grace. Thus through performing the will of God in works of charity, man could assist himself to secure forgiveness for his sins. In 1676, describing the impulse behind charitable visits to the poor, the Jesuit Amable Bonnefons wrote:

> The first and foremost motivation you must have in making these charitable visits is to celebrate the great glory of God ... The second is the honouring of Jesus Christ, seeking to laud his sacred humanity in assisting his afflicted children ... The third is to satisfy the Lord's justice for the sins that we have ... The fifth is to make these charitable visits for the

---

35 Bourdaloue, 1900, tom. IV, p. 13. After serving as a priest in the provinces, Louis Bourdaloue (born 1632) was called to Paris by the superiors of the Society of Jesus in 1669. He quickly gained a prestigious audience and was invited to preach before the court in 1670. He became one of the most influential church figures during the reign, preaching often at the court before being sent to Languedoc in 1686 to assist in the conversion of Protestants after the revocation of the Edict of Nantes.

36 Ibid., p. 26.

benefit of those souls in purgatory ... The tenth, remembering at last that by performing such deeds of charity you shall earn great indulgences ... say 'I know only too well, O Lord, that my sins merit some punishment and I seek from you some remission of them by virtue of the good deed that I am attempting to do.'[37]

Jesuits argued that an individual who led a pious life, accepted the sacraments and did penance through performing good works could assure a place in heaven.

There was nothing new in the link made by the Jesuits between religion and charity. They followed the tradition of the church which perceived Christian duty and charity as inseparable. By the seventeenth century, Catholics were accustomed to believe that God commanded them to give to the poor and afflicted as part of their general duty as Christians.[38] Louis Bourdaloue preached such a message in his sermons on charity. He emphasized his belief that Christians were put on earth to serve God's will:

> I have wealth, but God is the first master of it, the principal owner, and I am truly only the manager and distributor of my wealth; so that if I give it away I must not do so according to my will or do only as I see fit but distribute it according to the Lord's will and by his orders.[39]

He also reminded his audience that to thwart the will of the divine was to commit a grave sin. At the final judgement, God would know who had done their duty and who had not:

> I have wealth, but I must render a final account of it and a very rigorous account. The day will come when I will be called before the judgement of God and when He will say to me what was said to the tax collector of the Gospel: *Redde rationem vilicationis tuae* (Luke 16). Show what has been given to you by God and how you managed it. In this account I will not be able to excuse my actions and I must submit absolutely to His judgement.[40]

The commitment to God included a responsibility to perform works of charity. The argument that both contemporary Catholic thought and scriptural precedent sanctioned good works must have convinced many devout Catholics to give their time and money.

Molinist theology was only one of the reasons the Jesuits encouraged charity. The order had been founded in the sixteenth century in order to check the spread of Protestantism and win back converts. Poverty was seen as a breeding ground for heresy. If the threat that Protestantism posed was to be extinguished permanently, then it was necessary for the population of France to be properly Christianized. As well, many local superstitions and rituals which conflicted with orthodoxy had to be eliminated. The founder of the Society, Loyola, had first begun missions to improve Catholic understanding among the peasants and the poor of Europe in 1535, and throughout the sixteenth century such missions were regarded by the Jesuits as a tool

---

37 Bonnefons, 1676, pp. 15–19.
38 Ibid., pp. 2–4.
39 Bourdaloue, 1900, tom. IV, p. 4.
40 Ibid.

to prevent the spread of heresy.[41] In France, Jesuit missionaries undertook what Louis Châtellier calls the 'Grand Design' to challenge the religious peace of 1648, focusing on regions where the Catholic and Protestant communities lived in close proximity, such as Languedoc.[42] Charity was important to this drive. Jesuits recognized that the needs of the poor must be addressed to win them over, but there was little point to curing poverty if they remained in a state of ignorance which would leave them always prone to falling victim to heresy. It was important to provide for the poor in order to offer them material evidence of the proper course to take. One of the difficulties which the earliest missionaries had faced was the inability to coerce the poor to attend mass.[43] The Order found a solution in institutions of confinement, where the poor could be instructed in religion and their moral behaviour observed.[44]

In theory, the Jesuits looked on the poor as the image of Jesus Christ. This was an image common to many groups of Catholics.[45] The choice of Christ to appear on earth to minister among the lower orders gave special significance to them.[46] When thought of in terms of helping the representatives of Christ himself, charity took on great meaning. Bourdaloue reminded his audiences that 'He [Jesus] has established them [the poor] among you as substitutes for him.'[47] The image of the holy poor had carried a great weight in popular Christianity during the Middle Ages. The prayers of the poor were considered to be of more worth than those of the rich. Therefore, it was common for the rich to leave money for the poor in their wills. The Jesuits changed the emphasis on this sort of charitable bequest, placing it on helping the poor while the benefactor was still alive. Calls were made for the rich to consider themselves as the servants of the poor:

> Christian souls, you will not be offended by this quality of servant and you will excuse the use of this word as a part of my zeal as soon as you understand what I mean by it. To be the servants of the poor, that is to be servants of Jesus Christ Himself ... and Jesus Christ himself said unto you that all that you do for the poor it is for Him that you act.[48]

The identification was made between the saviour and the poor, but this concept gave little thought to them as human beings.

Although the poor were believed to be the representatives of Christ on earth, the Society of Jesus argued that they were only to be considered as such in the abstract. There was no belief that the poor were a form of living relics, with some element of sacredness attached to them. They simply represented Jesus. They were, in effect,

---

41 Châtellier, 1997, pp. 10–17.

42 Ibid., pp. 49–52.

43 Kleinman, 1962, pp. 80–81. Châtellier, 1997, p. 19. François de Sales, among others, complained during his mission to Chablais in the 1590s that he had been hampered by the failure of the secular authorities to compel their subjects to attend his services.

44 Bourdaloue, 1900, tom. IV, pp. 48, 55–67.

45 The Edict of 1656 which established the Hôpital Général of Paris described the deserving poor in these terms.

46 Taveneaux, 1980, pp. 204–209.

47 Bourdaloue, 1900, tom. IV, p. 6.

48 Ibid.

ciphers on which the pious could demonstrate their worthiness to themselves and, hopefully, to God. Elites were neither being called on to be real servants to the poor nor to care constantly for them. The Jesuits asked them to give a small amount of their wealth and time in order to demonstrate their faith. A certain amount of money given to a charitable institution and some time spent examining the results were usually all that was required by confessors and spiritual advisers. Occasionally a noble might take to heart the call to serve the poor and might perform some ceremonial task, usually on a particular feast day.[49] An active demonstration of piety through providing for the poor had replaced any consideration by the nobility of the state of poverty. The poor as individuals were treated as children who had to be forced to conform to accepted standards inside charitable institutions, or else as incorrigibles who should be punished in order to cure them of their faults.

When thought was given to the causes of poverty, the Jesuits blamed weaknesses in an individual's character. It is not surprising that, considering the importance the Jesuits placed on charity, religious reasons for poverty abounded. The concept that the poverty existed because of the ignorance of the poor of the true tenets of the Catholic faith was quite common among the devout. French society in the seventeenth century was a strict hierarchy organized from the top down. From the Jesuit point of view, it was religion that kept society bonded together.[50] The hierarchy was the method used by God to carry forth his plan for the kingdom. Individuals who were truly pious in nature would not slip out of it. Those who did, but who showed repentance and a willingness to accept correction, should, in the belief of the church, be assisted. Beggars, however, who seemed to choose to go against the accepted order, should not be helped.

According to Jesuit missionaries, destitution and starvation were not the worst problems that the poor faced. The ignorance that created the distress from which they suffered also led them to greater evils such as the heresy of Protestantism. These evils in turn led to eternal damnation. The ideas of the Counter-Reformation were strongly held by many in the church in France during the reign of Louis XIV. Everywhere they looked, the advocates of reform saw a poor country as they would define it. Religious rituals were being performed improperly and provincial priests preached out of ignorance while the elites spent their wealth and energy on frivolous entertainment.[51] It was no wonder that so many members of the kingdom could be subject to a sudden plunge into poverty. If the people were poor, then that fact should be perceived as the judgement of God on the country. This is why charitable drives for missions, new seminaries and aid for converted Protestants were so important to the Jesuits. A desire to see Catholicism triumphant in France underlay much of their call for greater efforts at charity.

The second half of the seventeenth century saw an Augustinian challenge to the Molinist theology of the Jesuits. This alternative theology was named Jansenism by

---

49   For example, the benefactresses of the house for female orphans in Grenoble would demonstrate their piety by imitating Christ by washing the feet of the young girls in their care: See Norberg, 1985.

50   Bélin, 1875, pp. 2–5.

51   Ibid., p. 21.

its opponents after Cornelis Janssens, its most famous early theorist. It was marked by its pessimistic attitude in contrast to the optimism of the Jesuits. Its fatalistic outlook on the prospects of the salvation of man might seem to have prevented it from formulating positive ideas about charity; however, it too stressed the need for charity as part of a Christian life.

The history of Jansenism as a social force in France began with the reform of the Benedictine abbey of Port-Royal by Marie Angélique Arnauld in the early years of the seventeenth century. Mère Arnauld, appalled by the laxity of the house of which she had been made abbess at the age of eleven, enforced a rigorous observance of the Benedictine rule. The austerity and piety of the house inspired the reform of others in the early decades of the century and drew admirers from among the laity to seek spiritual guidance. Before the Frondes, it was closely associated with many of the chief theorists of Christian charity, as Mère Arnauld developed friendships with François des Sales as well as many of the founding members of the Parisian Compagnie du Saint-Sacrement.[52]

Jansenist theology was marked by its adherence to an Augustinian concept of grace. The *Augustinus,* written by the bishop of Ypres, Cornelis Janssens, and published in 1640 after his death, was an attack on the Jesuit theologians, Molina and Lessius, in an attempt to vindicate the doctrine of Augustine. It emphasized the beliefs of Augustine on sin, predestination and divine grace. It was an appeal for true Catholics to lead a pious spiritual life.

Jansenism owed much to the experience of the world as a place full of misery and wretchedness for evidence of the truth of its message. The daily tragedies which faced many in the seventeenth century were, for them, a sign of the inability of man to overcome his sinful nature. These were physical proofs of the impossibility for an individual to win grace from God through his own deeds. God had denied man freedom of action. An individual could avoid a sin at any given moment, but Jansenists believed it was impossible for one to do so all of the time. Man often sinned without knowing, his ignorance being no defence before the eyes of God. Jansenist authors argued the Augustinian concept of grace meant that God elected a few individuals to be saved. Others might receive temporary grace, inspiring them to acts of piety and charity, but only those who received his true grace could enter heaven. Jansenists even used this concept to explain their own doubts about their state by arguing that God often temporarily withdrew his grace to keep his chosen humble.

The Jesuit notion of efficacious grace was mocked by the Jansenists. Blaise Pascal criticized the laxity of Jesuit theorists in regard to their belief that charity motivated from self-interest could have any value in the eyes of God:

> You [the Society of Jesus] will publish, with the approval and privilege of your theologians, that we can be saved without ever having loved God, and you will shut the mouths of those who defend the truth of the faith by saying that they will wound the charity of the faithful by attacking you and will blemish the modesty of Christians by laughing at your maxims?[53]

52 J. Racine, *Abrégé de l'histoire de Port-Royal*, in Racine, 1952, tom. II, pp. 37–54.
53 Pascal, 1965, pp. 200–201.

Pascal rejected the idea that a man could have a say in his ultimate fate. He believed that a man in a state of sin had no power to help himself. Such an individual could not even sincerely pray for help without some form of divine assistance. He believed that the actions of man were guided by self-interested motivations. A sinful man would undergo confession not from real contrition, but from fear of his damnation. Neither prayer nor the performance of good works could win salvation for the individual who was not given the grace of God:

> In truth, my Father, I know that the devotions made to the Virgin are an important method for salvation and that the least of them bear a great merit for the devout, but only when they come from a movement of faith and of charity as was the case of the saints who said them as well. But to imply that those who say these prayers without changing their wicked lives will be converted at the moment of their deaths, or that God will grant them resurrection is wrong. It is this belief that I have found very commonly used by sinners to justify their sins by the false peace that this promise recklessly brings them, it takes them away from the true conversion that grace alone can bring.[54]

Jansenists viewed with suspicion the motivations behind charitable enterprises. They did not believe that an individual could amass grace by means of good works. They argued that man was so insignificant in relation to God, so flawed in his perceptions that he had no way of understanding his motivations. Man's ignorance of himself and the universe was so total that it nullified the effects of any charitable action made without first being in a state of grace.

Despite their suspicion of motivations, Jansenists were not hostile to charity; in fact they greatly approved of it. Pierre Nicole argued that, while charitable works might not win grace without the approval of God, the performance of such deeds could calm the individual's anxiety. He advocated the undertaking of works of charity because, although leading a Christian life would not earn grace, it was preferable to a life of negligence, sloth and ease.[55] Although Jansenists disapproved of what they believed were extravagant claims made by Jesuits that charitable works could contribute to winning personal salvation, they accepted charity as a part of the duty of every Christian because of its biblical sanction. The ministry of Jesus among the poor was their model for emulation. An early biography of Pascal, written by his sister Gilberte, might verge upon hagiography, but it shows what its Jansenist audience expected in the life of a true Christian:

> This love that he had for poverty brought him to love the poor with such a great tenderness that he could never refuse giving alms even though he had his own needs, not being wealthy and being obliged by these gifts to make an expense that exceeded his revenues on account of his own infirmities.[56]

While the motivations behind charity might be challenged by Jansenists, none questioned that it should be part of their lives.

---

54   Ibid., pp. 160–161.
55   James, 1972, pp. 101–103.
56   G. Périer, *La vie de Pascal*, in Pascal, 1964, tom. I, p. 588.

Although they dismissed the Jesuits' claims that charity would assist the individual to gain admission to heaven, many Jansenists concurred with the foundation of institutions to care for the poor. Godefroi de Hermant applauded the creation of the Bureau des Pauvres in Beauvais in 1655, citing that examples of individuals giving alms to the poor in the streets were worthy:

> You must swear nevertheless that they are not comparable to the sacred gathering of several individuals who are united by the duties of Christian piety not only to offer solace to the wretched, but also to help end the causes of their misery, and who are found surrounded by a great host of the poor employing all sorts of methods to ensure that no poor live without assistance ... and it is for this reason that the wise man gave us this excellent rule to govern our almsgiving: 'Give to the worthy man and do not receive the sinner. Do good deeds for the humble but give nothing to the impious.' He taught us with these words not to wholly abandon the wicked who are still joined to us by nature, but to take care that our gifts may not be as nourishment for their crimes nor the instrument of further bad deeds.[57]

Other Jansenists advocated simpler forms of charity from their Jesuit opponents because of their different, more private and individual, motivations. The most austere, like Pascal, did not believe that everyone was called to participate in public demonstrations of personal piety, preferring for many like himself confidential well-intentioned gestures towards the deserving poor:

> He [Pascal] believed that the method of serving the poor most agreeable to God was to do so humbly, that's to say each according to his ability, without being filled with the spirit of these grand designs which detract from this excellence by deriving from the sort of worldly ambitions that he detested. That is not to say that he disapproved of the establishment of hôpitaux-généraux; to the contrary he had a great liking of these institutions, as is witnessed from his final testament. However, he said that these great enterprises were reserved for certain individuals who had been destined by God to undertake them but that such endeavours were not for everyone. The greater part of the world was summoned to give daily assistance of poor individuals.[58]

Individuals should not try to exceed their limitations but help those they could. Antoine Arnauld concurred with this idea, stating that: 'In theory, all Christians are obliged to feed the all the poor who are among them. But each Christian as an individual is not charged with assisting all of them.'[59]

The nuns cloistered at Port-Royal were expected to continue the Christian tradition of charity. Both the houses in Paris and Port-Royal des Champs offered services to the poor in their parishes:

---

57 Hermant, 1655, pp. 5–6. Hermant was born in Beauvais in 1617, educated by Jesuits before attending the University of Paris. In 1650, he became a doctor of theology at the Sorbonne. Although already defending the writings of Jansenist theologians in the 1650s, he attended the same salon at the home of the Premier Président of the Parlement of Paris, Guillaume de Lamoignon, during the 1660s which was often attended by Louis Bourdaloue.

58 Ibid., p. 590.

59 A. Arnauld quoted in Taveneaux, 1980, tom. I, p. 215.

It is scarcely believable how many poor families both in Paris and in the countryside subsisted on the charitable gifts that one or the other house provided for them. The nuns at des Champs had employed a physician and a surgeon for a long time. These men had almost no other work than to treat the sick poor of the region on behalf of the nuns and they went into all the surrounding villages to bring remedies and other necessary relief. And when this house was no longer in a position to employ either a physician or a surgeon, the nuns themselves were not able to carry on the same services [those of treating the sick poor in their own homes]. There is in the convent an infirmary where the poor women of the neighbourhood were received to be bled and treated by the Sisters deputed for that job and who acted in that employment with great skill and incredible devotion. In the place of all the frivolous activities, at which the most other orders of nuns are occupied much to the amusement of the people of this century, one would be surprised to see with what industry the nuns of Port-Royal worked to gather together the most minuscule clippings of cloth in order to clothe those children and poor women who had nothing with which to cover themselves, and by how many ways the nuns' charity made them appear ingenious at helping the poor all by themselves. God, who saw them act in secret, knew how much they had given of their own selves and how many times they had taken the bread from their own mouths in order to give it to those who were hungry.[60]

They offered simple, yet important services to the poor of their area, which earned them the loyalty of those who benefited.[61] Many Jansenists approved of such efforts as those at Port-Royal, relishing such self-sacrifice which was performed with no desire for spiritual gain.

Jansenists postulated that the poor were responsible for their own poverty. The wretchedness of everyday life influenced their theology. Destitution was a proof of God's withdrawal of grace. Jansenists, in their writings, spoke often about the love of poverty the Christian should have. The poverty they referred to in this sense would be better defined as austerity. They did not believe that their adherents should give up their money to become penniless friars, but they preached that men should lead a simple life, taking no more than they needed. For them the poor possessed no virtue themselves, but they served as reminders to keep the elect humble. The poor were a constant reminder of the wretchedness of man before God. They were physical representations of the innate weaknesses and faults of man.[62]

Jansenism was a rigorous and austere movement, but it was also a movement of the Counter-Reformation. While it might deride what it considered the extravagant claims of a Jesuit like Bourdaloue of winning salvation through good works, it did not criticize his efforts at converting Protestants. Mme de Sévigné believed in the validity of Jansenist theology, approving of the ideas of Pascal and Saint-Cyran.[63] At the same time she was able to applaud the efforts of noted Jesuit attempts to convert:

I still love Father Rapin [a noted Jesuit]; he is a good and honest man. He was often supported by Father Bourdaloue whose spirit is charming whose personality is one of easy

60 Racine, 1952, pp. 57–8.
61 Thiers, 1676, pp. 278–9.
62 Ibid., pp. 255–6.
63 Rabutin-Chantal, 1953–57, tom. I, pp. 353–6.

friendliness. He has been sent, by order of the king, to preach in Montpellier and in those provinces where so many men have been so recently converted (following the Edict of Nantes in 1685) without understanding why. Father Bourdaloue will teach them the faith and will make them into good Catholics. The dragoons have been very good missionaries up to now: the preachers will make the conversion complete.[64]

Jesuits and Jansenists disputed between themselves over many theological issues, but they had similar views on the issue of destroying Protestantism in the kingdom.

Noble paternalism

The elite order in French society, the nobility, underwent a period of redefinition in the seventeenth century. It remained the most powerful group in France, but it was consumed with a fear that the order was being invaded by commoners who advanced, not because they demonstrated their worth, but because they could buy titles and social position. It feared that the distinction between the old warrior order and newer men was becoming blurred. Wealthy non-nobles could put on as much of a display of wealth as members of the nobility. The old nobility feared even more the rise of individuals from newer noble families within the royal administration to assume places higher in the hierarchy of command than themselves. A paternalist approach to the relationship between elites and non-elites was promoted as a way to separate the truly noble from the self-interested rich.

Seventeenth-century France was a structured hierarchical country. The religious motivations of charity took this fact into account. The devout believed that social divisions were all part of God's plan. The king and the nobility were placed as rulers in society in order to watch over the rest of the kingdom. The rich were put on earth with a duty to look after the poor:

This wealth that the rich man has received, for what purposes has he been granted it and for what purposes must he use it? It is for the poor that this wealth has been confided to him and it is for the subsistence of the poor that God has given it. From this it follows that the rich man is not rich for himself but for the poor. That is to say that he is not rich in order to satisfy his own ambitions, to gratify his cupidity, to keep up a luxurious manner of living, to raise himself up, or to dominate but he is rich in order to take care of the needs of the poor, to offer solace for their misery, to give them bread and to feed them. This is the design that Providence has made for the rich.[65]

The idea that the nobility should recognize that in a hierarchy it had an obligation to look after those below it in society was developed by secular writers into a criticism of bourgeois behaviour, helping to reassert traditional beliefs about the nature of true nobility.

Nobility was associated with the qualities and social standing of a man, his family and his ancestry, rather than his wealth or office. In the code of noble discourse the word bourgeois was a great pejorative. By naming a particular characteristic

---

64 Ibid., tom. III, p. 114.
65 Bourdaloue, 1900, tom. IV, p. 5.

bourgeois, one denoted that it was the opposite of nobility. The nobility upheld elements of its traditional definition which separated itself from robe and ministerial pretenders. It identified itself as an honourable military and landowning elite. The qualities most associated with the affairs of business and administration became bourgeois qualities. Nobles thought the bourgeois to be consumed by their ambition for power and wealth, while they themselves were restrained through their use of reason. La Bruyère criticized his contemporaries for praising qualities which only benefited the individual and not society at large.[66] The *noblesse d'épée* complained that men were only measured by their wealth instead of their role in society. Great wealth did not necessarily denote nobility. The rich and successful were often the men who possessed the greatest luck or connections, leaving the men of virtue, talent and worthiness behind. Men strove for wealth and power because they allowed their passions to rule their lives. The fact of success gave men the appearance of noble qualities that they did not really possess. La Bruyère wrote that 'passions tyrannize the successful man and his ambition suspends in him his other passions and gives him for a time the appearance of all sorts of virtues.'[67] Allowing one's passions to rule was ignoble because it was self-centered, placing self-interest before the lives of one's inferiors:

> There are some miseries on Earth that seize the heart; some people lack simple necessities, they dread the winter, they fear living. Elsewhere one eats early fruits, one forces the soil and the seasons to provide him with delicacies. There are some bourgeois, only because they are rich, who have had the audacity to swallow up in a single mouthful the daily portion of one hundred families. Desire to be against such great extremes. I do not wish to be, if I have the power to decide, either happy or unhappy. I reject my wants and hide myself in mediocrity.[68]

A man who possessed true noble qualities did not allow his passions to rule him. He approached life in a rational manner. A truly wise man was one who 'neither allowed himself to be ruled nor sought to govern other people, he wishes only that reason alone will always govern him'.[69] Since wealth could be made by those without noble qualities, a great display of it was considered bourgeois by La Bruyère. A true noble would rather live an honourable life than one of gauche ostentation:

> In all conditions the poor man is right next to the man of wealth and the opulent man is scarcely separated from frivolous things. Knowledge and ability do not inevitably lead only to enormous wealth.[70]

Those born noble possessed a duty to place the interests of others before their own. It was felt that social climbers, because they were ruled by selfish passions, would not comprehend this fact. A good man, a noble, demonstrated his nature by considering others before himself:

---

66 La Bruyère, 1981, p. 119.
67 Ibid., p. 131.
68 Ibid., p. 129.
69 Ibid., p. 95.
70 Ibid., p. 128.

This man is good who does good for others, if he suffers for the good that he does then he is very good. If he suffers at the hands of those for whom he does this good deed he has such a great benevolence that cannot be increased except in the case where his own sufferings will come to grow by his actions. And if he dies by doing good, his virtue shall not go unknown, it is heroic, it is perfect.[71]

Nobility became synonymous with recognizing the obligations of the elite to its people and to the kingdom.

A paternalist argument in favour of charitable works developed from this criticism of the unworthy rich during the seventeenth century. A true noble naturally understood his duty towards those beneath him. The peasants of a seigneur's estates were considered to be like his children, depending on him for solace in times of trouble. The first duty of the seigneur was to ensure his own tenants did not fall into poverty:

Sell grain only in the marketplace and not elsewhere. Sell it to the poor who buy it at the commencement of the market day before you sell it to your other customers ... Do not keep too much grain in your granaries in order to sell it during a shortage ... In August, seigneurs should have published by their officers orders commanding all persons of both sexes to be put to work at the harvest and should provide them with reasonable salaries. Seigneurs should prevent the able-bodied from gleaning the fields after the harvest, only permitting the elderly or the crippled and little children and those who do not have the strength or health to provide for themselves to do so.[72]

The cause of poverty, in this argument, ought to matter little. The obligation of the nobility towards the peasantry, like that of parents towards their children, did not involve blame. A noble had to help those in his care to lead a moral Christian life. If they found themselves in trouble, the noble had a duty to put them back on the right path.

In the opinion of members of the nobility, the bourgeois who bought seigneuries and refused to help the tenants of their lands were beneath contempt. The duc de Luynes had written his *Instruction pour apprendre à ceux qui ont des terres dont ils sont seigneurs* in order to teach true noble duties to those bourgeois and robe nobility who had purchased estates around the towns in which they lived. The *noblesse d'épée* criticized non-nobles for not understanding the paternalist responsibility of the landowner, weighing up degrees of fault and refusing help to all but the most blameless. Members of the noble order felt that they should offer solace to their tenants in times of crisis. Their charity did not tend to take the form of funding urban institutions confining the poor, unless they held residences in the city, preferring to aid their own peasants according to their needs. The duc de Luynes argued that the nobility should establish well-regulated hospitals on its lands to offer material and spiritual care for the poor too infirm or old to work.[73]

---

71 Ibid., p. 66.
72 Albert, 1658, pp. 47–8.
73 Ibid., p. 67. If the noble did have a townhouse in Paris or a provincial capital, it was his duty to care for the poor of his parish: 'il sera bon qu'il garde encore quelque chose tous les ans pour donner aux pauvres malades et aux honteux de sa paroisse.'

Charity in this form was traditional. Nobles had commonly given alms to the poor of their estates and localities. Nor was almsgiving the only form it could take. The seigneur had a range of options to provide relief for his poor:

> There are some poor who cannot work either because of their extreme youth or their old age or from their infirmities or from being overburdened with children or finally because the little work they are able to do is still not enough to provide for the basic needs of a family which has too many mouths to feed. The state of the poor being precisely identified, the seigneur should take care to have them assisted with charities suited both to their needs and to his ability to give be it by providing them with clothes at the start of the winter or by taking care of the needs of their children or by furnishing them with grain or by purchasing for them some tools that will help them to earn a living according to what skills they might possess or finally to give them some money from time to time according to the seasons and the bounty or scarcity of the year.[74]

Rents could be forgiven or renegotiated if a family fell into hard times. The basis of paternalism was a moral economy practised in the countryside. Peasants, in theory, gave deference to their lords in return for the surety that they would be protected and cared for in hard times.

Nobles thought that the reasons behind poverty lay with the poor themselves. They believed that the lower orders were born hopelessly flawed. The poor were damned by their weaknesses and ignorance. Their innate miseries, however, were made worse by their betters ignoring their duty to society. La Fontaine believed that poverty could arise from the idleness or foolishness of the poor, but he also held that men could be made poor through no fault of their own. His fable of the two bulls and the frog reminded nobles that 'one sees that in every age the little people have been flattened by the follies of the great.'[75] La Bruyère, too, understood that the cupidity of those in power could force people into destitution. 'Champagne,' he wrote, 'at the end of a long supper which filled his stomach and breathing in the soft scent of a wine from Avenay or Sillery, sings an order that is presented to him which denies an entire province of its bread.'[76] It was the responsibility of the elite to help the poor regardless of what had reduced them to their state. It was not truly important what caused poverty, but it was necessary to help alleviate their suffering.

While such works were aimed at a noble audience, families from the urban elites emulated their social superiors. Wealth in the seventeenth century was not a end in itself. The socially ambitious urban elites eventually hoped that their families would rise to a position where they would pass into the nobility. They adopted the paternalist definition of nobility, using their wealth charitably in an urban context in order to ensure their descendants would be eased into the nobility by proving their worthiness.

---

74 Ibid., p. 63.
75 La Fontaine, 1898, p. 45.
76 La Bruyère, 1981, p. 122.

The Compagnie du Saint-Sacrement

The concepts of economists, theologians and social theorists were spread directly to their audience through their publications. More important, however, in disseminating these ideas were the confraternities which sprang up in French towns in the early seventeenth century. The Counter-Reformation helped to increase the numbers of devout Catholics actively engaged in charitable endeavors. In the early decades of the seventeenth century, many new lay companies dedicated to the fight against ignorance, immorality and heresy were created throughout the kingdom. The best known example of these organizations was the Compagnie du Saint-Sacrement which was composed of the lay and religious elites of the localities in which it was established. The Compagnie identified the poor as a breeding ground for heresy and it merged the economic, religious and social strands of poor relief theory as part of its struggle to defeat Protestantism. As a consequence of the mixture of theories about putting the poor back to work and ideas about the place of charity in a Christian life, these confraternities saw their struggle to create a more Catholic kingdom and the effort to rid France of beggary as inseparable.

Established in Paris in 1629, the Compagnie du Saint-Sacrement was the largest and most influential example of a seventeenth-century charitable confraternity. The Compagnie evolved from the regular meetings of the devout duc de Ventadour and the circle of his friends into a confraternity with set rules dedicated to the flowering of charitable works, the reform of morality and the extirpation of Protestantism in France. In general, it was modelled on other religious lay confraternities and, in terms of religious obligations, it demanded two things from its members: personal spiritual improvement through prayer and devotion to works of charity.[77]

The lay membership of the Compagnie in Paris was dominated by individuals from a patrician background. Lay membership made up about fifty per cent of the total, comprising figures in the Parlement, the Chambre des Comptes, and the Cour des Aides, along with the presence of a number of bourgeois, wealthy merchants and members of the liberal professions.[78] To this group, a small number of aristocrats was added, such as the duc de Liancourt, the duc de Nemours, the marquis de Laval; and even a prince of the blood, Conti.[79] However, the participation of these members should be qualified. Besides the occasional attendance of these exceptional men, the greater part of the organization was recruited from the wealthiest sectors of the citizens of Paris: the judges of the sovereign courts and their clients.[80]

Provincial chapters of the Compagnie du Saint-Sacrement reflected the urban elites of the locality in which they were established. In Grenoble, for example, the lay membership of the society founded in 1642 reflected the dominance of the

---

77 Allier, 1902, pp. 10–23.

78 Tallon, 1990, p. 7.

79 Allier, 1902, pp. 38–40. Unlike many of the provincial companies, no official record of the Parisian company survived. Allier's list of members is derived from individuals who were mentioned in the correspondence of the provincial companies or were given memorial masses by the companies at the time of their death.

80 Tallon, 1990, pp. 7–12.

judges and lawyers of the sovereign courts within that city.[81] The ecclesiastical membership was recruited from noble backgrounds and included men in substantial church offices, such as canons of the cathedral chapter.[82] The Lyon Compagnie, with a greater number of merchants and bourgeois amongst its participants, reflected the social and economic hierarchy of the city. The list of new members joining it in 1645 included two *marchands-drapiers*, one bourgeois, a master apothecary and a surgeon. Among the other new recruits whose occupation was noted down were two of the prosecutors in the municipal court.[83] There were no new participants listed with any title of nobility except Jean de La Poyppe, comte de Lyon, who joined in 1658.[84] The laymen of the Lyon chapter who joined in the years between 1645 and 1660 were mostly described as merchants or bourgeois, demonstrating the dominance of those families who had grown rich from the profits of commerce and industry in the city. Interspersed among the rich bourgeois of the city were new members who came from the civic courts and the city administration.[85]

In Marseille the lay membership of the local Compagnie, founded in 1639, was recruited from the consulate, from the courts, or from the bourgeois and merchants of the city. The first laymen listed were Francoys de Foresta, juge du Palais, and Pierre de Bausset, sieur de Roquefort, followed by several men who were either current or future consuls of the city.[86] The list of new members demonstrated the leadership of the urban elites throughout the existence of the organization.[87] The confraternity stressed its egalitarian nature, but it tended, in fact, to mirror the social composition of the elites in whichever town or city in which it was established. The organization devoted itself to the problems generated in seventeenth-century towns. The poor congregated in towns and cities looking for relief. It is not surprising, therefore, to find concerned individuals of the urban elites banding together to confront such issues.

The Compagnie demonstrated an impressive organizational skill in establishing itself throughout the kingdom.[88] The statutes sent out to the fledgling provincial companies drove home the need for a collective and directed action on the part of their members to accomplish in each city what could not be attempted by individuals on their own. Each chapter of the Compagnie met on a regular basis (in Lyon, for example, it was required to meet every Thursday at one in the afternoon).[89] Every three months it assembled to elect its executive: a superior, a spiritual director

81 Norberg, 1985, pp. 29–30.
82 Ibid.
83 Guigue, 1922, pp. 76–9.
84 Ibid., p. 84.
85 Ibid., pp. 76–84.
86 Allier, 1909, pp. 2–3. Pierre de Bausset was almost certainly a bourgeois of the city who had bought a seigneurie in order to claim a nobility of a sort.
87 Ibid., pp. 88–110. The Compagnie of Marseille appears to have ceased to meet after 1697.
88 See Tallon, 1990. Tallon argues that the Compagnie had established 64 chapters in important provincial towns by 1660.
89 Guigue, 1922, p. 3.

and six councilors.[90] The executive had the greatest impact over the organization by regulating who was accepted and who was dismissed from the membership. Existing members were required to introduce their candidates (often their clients) to the Superior who would undertake an investigation of the moral worth of each one and pronounce on his suitability to the general assembly.[91] The constitution of the group stated that it would not suffer the presence of those who did not live a devout Christian life.[92]

The primary goals of the Compagnie were to improve the understanding of the Catholic faith, to reform morality and to combat Protestantism throughout the kingdom. The members believed that if it was successful, then heresy would be wiped out and France would become a more Christian society.[93] The conflict between Catholicism and Protestantism was always present in the ideas of the participants. Charitable relief distributed to the poor was a means to protect them because they appeared to be an ideal recruiting ground for Protestantism. As such, the quality of services and care offered by local hospitals were important issues. In 1644, the Marseille chapter of the Compagnie required its members to find out if Protestant ministers had entered the city hospital in an attempt to convert Catholic patients.[94] The toleration granted to Protestants as a result of the Edict of Nantes was a constant thorn in the sides of the devout members of the organization, both in Paris and in the provinces. In 1660, for example, the Marseille society resolved to prevent Swiss Calvinists in the Guard regiment of Marseille from the public exercise of their religion – presumably to prevent impressionable citizens of the city from being swayed by what it considered as a false religion.[95]

Beyond the desire to reverse the settlement guaranteed by the Edict of Nantes, the Compagnie wished to protect the poor from falling into heresy. It believed that ignorance of the true faith brought the poor to the low state in which they found themselves. Influenced by François de Sales, it viewed Protestantism as a rebellion against the divinely inspired order of society. The confraternity argued that the poor, who existed with no real place in the social hierarchy, would be easy prey for Protestant proselytizing unless they were properly instructed in the Catholic faith.[96]

The ignorance of the poor could only be defeated by proper examples of religion and instruction. The Compagnie required its members to celebrate religious ceremonies according to proper Catholic practices as set forth by the Council of Trent. It instructed them to honour the name of the Compagnie du Saint-Sacrement by demonstrating the proper method of celebrating the festival of the Holy Sacrament. Through the correct participation of members of the local elites in such festivities,

---

90 Ibid., pp. 1–2.
91 Ibid., pp. 3–5
92 Ibid.
93 Allier, 1902, p. 10 and Guigue, 1922, pp. 1, 5–6, 148–52. The statutes of the Lyon, Marseille and rural chapters were so similar that they must have been modelled closely on those of the Paris chapter, suggesting that the mother house must have shared its religious ideals.
94 Allier, 1909, p. 48.
95 Ibid., p. 63.
96 Ibid., pp. 48–9.

it sought to encourage the accurate observance of Catholic ceremony among other citizens. The executive urged its membership to look for and to prosecute the perpetrators of what it considered to be the worst crimes committed against God: 'athées, déistes, libertins, hérétiques et schismatiques, jureurs et blasphémateurs du sainct nom de Dieu et autres impies'.[97] The author of the *Mémoires et instructions sur l'esprit de la Compagnie* outlined its duties to perform God's work:

> not only as part of the common duties toward the poor, the sick, prisoners and others, but also in missions, the seminaries, in the conversion of heretics, in the propagation of the faith in every part of the world, to condemn all scandals, impieties and blasphemies. To put simply, it is to anticipate all the injuries where it will bring remedies, to give all necessities both general and specific, to embrace all pious endeavours however hard or lonely they might be. It must apply itself to the needs of the next world.[98]

With these goals, the organization became an important aspect of Catholic Reform in seventeenth-century France, advocating a general revitalization of the efforts of the church and the devout to correct the ills of society.

The Compagnie attempted to improve the quality of religious knowledge among the laity throughout the kingdom. At the first meetings of the Toulouse chapter, in 1630, members were delegated to discuss plans with the archbishop about teaching the catechism in poor parishes of the city. The organization was concerned that the poor in the care of charitable institutions should receive religious instruction. The participants undertook the teaching of the poor in the hospitals themselves when they made the visits to such institutions required by the rules of the Compagnie. In their role as concerned members of the urban elites, they lobbied administrations of charities and municipal poor relief organizations to ensure that religious instruction continued to be given at other times.[99] In 1668, after the Paris group had been disbanded and the correspondence network with provincial branches which relied on it had ceased to function, the Lyon society continued to push for the catechizing of the poor. It proposed a plan to establish regulations for the rectors of the Hôpital de la Charité and the Hôtel Dieu to follow in catechizing the poor in their care. It wished to reserve bread bought through charitable contributions only for the poor who could demonstrate that they had been properly instructed in Catholic doctrines.[100] Its desire to see them properly instructed in Catholic ceremony was a result of the fear that the poor would spread religious ignorance and heresy.[101]

The Compagnie believed that the use of charity was a major weapon in combating the spread of religious indifference and ignorance. It approached charity with the Bible in one hand and bread for the poor in the other. Agreeing with the prevailing political and economic thought of the time, it rejected the common practice of individual almsgiving for a more effective collective effort.[102] It assessed the

97 Guigue, 1922, pp. 7–8.
98 Ibid., p. 34 and Allier, 1914, p. 39.
99 Allier, 1909, p. 49.
100 Guigue, 1922, pp. 64, 107–109.
101 Allier, 1909, p. 51.
102 Ibid.

writings of authors such as Montchrétien and Barthélemy de Laffemas and rejected the medieval notion of the poor as a permanent element of society. Influenced by economists who encouraged the poor to be retrained by forced labour, the Compagnie viewed poverty as a disease of ignorance which could be cured.

The confraternity's statutes were full of qualifications about which type of poor to assist. The members were not authorized to help anyone whom they found begging in the streets. A procedure was established to guide their choices about which sorts of poor should be assisted. A requirement of membership in the Compagnie was to keep vigilant in order to hunt out the poor that inhabited the towns. When a member found a poor family which he believed was deserving of aid, he presented the facts of their case before the weekly assembly, then the Superior would decide on the urgency of the need of the family. If it was pressing, then he was authorized to give them emergency assistance. Normally, however, the case would be deferred to the next week when, after inquiring about the worthiness of the family himself, the Superior would put the case to a vote before the whole assembly.[103]

It was because the Compagnie wished to end poverty, and especially vagrancy, that it took great care about who was to receive support. If support was given to anyone who asked, then, it was thought, the roads would be filled with people travelling to the cities and towns of the kingdom in order to lead an easy life by receiving casual alms in the streets. In this, the organization was influenced by the ideas of mercantilist authors in believing that such individuals were lazy by nature and had to be forced to work. It did not believe that the poor should be helped without qualification. Proper religious training was a necessary part of their charity. If the poor wished to receive aid from the Compagnie, they had to demonstrate a certain level of humility. The Marseille society took action to ensure that the poor of the various hospitals and hospices of the town were regularly confessed and, because they were ignorant of the principal mysteries of the Catholic faith, taught religion by the rectors.[104]

The religious component of its charity reveals the dualism of the Compagnie in regard to the causes of poverty. The society demonstrated an understanding of the social and economic circumstances that caused poverty concurrent with a belief that religious or moral weakness was the ultimate cause of long-term destitution. Its members saw disease and long-term misfortune as signs of the displeasure of God. In Lyon, it requested doctors to direct their patients to seek religious aid if they were not healed after the second visit. It viewed confession as a real solution to misfortune. A truly repentant sinner would be saved if given a proper chance.[105] Some of the most successful charitable efforts of the Paris chapter were initiated to meet the challenges of the Frondes. The assistance it gave to the missions of Vincent de Paul in the regions of the fighting, the centralized charitable donation and distribution centres, the Magasin Général, and their gazette, the *Magasin Charitable*, were all brought about in response to the reports of widespread destitution. This poverty might not have appeared to members of the Compagnie as having been

103 Guigue, 1922, p. 3.
104 Allier, 1909 p. 49.
105 Guigue, 1922, p. 65.

caused by the bad morality or the religious ignorance of the refugees, but they seem to have regarded the continuation of the war with Spain after 1648 and the civil war of the Frondes as a visitation of God's displeasure on the whole kingdom:

> From whence come these changes [the social disorder of the early 1650s] that are so wicked? From the war and what has lit the fire of conflict? Your sins. What has fed this disorder for the last twenty years? Your sins. Thus atone for your sins through your acts of charity. Drown these sins with this water and very soon you shall see the fire of the war extinguished across Europe.[106]

The poor were a sign of worse things to come if the state of belief in the kingdom was not improved.

Reforming poor relief in towns and cities so that the poor could be taught the proper observance of Catholicism at the same time as they received assistance was the cornerstone of the Compagnie du Saint-Sacrement's plans. The Compagnie merged the economic and religious in a theory of confinement known as *enfermement*. The difficulty of compelling the poor to undertake moral and religious reform would be overcome by confining them in hospitals. The deserving poor would be assisted and monitored in hospitals of confinement and assistance to the undeserving would be made illegal. Members the Compagnie in their roles as leaders in civic governments and the courts passed laws outlawing casual giving to the poor in the streets. At the same time the membership petitioned others among the urban elites to improve the services offered by existing hospitals for the sick poor and to establish new ones to confine the able-bodied. The Compagnie's plan to rid the workforce of the kingdom of its idleness through forced labour and constant observation complemented its goals to reform France religiously. In such institutions, the behaviour of the poor could be monitored. Its members would be assured that those confined would be instructed in proper Catholic doctrines without being given the opportunity to indulge their corrupt moral natures. Paternalist theories were employed to promote the reform of existing hospitals for the sick poor and the foundation of confinement institutions among socially ambitious members of the urban elites who came to view poor relief as an urban reflection of a seigneur's obligations toward his peasants. For much of the seventeenth century, provincial chapters campaigned in their towns to build confinement hospitals of various sorts. In 1656, the Compagnie made its greatest impact when the Hôpital Général of Paris was created to implement *enfermement* in the city. Many of the directors chosen to serve on the hospital board were either members of the Compagnie or directly influenced by them. Although the Paris chapter was outlawed in 1667, its members continued to work on the boards of such hospitals and the provincial chapters carried on until well into the eighteenth century. Those Jesuits who had been members of the Paris company took up the campaign to establish confinement hospitals in the name of the Society of Jesus during the 1670s, providing a continuity with the Compagnie du Saint-Sacrement. The Jesuits formed an easy alliance with the governors of the Paris hospitals (many of whom had been members of the Compagnie) and petitioned both the central government and local

---

106 Godeau, 1652, pp. 29–30.

elites in the provinces to continue the reform of urban poor relief during the reign of Louis XIV.

Orthodoxies developed during the sixteenth and seventeenth centuries regarding poverty and poor relief. Poverty came to be seen by both religious and secular writers as being caused by faults that lay within the individual. It was commonly believed that there was enough employment for those who desired to work. Failure for the able-bodied with no physical barrier to employment to find work was perceived to be the fault of either innate laziness or moral or spiritual defect within the poor themselves. The spread of Catholic Reform ideas among the elites of France during the early seventeenth century, such as those of François de Sales and Vincent de Paul, added a renewed charitable obligation by individuals to humanist ideas on the economy, such as those of Laffemas and Montchrétien. Humanists had argued that society could recover much of the lost potential of the poor through training the healthy to acquire good work habits or providing health care to cure the sick. At the same time, ambitious patrician families sought to emulate the paternalism of the old nobility by caring for the poor urban population. The three trends merged to promote an idea of confining the poor in public institutions, the theory of *enfermement*, where they could be observed and trained.

Chapter Two

Hospitals and the State

Historians have often been eager to accept that the reforms of poor relief and charitable health care in France during the early modern period were led by the state. From the reign of Louis XIV onwards the crown was eager to associate itself with charity and poor relief reforms. Patronage of the Paris hospitals evolved into a claim of foundation by 1700.[1] The government's claim to have led the drive to eliminate beggary in the seventeenth century has strongly influenced historians. In separate works published at the beginning of the twentieth century, Léon Lallemand and Christian Paultre argued that the crown led the reforms to poor relief during the early modern period. In the 1960s, Michel Foucault claimed that the Hôpital Général of Paris and the development of a network of confinement hospitals was an attempt by the growing absolutist government to segregate social deviants and force them to conform to the values of middle class society. Since his work, historians such as Jean-Pierre Gutton, Cissie Fairchilds, Colin Jones and Kathryn Norberg have placed the religious motivations behind assistance ignored by Foucault at the forefront of social welfare changes. These historians, however, have accepted as fact the argument that the crown assumed authority over the hospitals of the kingdom and led the reform to their services during the seventeenth century. Gutton, in an article tracing the origins of the ministries of Public Assistance and Health, stated the reason for the central government's inability to establish a nationwide system of hôpitaux généraux in the 1660s was not the lack of initiative, but the division of the administration of the provinces between the four Secretaries of State, making each a de facto Minister of the Interior in his region of responsibility. Likewise, Jean Imbert has claimed that the crown assumed control over social welfare during the period from 1505, with the secularization of the Hôtel Dieu de Paris, and the Revolution in 1789. In his opinion, sixteenth- and early seventeenth-century kings were not in a position to impose their power over the localities, but Louis XIV was strong enough to implement a fully national legislation. He identified the Edict of 1662, which called for the establishment of hôpitaux généraux in every town in the kingdom, and subsequent campaigns to enforce that legislation by the Jesuits in the 1670s as real attempts to impose a uniform national social policy. Most recently, Daniel Hickey has charted the resistance by administrators of small local hospitals to royal efforts to rationalize poor relief funds, but he too assumes that legislation concerning the foundation of large confinement hospitals (which was in fact designed to allow the crown to help the municipal leaders of Paris finance and manage their hospitals)

---

1   *Médailles sur les principaux évenements du regne de Louis le Grand* (1702), p. 42.

reflected an initiative of the central government.[2] Over the course of the sixteenth and seventeenth centuries the state issued several important edicts concerning hospitals and poor relief. At their heart, these edicts all maintained that individual localities were responsible for the assistance of the poor both by natural law and by the traditions of the kingdom. While the crown recognized that poor relief in the cities and towns of the kingdom was important, it only took an active interest in the distribution of aid in the capital. During the seventeenth century, the central government kept to its traditional role as an arbiter between localities, attempting to make sure that each lived up to its duties to care for its own poor.

The establishment of traditional royal policy

Prior to the spread of the bubonic plague throughout the kingdom during the mid fourteenth century, the crown had no established position in regard to poverty and assistance. In the early medieval period, poverty was considered to be a natural part of society and the charitable relief of the poor was a responsibility of the church. However, the outbreak of the plague created a situation in which the crown was obliged to act. It was feared that many poor would flee the countryside and small towns to seek help in hospitals and religious houses in large cities (most notably those of Paris). The crown issued its first statement concerning the poor in 1351. The poor were forbidden from leaving the parishes of their birth.[3] The roads to Paris were to be kept from the beggars in an ultimately fruitless attempt to prevent the spread of the disease.

The 1351 edict established for the crown a position that would remain in force, albeit with subsequent change and development, until the eighteenth century. The localities would have the responsibility for relieving poverty and assisting the sick.[4] The crown would intervene only when localities were perceived to be neglecting their duties toward the poor and unjustly burdening their neighbours. In most cases during the early modern period this intervention was quite limited and the state would only act in the interests of Paris to try to stop other towns from encouraging their poor to seek succour in the capital.

The medieval period witnessed an outpouring of charitable spending in French cities and towns. Many localities built hospitals during the twelfth, thirteenth and fourteenth centuries. A wide variety of such institutions from hospitals for the sick poor to leper houses were established throughout France.[5] While many were founded by lay benefactors, the majority of these hospitals were administered and staffed by religious hospital orders. The control of hospitals by religious orders posed a problem for some laymen. It was feared that charitable donations were used by the religious to support themselves, rather than for the purposes originally intended. Complaints were occasionally made against religious administrators about

---

2   See, for example: Lallemand, 1909–12; Paultre, 1906; Foucault, 1961; Gutton, 1970; Fairchilds, 1976; Norberg, 1985); Imbert, 1993; Hickey, 1997.

3   Geremek, 1987, pp. 29–30.

4   Ibid.

5   See Imbert, 1996.

corruption and misuse of hospital income.[6] One way in which the crown chose to
allay such fears and to support those whose families had given funds was to claim
authority over all hospitals which had no patron. Those hospitals whose founders
had retained the right for their descendants to nominate administrators were left
untouched. Hospitals which had no patron were decreed to have the king as patron
and could be inspected and reformed by the Grand Aumônier du Roi.[7] In effect, royal
patronage brought such hospitals within the jurisdiction of the royal courts, allowing
some legal recourse for their benefactors.

The crown seems to have seldom exercised its newly claimed powers of inspection,
however.[8] Over the course of the fourteenth and fifteenth centuries many small
hospitals became defunct as the great medieval monastic hospital orders declined
or drifted away from the purposes for which they were founded. The effects of the
plague and the Hundred Years War disrupted the collection of revenues, leading to the
cessation of many charitable services. As well, by 1500 a large number of hospitals
set up to isolate sufferers of leprosy had ceased to exist owing to the disappearance
of the disease from the kingdom.[9] Commonly, the revenues for these institutions
continued to be collected. However, the incomes of such defunct hospitals were
used to support the religious staff without any assistance being given to the poor. By
the sixteenth century, few of the kingdom's hospitals for the sick poor possessed a
staff beyond a porter and a small number of servants. Many town hospitals ceased to
function as anything more than warehouses for the poor, and by the late fifteenth and
early sixteenth centuries many municipalities, unguided by the crown, had begun to
take action to reform them.

The early sixteenth century was a period of municipalization of urban hospitals
as town governments formed lay hospital boards to replace religious control. This
municipalization was not an effect of the Reformation. In most cases the process was
either complete or well underway before 1517.[10] Local communities worried about
corruption, and often influenced by Christian humanist ideas that emphasized that
the individual could be rescued from both poverty and damnation, took control over
institutions of poor relief. For example, Lyon's city government took over control of
its hospital for the sick poor in the late fifteenth century and the Parlement of Paris
removed the administration of the Hôtel Dieu from the cathedral chapter in the first
decade of the sixteenth.[11]

At the start of the sixteenth century many cities and towns had embarked on
the reform of hospital administrations, bringing institutions under local lay control.
However, the poor relief in many urban centres was disrupted by the civil wars of the
second half of the century.[12] In the context of sectarian strife, poverty was believed

6   Jones, 1999 p. 219.
7   Ibid.
8   Ibid.
9   See Le Grand, 1898.
10   Imbert, 1993, pp. 9–13.
11   Ibid. and AAP HD 864.
12   See Holt, 2005 and Knecht, 1996 for the best introductions to the Wars of Religion in
France.

by both sides to be a breeding ground of ignorance and heresy. Both Catholic and Protestant faiths worried that the poor were a potential source of strength for the other side. The Wars of Religion proved to have serious consequences for civic poor relief programmes as fighting could periodically cause lengthy interruptions in the provisioning of welfare, such as happened during the siege of Montpellier in the early 1560s. For much of the period after 1560, the crown attempted to keep its own freedom of action by manoeuvring between Catholic and Protestant activists. The crown hoped to bring the Huguenots back into the fold. However, the international nature of the Catholic Church made moderation difficult in the area of poor relief and charitable health care. At the twenty-second session of the Council of Trent in 1562 the Catholic Church decreed that bishops would have final authority over all of the hospitals in their diocese. This decision created an untenable situation for those localities that had a Protestant majority or significant minority. Bishops would be able to force hospitals to become more Catholic and to either shut out the Protestant sick or to be used as institutions of their conversion. The French crown attempted to solve this problem with the Edict of Moulins in 1566.[13] The edict outlined the kingdom's tradition that each locality was responsible for its own poor, reinforcing the earlier Edict of Orléans of 1561 that stated that hospitals should be managed by local lay elites. The central government attempted to tread a line between Counter-Reform activists and the Huguenots in 1579 with the Ordonnance of Blois, which again forbade the nomination of ecclesiastics to the administration of hospitals but allowed the establishment of new hospitals only with the approval of both the local bishop and the crown.[14] The crown's insistence to remain true to the traditions of the kingdom, even if it went against the wishes of the Catholic Church, would placate localities, it was hoped, by allowing majority populations (whether Catholic or Protestant) to keep control over poor relief. Protestant towns and cities would not be forced to allow hostile religious figures on to hospital boards.

Following Henri IV's succession to the throne and the religious settlement of the Edict of Nantes in 1598, the state turned its attention to defunct and ineffective hospitals as a source of income to supplement care for its own agents. The increased costs of the military forced the government to look for new revenues and to maximize the tax base. The income of defunct and corrupt hospitals caught the attention of the state. In 1606, it set up the Chambre de la Charité Chrestienne to divert these proceeds away from leper houses and poorly run hospitals to retired and incapacitated soldiers.[15] The Chambre was successful in securing places for ex-soldiers, but was largely stymied on legal grounds when it faced any local opposition to the transfer

---

13   The texts of the sixteenth-century royal edicts on hospitals used in this work come from the laws registered in the royal courts in Saint Brieuc, ADCA B24, and from seventeenth-century copies made by the governors of the Paris Hôpital Général, AAP HG 2. Edited copies of these edicts can also be found in Isambert, 1821–33.

14   Imbert, 1993, pp. 9–15.

15   The history of the campaign to transfer the revenues of defunct hospitals to army veterans is best covered by Hickey, 1997. Although the Chamber was renamed in 1612 by Louis XIII as the Chambre de la Réformation générale des hôpitaux, it continued to function in a similar manner.

of funds away from their original purpose.[16] The crown argued that the Chambre was part of its function to ensure that institutions lived up to their obligations. The Chambre was successful where there was a general agreement between locals and the government that the revenues of defunct hospitals could be put to better use.

As Daniel Hickey has shown, local hospital governors were successful in blocking attempts to close hospitals that were functioning well. As well, the state does not seem to have had much desire to close hospitals which did live up to their obligations. The problem of what to do with the income from estates and *rentes* left to institutions such as leper houses which no longer had a purpose remained unsolved throughout most of the century. Louvois, as Minister of War, established a systematic approach to divert these funds directly to army veterans. The income of defunct hospitals was seized and given to the religious Ordre de Notre Dame de Mont Carmel. Retired army officers would be made priors of the Order, enabling them to collect pensions. However, the scheme fell apart after Louvois' death and the revenues of the Order were granted to existing hospitals in 1698 in an effort to return charitable bequests to some purpose similar to their original aim.[17]

Royal policy toward the poor during the seventeenth century

Following the restoration of civil order in 1598, poor relief took on renewed interest among urban elites. Charity, poor relief and the poor became important issues during the seventeenth century for many in town governments who wished to eradicate the visible signs of poverty. To rehabilitate the sick poor, hospital boards undertook the medicalization of provincial hôtels dieu by securing visits from local medical men and, perhaps more importantly, by contracting the services of the new nursing orders in the wards.[18] With the founding of the Compagnie du Saint-Sacrement in 1629, periodic campaigns to spread the idea of confining the able-bodied poor took place in many urban centres. A number of hospitals of confinement were built in towns and cities during the first half of the century, although most urban centres found it either unnecessary or too expensive to do so. As well, most of the hospitals established in the period before 1662 confined only small numbers of the poor. Institutions built in the wealthiest urban centres, such as Paris or Lyon, wound up attracting the able-bodied poor from areas where little or no poor relief was available.

During the seventeenth century the crown hoped to maintain its traditional role in poor relief, but after 1656 it was called on several times by the Parisian elites to aid the survival of the capital's hospitals. The central government was first drawn into making a statement concerning reform of poor relief by the governors of the Paris hospitals in 1662. The urban elites of Paris had established an Hôpital Général to confine all categories of the deserving poor in 1656, but the number of poor who

---

16 Ibid., pp. 36–44.

17 Ibid., pp. 64–8.

18 For example, Nicolas Fouquet contracted the Soeurs de Charité to serve at the hospital at Belle-Isle-en-Mer in 1658, ADM 8Hs1. The medical skills of the new seventeenth-century nursing orders are discussed in Jones, 1989, pp. 89–205. See also Chapters 5 and 6 below pp. 122–3; 148–9.

would seek assistance had been underestimated in the initial planning and the famine crisis of 1662–63 had worsened overcrowding. The Paris hospital governors accused other nearby towns of limiting aid to their own poor and of encouraging many to seek relief in the capital. The royal edict issued in December 1662 was an attempt to force towns close to Paris to comply with the kingdom's tradition to care for their own poor. It allowed all towns and cities of the kingdom to levy local taxes in order to found new hôpitaux-généraux and the edict further ordered those localities which already had institutions of confinement to assist their native poor, preventing them from travelling to the capital. In 1662 the Parisian elites convinced the crown that the capital's hospitals would only survive if the theory of *enfermement* was fully implemented by building a confining hospital in each town and region:

> We [the king] have also granted the Paris Hôpital Général our protection, and privileged it with our grace and approved the economy that the directors of the institution shall have been able to bring there: what care they have taken to seek the means to make the hospital survive, both by the counsel that they have presented [to the crown] and by the public support that they have procured from the city's curés and preachers, by the memoirs that they have had printed several times concerning the hospital's finances and its needs, and by the collection drives made first in our Court and then amongst the population of Paris by charitable ladies of the highest quality. Nevertheless the number of beggars who have arrived from many provinces of our kingdom has become so great that, although the directors of the hospital have only half of the revenue which is required for the normal care of between four and five thousand poor that they have had in previous years, they now house and feed more than six thousand individuals in the five buildings of the hospital and they also give food to a further three thousand married poor in six locations throughout the city, and besides all these poor, one still sees a great number of beggars in the city who can be neither housed due to a lack of space in the hospital nor fed because the institution's income does not cover one-half of its expenses which are made for this purpose. This is why, considering that unless the hospital buildings and revenues are augmented it will be impossible without this hospital to either house or feed all of the beggars who beg in all parts of this good city, some of them through idleness, others from a lack of work and the majority of them by the great need which reigns in the countryside. And it is under these circumstances that the poor, both they themselves and their children, grow accustomed to this unhappy idleness which is the cause of all social disorders and moral corruption. It is why the wealth of our countryside lies, in part, abandoned since there are not enough people to carry out the necessary work. Beyond that, it is not just that our good city of Paris alone should furnish the assistance that the other towns and cities of our kingdom ought to provide for their own poor, according to natural law and conforming to the orders of our royal ancestors.[19]

The edict authorized the building of new hospitals, but nothing was done at the time by the central government to ensure that all towns and cities complied, because there seems to have been no true desire on its part to create more institutions which could fall into debt like the Parisian Hôpital Général. The terms of the new law covered the whole kingdom because, while the hospital governors and the Parlement worried most about the towns and cities nearest Paris, the numbers of poor from all

---

19 AAP HG 2.

regions (and from other countries as well) had grown during the 1662 famine. While some French towns took advantage of the ability to raise taxes in order to build new hospitals or to convert old ones, many of the hôpitaux généraux built during the reign of Louis XIV were a result of the Jesuit order's campaigns of the 1670s and 1680s to spread the policy of confinement.

Beginning in 1670, the Jesuits took over from the disbanded Parisian chapter of the Compagnie du Saint-Sacrement in petitioning provincial towns to establish general hospitals.[20] This renewed campaign was undertaken by three priests: Calloet Querbrat, Honoré Chaurand and André Guévarre. These men have been described as royal agents;[21] however, they operated as independents with the king offering them inexpensive favour by being named as their patron. Querbrat and a committee composed of members of the Parisian hospital boards co-ordinated the activities of Chaurand and Guévarre in the provinces.[22] Querbrat explained in a letter to the bishop of Tréguier that the governors of the Paris Hôpital Général were the force behind the Edict of 1662 and the crown's subsequent reminders to provincial towns in 1670 and 1676 that each locality was supposed to look after its own poor.[23] Querbrat's group entered into an easy alliance with the governors of the Paris hospital because both sides greatly desired every town in the kingdom to build a confinement hospital. The hospital governors, believing that Paris was providing assistance to more than its fair share, believed that it was necessary for every locality to confine its poor. They hoped that if the Jesuits were successful in establishing new confinement hospitals, it would help to alleviate the financial difficulties of the Paris hospitals by lessening the numbers of poor they were forced to assist. The Jesuits believed that the general hospital offered the ideal place to conduct missions among the poor. The religious reform of the poor into good Catholics could be observed and enforced within the walls of the institution. The Jesuits acted as advocates and consultants, targeting towns likely to effect reforms and advising them as to the best way to proceed. However, in many cases the reforms amounted to little more than enlargement of existing hospitals or the foundation of small general hospitals with limited resources.[24] The hôpitaux généraux established conformed more to local needs and wants rather than to a theory of total *enfermement* favoured by the Parisian elites or the Jesuits. For example, Chaurand found that the town of Lamballe in Brittany was willing to establish a confinement hospital within its hospital for the sick poor, but no revenues were set aside to pay for it. Few beyond those poor of extreme age were

---

20 The Jesuit campaign can best be followed in Paultre, 1906. Hickey, 1997 also gives a good account of their efforts.

21 Brockliss and Jones, 1997, pp. 679–81.

22 The composition of the committee is found in Boislisle, 1881, pp. 415–17. All of the members besides Querbrat were directors of the Paris Hôpital Général.

23 ADCA G199.

24 ADF 5H89. Quimperlé in Brittany transformed its town orphanage into a general hospital on the advice of Chaurand in 1679 in order to make the hospital exempt from royal taxation. Besides issuing a proclamation outlawing beggars from the town, the new general hospital functioned exactly as before.

ever sheltered at the new hospital and it eventually merged with the town's Hôtel Dieu and ceased to care for the able-bodied poor.[25]

Royal paternalism

In their private lives, seventeenth-century royal ministers seem to have favoured the reform of poor relief and encouraged localities to make such systems more efficient. However, as agents of the crown they did not wish to assume the authority for managing poor relief or to encourage the creation of new institutions that could divert limited resources away from the crown's coffers. The preferred solution to vagabonds throughout Europe in the seventeenth century was to provide a harsh alternative to employment.[26] The idea that the able-bodied poor would return to useful employment if the alternatives to an honest life were harsh continued throughout the early modern period. Jean Baptiste Colbert, as Controlleur Général des Finances, was greatly influenced by mercantilist economists who stressed that the poor were an untapped source of wealth. Colbert attempted widespread reforms to the economy of the kingdom in an effort to maximize its tax base, and he seems to have believed that institutions of confinement were the best method to cure the poor of their idleness because they offered a way to instruct them in an environment away from the corrupting influence of the world outside. In such places the behaviour of the poor could be corrected by forcing them to work and pray, and their progress towards productivity constantly observed. However, beyond cajoling towns to comply with the Edict of 1662, he offered no material support. In 1670, he even reduced the incentives that the edict had offered for the establishment of new hospitals by removing the right of towns to levy local taxes to raise capital or to provide a steady annual income.[27] From that year on, hospitals were supposed to be financed strictly through charity so that they would not compete with the crown's sources of income. For example, Colbert approved of the decision of the *maire* and *échevins* of Chaumont-en-Bassigny, in January 1672 to lock up the able-bodied poor in the Hôtel Dieu of the town, providing work and instruction for them, because there was nothing better: 'to banish laziness and idle ways from among the people'.[28] However, no government funds were forthcoming to assist them. Colbert even hindered the foundation of general hospitals when they conflicted with the crown's interests. In 1679 he wrote an angry letter to the Intendant of Languedoc, Daguesseau, forbidding the town of Mende from building a new hospital unless it raised the capital through charitable means instead of impositions on the community.[29]

---

25 ADCA H Dépôt 1/4. In 1699 when local crops failed and the town council complained about the growth in numbers of the poor, the hospital housed only 11 men and 21 women.

26 B. Pullan, 'Catholics and the poor in early modern Europe,' in Pullan, 1994, pp. 15–19. Pullan demonstrates that this crossed confessional boundaries, creating more similarities between the ideas behind poor relief than differences between Catholic and Protestants.

27 The letters sent to the bishops at the bequest of the Jesuits and Paris hospital governors by Colbert in 1670 and 1676 can be found in ADG HG 2 and ADCA G199.

28 Colbert, 1861–73, tom. II, p. 656.

29 Depping, 1850, tom. I, p. 876.

While believing in the seventeenth-century orthodoxy that poverty was a result of faults within the individual, government authorities could also understand that short-term poverty could be caused by factors beyond the control of the people. Colbert, for example, was willing to concede that taxation could be too high for some to pay, reducing their families to poverty. He wrote to the Intendant of Tours in reply to the imprisonment of men who had been condemned for their failure to pay taxes, explaining that: 'the imprisonment of a man takes away from him the means to work and to feed his family who will undoubtedly resort to begging.'[30] Such matters ought to be dealt with by correcting the problem that affected the area. Colbert wrote to the Intendant of Alençon in 1682:

> you must examine with care from what origins this poverty comes so that you can then seek out the means to lessen it, either by the lowering of the *tailles,* by redistributing on to the other better-off *élections* that which you retrench on the poor, or by providing for the people the means of earning a living, or by examining whether their poverty comes from a natural idleness, because, in this last case, they do not merit much in the way of assistance.[31]

Neither royal ministers nor local elites could come to terms with the existence of able-bodied beggars in periods of peace and economic strength. They did not believe that men could be unemployed during such periods. Crown officials, as did local elites, tried to appear caring towards the poor, expressing a desire to save them from their idleness. Colbert, in March 1669, wrote to the Bishop of Chalon-sur-Saône that the founding of an hôpital général would enable the town to 'pull the poor from their idleness and give them the means to earn a living'.[32] However, the personal beliefs of a minister such as Colbert did not mean that the royal prerogative was extended to include social welfare programmes. The seventeenth-century state, even at its most robust under Louis XIV, lacked the apparatus to force unwanted reforms on localities. In order to secure its desires on pressing concerns, such as financing wars and diplomatic initiatives, the crown traded favours with local elites, supporting their needs in return for deference in matters of the royal prerogative.[33]

French monarchs personally offered little material support for poor relief institutions. Marie de Médicis gave her name as patroness of the Hôpital de la Pitié in Paris as a way to show her favour and to increase her own prestige among the Parisian elites. Louis XIV, as well, was named as patron of the Parisian hospitals for similar reasons.[34] He also seems to have enjoyed the ceremonial demonstrations of charitable giving such patronage allowed. However, his only direct responsibility in social welfare was in providing for retired and incapacitated soldiers. The Invalides was founded both as a means of expressing the glory and status of the king and a recognition of his obligations to the subjects who had risked their lives for him. The

---

30 Colbert, 1861–73, tom. II, p. 137.

31 Ibid., tom. II, pp. 208–209.

32 Ibid., tom. IV, pp. 45–6.

33 See Beik, 1985; Kettering, 1986; Mettam, 1988 and Collins, 1995 for the weaknesses of the absolute monarchy.

34 Brièle, 1888, p. 253.

aim of the Invalides was to care for the veterans of the wars of Louis XIV and to prepare them for a Christian death and salvation. André Corvisier argues that 'Louis XIV was preoccupied with the idea of assuring his veterans and his crippled soldiers that he would grant them all the means necessary for a decent retirement and a pious old age.'[35] The king was concerned for the final salvation of his valued servants, ensuring that the religious life of the pensioners was strictly regulated. In May 1675 a contract was signed between Charles-Maurice Le Tellier, the Archbishop of Reims, and Edmé Jolly, the supérieur général de la congrégation de la mission, to provide priests to give religious instruction to the men in the Invalides. Mass was said in the soldiers' chapel and confessions taken on Sundays. Care was taken that religious festivals were celebrated with proper decorum and attention paid to the details of rituals. Books of piety were often distributed in the Hôtel. The Invalides, in the years immediately before the Revocation of the Edict of Nantes, even became a weapon in the arsenal of the Counter-Reformation. Its charter allowed for the admission of Protestant veterans if they converted and remained Catholic.[36] Louis XIV made a striking but nevertheless symbolic gesture to his troops because the Invalides could provide assistance for only a fraction of those who had given him their service. However, the history of the hospital demonstrates the inability of the state to compel cities to act against their own interests. The Paris Invalides was meant to be a showcase copied in every provincial capital, but none were ever built outside the capital.

Plans for reform at the end of the seventeenth century

By the 1690s the directors of the Paris hospitals were still unhappy with the assistance given to them by the crown. They urged the central government to take a greater interest in matters of poor relief and to force towns and cities to reform their systems of assistance to conform with *enfermement*. The crown responded in 1699 with a call for the localities to imprison all of their poor, but doing little beyond granting tax breaks to those who returned to the countryside.[37] The calls made by the Parisian elites for the state to take more direct action in the area of poor relief were being echoed by those aristocratic reformers who believed the state had drifted away from its traditions. The last decades of the reign of Louis XIV were dominated by long wars. The effects of the king's foreign policies on the domestic situation of the kingdom led some to call for reform. A group of aristocratic writers centred in the entourage of Louis XIV's grandson, the duc de Bourgogne, called for a return to a society based on traditional values. These writers believed that the long-drawn-out wars fought against most of Europe had forced the king to turn away from his policy to maintain the traditional aristocratic nature of society. The abbé de Fénelon wrote

---

35 Corvisier, 1983, p. 216.

36 Ibid., pp. 217–18. Although its charter contained this qualification for admission to the wards, Louvois as Minister for War understood how heavily the army relied on Protestants for service. While maintaining a scrupulous watch on all other aspects of the institution, he does not seem to have investigated if Protestant soldiers in the Invalides attended mass.

37 *Code de l'Hôpital Général*, pp. 436–8.

that the king had been forced to turn the government over to unscrupulous ministers in order to pursue his goals:

> For the last thirty years your chief ministers have burnt and overthrown all of the ancient principles of the state so that they could raise your own authority to its maximum. That authority has become their own because it is exercised by them.[38]

The comte de Boulainvilliers echoed this idea, arguing that the whole social order had been corrupted from the top down because the natural elite of the kingdom, the nobility, had been constrained from providing a proper model for the lower orders. The crown had been forced to grant social and economic privileges to financiers in return for loans to keep the kingdom at war. Members of the *noblesse d'épée* could understand the granting of honours to subjects who showed exceptional valour in the service of the king, but they resented any attempt by financiers to claim noble status. Boulainvilliers argued that financiers' social success inspired otherwise productive groups to abandon commerce, manufacture and agriculture to participate in moneylending and speculation on the value of venal offices.[39]

The direct consequence of the king pursuing policies that were not in the best interests of the country and, to pay for them, allowing those not born to true nobility to manage the affairs of France, was the creation of widespread poverty:

> Instead of taking money from these poor wretches, it would be better to give them charity and to feed them. All of France has become nothing more than a great hospital left abandoned and without provisions ... if the king ... had the heart of a father to his people would he not rather put aside his own glory in order to give them bread and to let them rest after so much evil has befallen them than to hold on to some frontier towns which were the cause of the war?[40]

The idea that only the nobility truly understood the responsibility to care for the poor was repeated toward the end of Louis XIV's reign to inspire calls for social reform. The poverty of the realm was cited by reformers as evidence that the kingdom had been diverted from its traditions. Fénelon believed the origins and form of society were the product of God's will. He argued that God had created certain natural laws which had shaped the development of the kingdom and that civil laws had been constructed by men in order to force society to conform to His will.[41] Change itself was not wrong, if it helped society to conform in a better way to natural law, but when the system was changed in a radical manner, upsetting the natural order of things, society became corrupted. He believed that allowing social inferiors, who did not recognize the responsibilities that came with power, to rise to positions of importance had proved a disaster for France. He argued that the kingdom desperately needed social and constitutional reform to return to health. His planned reforms were not intended to be a return to a mythologized past that had been subverted for

---

38   Salignac de La Mothe-Fénelon, 1920, pp. 144–5.
39   Boulainvilliers, 1727, tom. I, pp. 13–16.
40   Salignac de La Mothe-Fénelon, 1920, pp. 150–51.
41   Ibid., p.92.

reasons of fiscal expediency, but the restoration of the aristocracy to an active role in a modern system of government.

The circle of writers around the duc de Bourgogne did not expect to bring about change during the reign of Louis XIV. They concentrated their efforts in convincing the eventual heir to the throne of the usefulness of their ideas. Fénelon's *Examen de conscience sur les devoirs de la royauté* was written in the form of a secular catechism to remind the future king of his duties, of which his responsibility to look after the welfare of his subjects was the most important. A good king ruled within traditional boundaries, without treading on the customary rights of his subjects:

> The study of history, the conduct and all of the detail of the ancient form of the government should not be regarded as an indifferent curiosity but rather as an essential duty of the king.[42]

For the duc de Bourgogne to understand properly his future duties as king, it was necessary for him to be taught everything about his kingdom. Besides material matters such as population and economic statistics, which the reformers felt were important, matters of the various rights and customs of the localities and orders in society were considered essential.[43] It was for this reason that Boulainvilliers compiled his *Etat de la France* in 1698, using reports made specifically for the education of the duc by the Intendants throughout the kingdom. In the paternalist hierarchy that Fénelon envisaged, the role of the king would be as a father and a guide to his people:

> He should work to make them just, wise and happy. He must believe that he only does his duty when he is, shepherd's crook in his hand, leading his flock to graze away from the gaze of the wolf. He should only believe that his people are well governed when all of them work, are fed and obey the laws.[44]

Boulainvilliers agreed with this sentiment: 'the king is the father of his subjects, and in this quality His Majesty is obliged to ensure their subsistence.'[45] The relationship of the king with his subjects reflected that between a father and his children. The subject was required to give obedience to the sovereign, but in return he expected that his interests would be protected. In essence, there were few differences between this concept of paternalism and the tradition represented by the writings of the duc de Luynes in the 1650s. The reformers believed that only by teaching the heir to the throne his duties would he be able to guard the welfare of his subjects.

The reformers did not believe that a properly educated king was enough to end the problems of the kingdom. They possessed a vision of France ruled by a king and the nobility in tandem, extending a paternalistic protection to their subjects. To set society back on the proper footing, they proposed to restore the finances of the crown to their traditional roots. They wished the king to contain his authority within his recognized prerogatives: leadership in war and foreign affairs. At the top the

---

42   Ibid., p. 35.
43   Ibid., pp. 36–7.
44   Ibid., p. 164.
45   Boulainvilliers, 1727, tom. I, p. 70.

king would be required to maintain himself and his government from the income of the royal domains, except in times of emergency. When a crisis that threatened the welfare of his subjects arose, the king would be able to request new taxation from the population via the mechanism of an Etats-Généraux.[46] Each province of the kingdom would have its own Etats to look after its interests as well as defending it from interference from the centre. The military nobility would resume its rightful place as the primary servants of the king, displacing the grasping social climbers whose cupidity had created the problems of the kingdom.[47] The reformers advocated a novel idea to secure the position of the nobility in both status and in wealth. It would be allowed to assume a role as leader in commerce as well by being permitted to participate openly in trade, a role which would assure that its place at the top of the social ladder would be unchallenged by rich bourgeois. The reformers of the early eighteenth century believed that with the *noblesse d'épée* – men born to wield authority – restored to its traditional place in society, with its customary privileges defended from encroachment, the kingdom would be restored to health.

The proposed reforms were not a self-interested attempt by the nobility to have all the privileges it claimed without assuming its traditional responsibilities. The fact that the burden of taxation in the country fell heaviest on the part of society least able to pay was recognized by the writers of Bourgogne circle. They wished to see a fundamental reform of the tax system, shifting the weight of the *taille* off the poorer elements. This idea was not new. A similar reform had been proposed in the sixteenth century.[48] However, the advocates of reform planned a novel change to the way in which poor relief was handled in the localities. Boulainvilliers recommended the establishment of a new method to prevent both widespread and long-term poverty. His plan was to create agencies at both national and local levels to help stimulate manufacture, agriculture and trade. The central and local governments would intervene in the economy in order to maintain full employment, ensuring that only those who really deserved help would receive it.[49] His desire to abolish the idleness of the labourers of the kingdom was as passionate as that of Jean-Baptiste Colbert. Colbert, however, had wished to increase the productivity of the kingdom in order to augment the tax base, while Boulainvilliers' intention was to increase overall wealth.

The reformers wished to end poverty, regarding the poor as children who suffered because of their ignorance or moral weakness. They felt that the poor had to be kept at work to be prevented from falling into their natural idleness, their children given a rudimentary education and a skill. Boulainvilliers believed that many workers became poor because their lack of education prevented them for preparing for bad times:

These common people are like the soldier who eats everything and who saves nothing of his pay. Now from the soldier's pay we hold back the costs of his clothing and his

46 Ibid., p. 8; Salignac de La Mothe-Fénelon, 1920, pp. 47–8.

47 Rothkrug, 1965, p. 278.

48 Ibid., pp. 135–8. Rothkrug cites the influence of sixteenth-century authors such as Jean Bodin on the tax-reform plans of the Bourgogne circle.

49 Boulainvilliers, 1727, tom. I, p. 62.

weapons, and he does not think about these matters only being concerned with the little that is remaining to him. It is the same for the journeyman artisan: As soon as he receives his daily wage or the payment for what he has made, he will go spend it in the cabaret and he will have scarcely enough left to support his family. Thus it is difficult to make this type of person pay the least amount of taxation. Instead of this situation we should hold back a part of his daily wages or *sales* both to pay his taxes and to provide for his children's education, and to assist him and his family during the sicknesses that befall them. It is certain that none of these men could be opposed to this plan.[50]

Because Boulainvilliers shared this opinion of the moral weakness of the poor with most other members of the elites of the kingdom during the early modern period, he called for the leadership of the crown in assisting them.

Those of the Bourgogne circle did not criticize the crown for overstepping its bounds with the Edict of 1662, but for not going far enough to ensure that each locality took care of its own poor. Boulainvilliers planned to rationalize the distribution of poor relief throughout the kingdom. While he advocated a reform which would convince local authorities to comply with crown regulations, his plan confirmed their traditional authority over the distribution of poor relief. Each parish would be required to build and administer a *bourse commune* which would act as workhouse, hospital and vocational school.[51] Local labourers would then register to receive the benefits of the *bourse*, namely becoming exempt from the *taille*, receiving an education for their children up to the age of ten and assurance of care should they fall sick. These benefits would be paid for by diverting a small portion of each man's income to a welfare fund. The primary goal of the plan was to limit the expenditures of the *bourse* by keeping the population at work. The local authorities would have the responsibility to ensure that the poor were kept employed:

> The council and executive of each parish, or the people proposed to make up the *bourse*, will take care that those who will be inscribed in the book of the Commissaire Inspecteur will have work and will be employed in preference to those who are not so registered. They will ensure that none of the residents, nor anyone else, beg for a living and if there is someone engaged in that idle life, they will have him arrested and sent to prison. To do this the Prévôts and Officers of Justice will be ordered to assist the *bourse* without charge.[52]

Boulainvilliers believed that the utility of his project would become self-evident to the lower orders. Since the worker paid into the scheme a set percentage of his earnings, there was no disincentive to earning more, nor were those who earned little punished. He felt that the benefits to the poor would make the *bourses* a popular institution. He believed that the crown would benefit from the scheme for several reasons. Full employment was thought by most to be a guarantee of a stable society. By teaching poor children a skill, he thought the *bourses* would offer a way to break the circle of destitution that afflicted their parents. The localities would benefit financially by taxing the *bourses* on their profits. Perhaps most importantly, the crown would be able to ensure that there would be an efficient system of poor relief

---

50 Ibid., tom. I, pp. 63–4.
51 Ibid., pp. 65–6.
52 Ibid., pp. 68–9.

in small towns and the countryside, dissuading the poor from taking to the roads and flocking in great numbers to larger towns.

Charitable works were not excluded from this plan. Although the reformers seem to have been hostile to some of the great schemes of the reign, local elites, especially seigneurs in rural parishes, would be encouraged to demonstrate their status in society by contributing gifts to the *bourses*. [53] The system might provide for the working poor of each parish, but there was still an obligation for the nobility to care for those who had nobody to support them. Besides the need of the poor, there remained a desire on the part of the nobility to demonstrate their virtues by means of charitable gifts.

Boulainvilliers' proposals were never implemented. However, the combination of pressure from urban elites seeking state assistance in financing hospitals added to aristocratic calls for the king to act according to paternalist principles led to a change in government policy during the minority of Louis XV. For the first time the state would take the initiative in implementing poor relief. Although the *bourses communes* were not to be built, the central government took to heart the duc de Bourgogne circle's ideas about an informed and planned reform. Following the example of the *Etat de la France* of 1698, the Intendants in the provinces were asked to make an inquiry into the size and condition of the kingdom's hospitals. With the Edict of 1724 putting the *Grand Renfermement* into motion, towns and cities were compelled to provide space for the sick poor in hôtels dieu and to confine the able-bodied poor in general hospitals. The innovation of the new policy was that the crown would pay the extra costs involved with imprisoning greater numbers of the poor. However, the project failed as the price of confinement exceeded even the most pessimistic estimates and the crown ceased payments to hospitals by the early 1730s.[54]

The state did not take an active lead in the reform of poor relief in the seventeenth century. The crown's position on poor relief had developed during the medieval period. Poor relief was the responsibility of the localities. The central government acted as a moderator between different towns only when it became necessary to force a locality to live up to its obligations. The administration of poor relief and the form it took was left up to individual towns and cities. While secular elites in many towns took control over hospitals and other social welfare institutions, they did so on their own initiative and, as much of the municipalization of the kingdom's hospitals was accomplished well before the Edicts of Orléans and Moulins, they did so without any real assistance from the state.

Although many attempts were made by various governments to reform the economy of France in the seventeenth century, the position of the crown in regard to the poor remained largely unchanged during the period. Important reforms were made to hospitals and to the services they provided to their communities. Over the

---

53 Salignac de La Mothe-Fénelon, 1920, p. 100. Fénelon was opposed to using the Invalides to house wounded soldiers, preferring to provide small pensions to each veteran in his own village as a reward for his services.

54 ADIV C1285–90.

course of the century hospitals for the sick poor gained medical practitioners in the form of nursing orders of nuns and professional medical men, such as surgeons and physicians, in some cases. Poor relief to the able-bodied poor became institutionalized in hôpitaux généraux in many towns and cities. While ministers such as Colbert might privately concur with these changes, they did not move to increase the scope of the royal prerogatives to include social welfare. The state did little to assist locals to effect these reforms beyond lending its name to the attempts to spread the idea of confinement by the Parisian elites and the Jesuit Order.

Although the central government did not take over responsibility for poor relief, the seeds of change were sown. Calls for more crown involvement by the elites of Paris who governed the capital's hospitals were echoed by an aristocratic critique of the king's lack of paternalist leadership. Change would come in the eighteenth century as the crown began to recognize that it could emphasize its own leadership at a national level through the provision of poor relief.

Chapter Three

The Reform of the Paris Hôtel Dieu

During the early modern period, Paris possessed the largest hospital for the treatment of the sick poor in France. Over the course of the sixteenth and seventeenth centuries, the institution remodelled its medieval wards, doubled in size and built new satellite hospitals to isolate victims of epidemic disease and to provide care for the incurable. Importantly, during the same period, the hospital for the first time created permanent paid positions for both physicians and surgeons. By the end of Louis XIV's reign the Paris Hôtel Dieu had the largest medical staff in the kingdom and had transformed itself from an institution that provided food and shelter into one which provided the charitable services of physicians and surgeons to the sick poor.

At the beginning of the twentieth century, Marcel Fosseyeux examined the history of the Hôtel Dieu during the seventeenth and eighteenth centuries. He viewed the hospital administration in that period as a conservative group who tried to maintain the essentially religious quality of the medieval institution. While Fosseyeux cites the increase of the medical staff during this period, he does not examine why the number of practitioners grew.[1] Beginning in the 1960s, historians such as Michel Foucault, David Vess, and John Frangos, whose works have centred on the thesis that the origins of the modern medical hospital lay in the French Revolution and the opportunities for change that a break with the past brought, continued to see the Paris Hôtel Dieu as a medieval institution. In their opinion its primary aim was to shelter the sick poor, a role which remained largely unchanged throughout the early modern period.[2] They argue that the hospital at this time was more concerned with religious obligations and poor relief then medical services. In regard to the Paris Hôtel Dieu before the late eighteenth century, all contend that the hospital was more preoccupied with providing the sick poor with religious training and a good death than in healing them.

Historians who have studied French provincial hospitals have, since the 1980s, raised questions about the veracity of the revolutionary model of hospital medicalization. The work of Colin Jones, in particular, has done much to debunk the 'black legend' of early modern French hospitals.[3] As Jones has claimed, there was more medical treatment at provincial hospitals aimed at the healing of the sick and

---

1   Fosseyeux, 1912, pp. 1–93.

2   Most notable among those who advocate revolutionary change to hospitals at the end of the eighteenth century are: Foucault, 1973; Frangos, 1997; Vess, 1974. Frangos argues that hospitals in Paris functioned to separate the sick poor from the rest of society, not to cure them, p. 17.

3   See, for example, Jones, 1989, Brockliss and Jones, 1997. Other studies of provincial hospitals in France include: Gutton, 1970; Fairchilds, 1976; Norberg, 1985. The 'Revolutionary

injured than had previously been suspected. However, despite evidence that French hospitals of the seventeenth and eighteenth centuries were, at least in part, houses of healing, the Paris Hôtel Dieu remains tarred by this 'black legend.'[4]

Toby Gelfand, in his examination of eighteenth century surgeons in Paris, argues that there were two major stages of change in the practice of surgery. Firstly, he suggests that there was a consolidation and strengthening of the surgical guild after 1660 and a subsequent separation of surgeons from barbers. Secondly, Gelfand believes that the Paris surgical guild was transformed between 1715 and 1750 into a monarchical profession tied to the central government under the authority of the king's premier surgeon. As a result of this, Gelfand argues that Paris surgeons became independent of the conservative medical faculty and sees the Paris Hôtel Dieu before the Revolution as a place of employment for surgeons, but largely unimportant in the development of the profession.[5]

During the 1990s, several studies on the motivations and expectations of the patrons and governors of early modern European hospitals have highlighted the importance placed on these institutions.[6] In particular, hospitals were used by urban elites not only to provide charitable relief and retraining for the poor, but also to boost the social prestige of their families and exert control over the lower orders of society.[7] Society in early modern Europe was hierarchical in nature. While few questioned the validity of the existing order, social and political power was not held by the elites solely through the use of force (although, at times of crisis, force would indeed be used). For the most part, power was exercised through coercion of interests from the highest ranks down the social ladder. The hierarchy relied on a negotiation for control in a deferential society. The lower ranks gave political and social deference to the upper in return for material benefit. In early modern Paris, as in other urban communities, one of these material benefits came in the form of charitable assistance at the city's hospitals.

An important method of assistance chosen by the patrons and governors of the Paris Hôtel Dieu after 1500 was to increase the number of medical services offered to the population of the city. Foremost among the reforms initiated by the hospital directors was the introduction of professional medical men to the staff and the eventual increase in their numbers over the course of the sixteenth and seventeenth centuries. Beyond the introduction and increase in numbers of professional medical men, the institution's governors sought to maintain the hospital's reputation and strove to keep the quality of care high (often coming into conflict with the interests of the medical practitioners themselves) according to the standards of the day. By fulfilling their social ambitions, the governors of the Paris Hôtel Dieu helped to change the expectation of what a hospital was supposed to be. Through a series of

---

thesis' of the rise of the clinic is challenged by historians who have studied developments in hospitals outside France. See Risse, 1986 and Risse, 1999.

4   Jones, 1989, p. 49.

5   Gelfand, 1980, pp. 6–31.

6   Cavallo, 1995; Hickey, 1997.

7   Ibid. and S. Cavallo, 'The Motivations of Benefactors, An Overview of Approaches to the Study of Charity' in Barry and Jones, 1991.

reforms to the hospital, they altered the goal of the institution from a place of shelter for the sick poor to a place in which medical services well beyond the means of many Parisians were to be found.

The hospital governors

From the introduction of written regulations for its governance in 1168 to the beginning of the sixteenth century, the Hôtel Dieu was a religious establishment administered by the cathedral chapter of the diocese of Paris.[8] For some time before 1500, wealthy laymen of Paris had given donations and bequests to the hospital to fulfil their religious obligations towards the poor. A disregard for the conditions placed on the Hôtel Dieu by its benefactors, however, led to secularization in the late fifteenth and early sixteenth centuries. The Parlement of Paris, the most prestigious law court in the kingdom, was shocked to receive complaints that travelling and convalescent clerics were taking up beds which should have been reserved for the sick poor. The judges claimed the right to enforce the terms of wills, many of which had been left by families of members of the sovereign courts of the city.[9] A dispute between the chapter of Paris and the Parlement developed over calls to reform the administration of the Hôtel Dieu, allowing the court to accuse the canon administrators of mismanaging the finances of the institution.[10] When the ecclesiastical administration of the Hôtel Dieu became divided over a crisis in the hospital's finances at the end of the fifteenth century, it was forced to turn to the Parlement and the city of Paris for assistance. To ensure the survival of the institution, the cathedral canons, as governors of the hospital, themselves asked the Parlement to take the task of reform in hand.[11]

After 1505, elite groups in the city, judges and lawyers of the sovereign courts and *échevins* and bourgeois of the municipality assumed the leadership of the administration.[12] These secular elites of Paris, which comprised the city's ruling classes during the early modern period, managed the institution unchallenged, remaining concerned to keep services and standards high in order to maximize their own social profits from their association with the hospital. The Parlement reserved the right to approve both the nominations of board members as well as to audit the expenses of the hospital. Furthermore, the Premier Président of the Parlement became, from 1505 to 1690, the de facto chairman of the administration. Although the spiritual side of the institution continued to be managed by the cathedral chapter of Paris, the religious took a secondary role to that of the secular board. The appointment of

---

8   Imbert, 1996, p. 9. AN K1024/5.

9   The Parisian sovereign courts held jurisdiction over roughly two-thirds of France. They included the Parlement of Paris, the Cour des Aides and the Chambre des Comptes.

10   AAP HD 864.

11   Imbert, 1993, pp. 9–13.

12   The term bourgeois here is used in its early modern definition of a non-noble citizen of the city living 'nobly' (that is, from investments in the city's *rentes* or land) and who had bought the title of bourgeois of Paris.

candidates to fill vacant positions among the clergy would henceforth be confirmed by hospital governors.

The secularization of the administration of the Hôtel Dieu by members of the Parisian sovereign courts took place concurrently with the establishment of the principle of venality for offices in those courts. While sovereign courts had been created by the crown during the Middle Ages, it was in the late fifteenth century and early sixteenth century that these judgeships fell firmly into private ownership.[13] The sale and purchase of office helped to establish the holders of these posts as a ruling class in the city of Paris. In the early modern period, the Parlement took a more direct role in the government of the capital, assuming control over municipal poor relief.[14] As the sovereign courts assumed great political power in Paris, the judges also increased their social prestige. With the introduction of the *paulette* tax in 1604 and the coalescence of a judicial nobility during the seventeenth century, the office of judge in the sovereign courts developed into a highly placed rung on the social ladder. Some families, such as the Colberts, the Le Telliers and the Lamoignons who achieved noble rank in this manner could go on to achieve even higher rank by using their positions in the sovereign courts to bring themselves to the notice of the crown. Thus these offices attracted candidates from a pool of dynastically ambitious bourgeois families who wished to legitimize money often made through socially unacceptable means such as trade or finance.[15] One way to do so was through patronage of or service at the Hôtel Dieu in order to prove family worth.

The board of the Hôtel Dieu changed little in form and function after its reform in 1505 until 1690. The board of directors was made up of eight members, all laymen by statute, and it selected its own members to serve for life. The Premier Président of the Parlement of Paris and the Premier Président of the Cour des Aides traditionally formed an unwritten upper echelon at the head of the board. There was no regulation stipulating that these judges be granted a place on the board until an administrative reform in 1690. However, the new Premiers Présidents were always invited by the board of the Hôtel Dieu to replace the old. The traditional inclusion of the Premier Président of the Parlement in the administration reflected the fact that, in the early modern period, the court increasingly assumed many of the responsibilities for governing the city and claimed authority over the management of the hospital in 1505.[16] The role which the Parlement played in the administration of the Hôtel Dieu was in accordance with the social position of the judges as the highest ranking office-holders of the city. The members of the sovereign courts might, in theory, have held their offices from the crown, but in relation to the hospital board they held their places because they were the most influential citizens in Paris. The remaining members of the board were all recruited from a pool of judges of the sovereign courts and worthy bourgeois of the city. The board of directors of the Hôtel Dieu increased in number from eight to fourteen in 1655 on its own authority because it

13   Shennan, 1968, pp. 116–18.
14   See Chapter 4, pp. 83–8.
15   See Dent, 1973.
16   AAP HD 864.

felt that, as the institution had grown in size, the responsibilities of administration required more attention.[17]

During the course of the seventeenth century, the hospital came to rely more heavily on local taxes and, in 1690, the board of directors felt a need to expand its size again in order to grant a voice in its administration to a larger portion of the city's ruling elite. The new administration was headed by an upper echelon of senior directors, composed of the Premiers Présidents of all of the Parisian sovereign courts and, for the first time, the archbishop of Paris. A lower tier, made of those lesser-ranked members, mostly judges of the sovereign courts and wealthy bourgeois of the city, was established to take care of the daily management of the hospital. These board members took their positions seriously, seldom missing the twice weekly meetings and personally inspecting the wards on a regular basis.[18]

Early modern Parisian elites, the holders of venal office and their bourgeois allies, saw in the physical embodiment of charitable institutions a way to stamp their familial and individual ambitions on the fabric of Paris. In the sixteenth and seventeenth centuries, the administration dramatically increased the size of the Hôtel Dieu in a series of building projects. The original fabric of the hospital, built between the twelfth and fifteenth centuries on the south side of the Ile-de-la-Cité, was enlarged during the middle decades of the sixteenth century in order to increase the number of sick poor who could be accommodated. The new wards extended from the Petit-Pont to the future site of the Pont-au-Double. In the seventeenth century, the hospital expanded to the left bank of the Seine, raising funds to build the Pont-au-Double itself during the period 1628 to 1632 to house more wards along the new bridge. Building commenced again in 1651, when two new large wards, the salle Saint-Charles and the salle Saint-Jacques, were built along the left bank of the Seine from the Pont-au-Double westward to a point halfway to the Petit-Pont. The completion of the wards on the left bank up to the Petit Châtelet was planned during the later decades of the seventeenth century, but was not undertaken until 1714 due to financial constraints during the reign of Louis XIV.[19] These building projects allowed ample space for the display of patrons' familial emblems and devices within the hospital wards.[20] Likewise, the increased number of sick poor sheltered and treated at the hospital created opportunities for more direct influence over them through the endowment of wards or individual beds that carried the obligation for patients to say prayers for the souls of benefactors.[21] Ambitious families from both the Robe (such as the Lamoignon, Harlay, Le Tellier and Nicolai) as well as the Sword (such as the duchesse de Guise and the prince d'Harcourt) associated themselves with

---

17 AAP HD 1438/22. The registers containing the minutes of the board of directors of the Paris Hôtel Dieu during the sixteenth and seventeenth centuries are contained in series 1438 and are invaluable for the study of the hospital. An edited version of the registers is also found in Brièle, 1881, tom. I.

18 Fosseyeux, 1912, pp. 66–70.

19 *Les hôpitaux disparus,* 1912.

20 Fosseyeux, 1912, pp. 315–16.

21 Fosseyeux, 1912, pp. 315–16, AAP HD 1414 and Brièle, 1866–82, pp. 340–53.

the hospital and its goals by leaving substantial donations in their final wills and ensuring that their gifts were made known to the public.[22]

Physicians at the Hôtel Dieu

Prior to the secularization of the Hôtel Dieu, the hospital had offered some medical provision to the sick poor in Paris through the service of its resident monks and nuns. This staff functioned as a group of irregular practitioners, providing medical and surgical services alongside their role as givers of spiritual comfort and instruction.[23] This religious staff at the Hôtel Dieu did not disappear with the secularization of the hospital administration. A staff of over 80 religious, composed of Augustinian monks and nuns, served day and night on the wards. However, their functions as autonomous medical practitioners were restricted as learned physicians assumed control over the medical affairs of the hospital during the sixteenth and seventeenth centuries.[24]

The introduction of medical men into the routine of the Hôtel Dieu dates from 1537. In that year, the board of directors, using its influence in Parisian civic society, secured a contract between the hospital and a physician from the Faculty of Medicine.[25] Originally, this contract stipulated that the physician need only visit the sick at the hospital when asked.[26] However, this arrangement did not prove satisfactory to the directors and, seeing an opportunity to extend services to the lower orders in Paris by providing the skills of an educated physician on a regular basis, the directors negotiated a new deal in 1547 to ensure that a Faculty physician attend the wards at least once per week.[27] This position was regularized in 1568 with the establishment of the first official post of medecin audit Hostel Dieu.[28]

Although the first steps toward establishing a staff of physicians at the Hôtel Dieu were taken during the sixteenth century, the medical authority of the physicians became complete only in the seventeenth. The hospital physician's duty during the late sixteenth century was wholly concerned with the supervision of medical

---

22 AAP HD 1414, Brièle, 1881, pp. 340–53 and Fosseyeux, 1912, pp. 404–406.

23 Brockliss and Jones, 1997, pp. 230–38 argue that the forms of medicine practised by amateur practitioners could be very similar, if not indistinguishable, from that of regular practitioners. For the medical roles played by the nuns at the hospital before the seventeenth century see Broomhall, 2004, pp. 71–95.

24 AAP HD 1438/13, 9 Dec., 1620. The religious staff of the Hôtel Dieu in 1620 was 5 monks, 4 secular priests, 40 nuns and 40 novices. By the end of the seventeenth century the total has risen to a total religious staff of over 120. Although, after secularization, the religious staff of the hospital had no autonomous authority over the treatment of the sick poor, the monks, nuns and priests were supposed to act as both ward managers and nurses, ensuring that the prescriptions of the physicians were carried out. AAP HD 1438/17, 15 July 1639.

25 AAP HD 1438/1, Feb., 1537.

26 Ibid.

27 AAP HD 1438/2, 2 Apr., 1547.

28 AAP HD 1438/4, Aug., 1568. The terms of the contract that established the official post of hospital physician did not change the requirements of a single weekly visit to treat the sick poor.

treatment of the sick poor as carried out by the religious staff. In effect, he filled the role of a professional advisor, prescribing courses of treatment for the nuns to follow. The enlargement of the hospital wards and the creation of the post of a hospital surgeon during the second half of the sixteenth century increased the importance of this supervisory role. After 1605 the physician of the Hôtel Dieu was required to attend and observe all invasive surgery that took place in the hospital.[29] This situation reflected the hierarchical nature of the medical community outside the walls of the institution, establishing the role of the hospital physician (later that of the chief physician of the hospital) as the predominant figure in the treatment of the sick poor.

By the early seventeenth century, learned medicine had become an important service offered by the hospital. The dominance of the physician over other groups within the staff of the Hôtel Dieu may be seen in a decision by the board of directors in January 1636 to excuse patients from fasting during Lent. The importance placed by the hospital physicians on using diet as a means to restore humoural balance to the sick allowed them to exert their authority over the religious staff. The chief physician, René I Moreau, argued before the hospital directors that the religious sanctions against the eating of meat during Lent ought to be excused on medical grounds. The assertion made by the priests of the hospital that the ill were allowed to eat fish and prunes during Lent was dismissed by the physicians who countered that such foods would too easily corrupt a weakened stomach.[30] The directors, as they would do on all subsequent matters of medical practice, sided with the physicians, ordering the nuns to provide meat on all days regardless of religious season.[31]

The first half of the seventeenth century was significant both for the expansion of the physician's duties and for the creation of new medical posts at the hospital. The numbers increased both because of the growth in the city's population and because, as the patrons of the Hôtel Dieu sought to express their civic pride and leadership through the enlargement of the hospital, the need for a greater medical capacity became apparent to both the physicians and the directors. In December 1615, the hospital physician, Simon Bazin, complained to the board that, as the number of sick poor in the institution numbered more than 800, he needed assistance, emphasizing his inability to see more than a fraction of the patient population during his weekly visit.[32] The directors attempted to solve this problem by offering Bazin a new contract, doubling his salary from 300 *livres* to 600 *livres* in return for visiting the wards for four hours every day.[33] Four years later, when René I Moreau was appointed to the

---

29 AAP HD 1438/11, 4 Mar., 1605. As the greater part of the surgeons' service at the Hôtel Dieu was devoted to non-invasive techniques such as bone-setting and general body maintenance, this condition was unlikely to have increased the burden on the physician. It did, however, confirm the status of the educated Faculty physician over the artisanal surgeon at the hospital during the early modern period.

30 AAP HD 1438/17, 25 Jan., 1636.

31 Ibid.

32 AAP HD 1438/12, 30 Dec., 1615.

33 Ibid.

62   HOSPITAL POLITICS IN SEVENTEENTH-CENTURY FRANCE

post, this salary was again doubled to 1,200 *livres,* in an effort to compensate a quality physician for time spent treating the poor.[34]

The appointment of René I Moreau, an influential member of the Paris Faculty of Medicine, to the post of hospital physician was important for the future development of the medical staff at the Hôtel Dieu.[35] He was able to use his reputation within the Faculty as a means to convince the hospital board that the workload was simply too great for a single physician to handle. He secured agreement from the directors to create a second post of physician in 1629 and for a third in 1638.[36] The creation of new posts came at the initiative of the board of directors itself in 1661, when the number of physicians was increased to seven.[37] This growth in staff numbers came at a time when the judges and lawyers of the sovereign courts were repairing relationships with the crown following the Frondes, consolidating their leadership in the city and re-establishing the prestige of Paris over other cities of the kingdom.[38] No other hospital in France could boast such numbers of educated practitioners offering service free of charge to the sick poor, a fact that the directors were keen to emphasize in official publications.[39]

The creation and development of permanent posts of physicians at the Hôtel Dieu increased the prestige of the hospital and its directors. From the start of the seventeenth century onward, Faculty physicians recognized that positions in the hospital would not hinder their private practices, but, in fact, helped to develop them. Throughout the century, physicians came to regard a position at the hospital as a means to supplement their income and to enhance their reputation. The post offered the basis of a good income for a physician while requiring only a few hours each morning.[40] More importantly, granting medical assistance to the sick poor at a charitable institution was seen by many wealthy clients as a mark of a good practitioner. Not only did this pious service appeal to the Catholic Reform values of many in seventeenth-century society, but it was seen as being beneficial to a physician's skills.[41]

The hospital physicians used their experience in the medical treatment of the sick poor to sell their services to wealthy clients. There was certainly no stigma attached to service at a charitable hospital. The fact that the hospital board was composed of the elite of Parisian civil society was used as a means to further a physician's career.

---

34 AAP HD 1438/13, 6 Sept., 1619.

35 René I Moreau (1584–1656) was noted for his anti-Fernelian (and anti-Paracelsian) opinions and was selected by the Faculty of Medicine of Paris to write an attack against the medicine of Théophraste Renaudot in 1641. Debus, 1991, p. 93 and Brockliss & Jones, 1997, p. 136.

36 AAP HD 1438/14, 18 July, 1629; AAP HD 1438/17, 10 Dec., 1638.

37 AAP HD 1438/29, 21 Jan., 1661.

38 See Hamscher, 1976 on the relationship between the Parlement and the Frondes. Disquiet between crown and sovereign courts continued sporadically throughout the 1650s and early 1660s.

39 AAP HD 879.

40 AAP HD 1438/13, 6 Sept., 1619. The post was paid 1,200 *livres* a year. This sum was subsequently raised over the course of the century to a figure of 3,000 *livres.*

41 AAP HD 1438/20, 4 Dec., 1648.

Hospital directors may have acted as patrons to these physicians, passing them up the social ladder to higher-ranked individuals in an effort to further their own social and dynastic ends. Indeed, several of those who filled the post of hospital physician left their office when the commitment to aristocratic patrons took them away from Paris. One of the hospital physicians during the 1640s, Dupré, accepted the position of personal physician to the prince de Condé in 1648,[42] and similarly, in 1681, René II Moreau, who had filled the post since 1661, resigned from the hospital's staff in order to devote his full attention to the dauphin and dauphine at court.[43]

From the middle of the seventeenth century, many members of the Faculty who possessed talent, ambition and good connections seemed to view time spent in the wards of the Hôtel Dieu as a form of career development. While the directors were concerned to keep a tight rein over who could treat the poor within the hospital, they were open to providing some work experience to high-calibre physicians. For example, in 1666 the board created an unpaid post for Guy-Crescent Fagon, who would go on to become the chief physician to Louis XIV himself in 1693.[44] Fagon's case was an exception and few others were granted such an opportunity, although others did offer to treat patients for free.[45]

The board was concerned with keeping a good reputation for the office of hospital physician and in maintaining its regard amongst the city population. Unlike many posts in early modern France, that of physician to the Paris Hôtel Dieu never became a venal position, although there must have been a temptation to sell the office during the periodic financial crises suffered by the hospital during the course of the seventeenth century. Throughout the period, the board retained its right to appoint and remove a physician for being unable to fulfil his duty.[46] The fact that there was no suggestion raised in the directors' meetings of selling these offices testifies to the board's desire to offer the best quality medical care available.

The decision to choose physicians of high regard improved the standing of those who held the post, generating great interest in securing the office when it fell vacant. The popularity of service in the Hôtel Dieu increased over the course of the century. In 1671, when one of the hospital physicians died, 30 applicants put themselves forward to succeed him.[47] Toward the end of the seventeenth century, this demand was recognized by the board who turned the desire of these physicians to the hospital's advantage. In 1689, the directors, in order to regulate the selection process,

42   Ibid.

43   AAP HD 1438/49, 19 Sept., 1681.

44   AAP HD 1438/34, 10 Dec., 1666.

45   Given Fagon's later career, he must have had both a perceived talent as a physician as well as influential connections.

46   AAP HD 1438/46, 29 July 1678. After 1678, the board carried out a yearly assessment of the hospital physicians and, in theory, could bar those who did not fulfil their obligations from office. However, no physician lost his office during the period under study. While the office of hospital physician was not venal, it did pass in several cases from father to son. But in each of these instances the candidate submitted to the same selection processes. See, for example, the appointment of the son of René II Moreau in 1681. AAP HD 1438/49, 19 Sept., 1681.

47   AAP HD 1438/39, 7 Aug., 1671.

nominated two physicians who would be in line to succeed when established posts became available.[48] This waiting list was soon transformed into an unpaid medical position at the Hôtel Dieu, the médecin expectant.[49] The médecins expectants served as physicians in the wards for free, working alongside those who possessed official posts. By the early eighteenth century, the waiting-list physicians had become an official part of the hospital staff, increasing in number to four, with their duties and rotation outlined by the board.[50]

Although learned practitioners exerted influence over all medical matters at the hospital, the directors kept a constant watch to ensure that the physicians did not take their offices for granted. In 1583, the board rebuked the contracted physician for not fulfilling his obligation to visit the hospital's sick during the outbreak of plague in the city.[51] In the early seventeenth century, there were frequent complaints from the sick poor themselves that the hospital physicians were neglecting them in favour of wealthy patients. In 1661, the board, concerned that the medical services that it secured for the sick poor were being eroded by the physicians' desire to develop their private practices, drew up the first official rules for the practice of medicine at the Hôtel Dieu.[52] The concern that the physicians were not fulfilling their duties properly was reflected by the criticism of them by Guillaume de Lamoignon, the Premier Président of the Parlement of Paris. He berated the hospital's chief physician that 'the number of physicians was not increased in order to relieve them of the care and devotion they owe to the sick, but in order to give them the time to examine each of them more fully.'[53] The new rules proposed an establishment of ward rounds by the hospital physicians. The seven physicians were to divide responsibility for the individual wards among them and spend at least two hours each day treating the sick.[54]

Although the rules were drawn up by senior members of the sovereign courts, the hospital physicians were not reluctant to voice their grievances over the enforcement of daily rounds. The chief physician, René II Moreau, replied to the board that 'if we are obliged to give two hours of our time to the Hôtel Dieu each day, we would have to abandon the greater part of our practice in the city, which a physician cannot afford to do, and thus the Hôtel Dieu would only be left with the least experienced

---

48   AAP HD 1438/58, 29 Apr., 1689.

49   Ibid. The physicians who were nominated as a *médecin expectant* clearly felt that the eventual rewards were worth the wait. The first man to be appointed as such, a physician named Doye, was put on the list in April 1689, only to succeed to the post of hospital physician in 1704. AAP HD 1438/73.

50   AAP HD 1438/78, 12 Jan., 1709. The Parisian medical community recognized the establishment of the *médecin expectant* as an official post by 1709. In that year, when one of the *médecins expectants* died, five Paris physicians presented themselves before the board to take his place on the waiting list and to practise medicine at the hospital for free. AAP HD 1438/79, 9 Feb., 1709.

51   AAP HD 1438/6, 23 Sept., 1583.

52   AAP HD 1438/29, 11 Feb. 1661.

53   Ibid.

54   Ibid.

people to treat the sick.'[55] Moreau consented to the creation of specified ward rounds to be followed by each of the hospital physicians, but he argued that a single hour each day should be enough to treat the sick. He blamed the patients' complaints on the inefficiency of the nuns in managing the wards overnight, stating that the sick were moved from one bed to another without the physicians' knowledge. He complained that much of his time was spent in looking for his patients.[56] In this instance, the board allowed the limit of one hour of service each day, but stipulated that one of the physicians must visit the hospital each afternoon in order to view new admissions to the wards and to oversee the movement of patients by the nuns.[57]

Despite the agreement made between the hospital physicians and the board over the introduction of ward rounds, tensions over the regulations did not disappear. In 1687, the younger hospital physicians complained that the requirement to rotate to a different ward every two months was disadvantageous for the care of the sick.[58] They argued that they were just developing new skills and knowledge when the rules required them to move to a new ward and a new set of patients.[59] The board, concerned whenever the treatment of the hospital's patients was queried, consulted with the senior physicians over the length of time needed for them to develop their skills in each ward, and it agreed to a new period of four months per rotation.[60]

Tensions over the hospital's need to make medical treatment available to those who were admitted after the physicians' daily visit were to prove difficult for the board to solve. In 1687, following repeated complaints that the sick who had been admitted in the afternoon could spend most of the day before being seen by a physician, the directors asked that the ward rounds could be made twice per day, once in the morning and once in the late afternoon.[61] The physicians, who did not wish to jeopardize their ability to grant their full attention to paying customers during the afternoons, refused the board's request.[62] The directors raised the issue again in 1691, when patients complained that they had no access to the hospital physicians after the morning ward rounds, and that, when illnesses grew worse, they had to wait until the following morning for treatment.[63] The directors, mindful that they needed to balance their own desire to utilize the physicians' medical services to negotiate their social position in Paris and the doctors' own need to make money from their practices and to create relationships with influential patrons, asked for a physician to volunteer to visit the hospital in the afternoon.[64] However, none of the physicians were willing to take that step.[65] A solution only came in 1715 with the expansion of

---

55 Ibid.
56 Ibid.
57 Ibid.
58 AAP HD 1438/55, 16 Apr., 1687.
59 Ibid.
60 Ibid.
61 AAP HD 1438/55, 2 May 1687.
62 Ibid.
63 AAP HD 1438/60, 17 Mar., 1691.
64 Ibid.
65 Ibid.

the number of médecins expectants to four, when the board required one of those on the waiting list to visit the hospital in the afternoon, rotating weekly.[66]

Surgeons at the Hôtel Dieu

The establishment of surgeons at the Hôtel Dieu began at about the same time as that of physicians. The first official position of hospital surgeon was established in 1568.[67] By the end of the sixteenth century, the post had become one of significant importance to the board's desired aim to provide charitable care to the poor of the city. Although the social position of the more artisanal surgeon was much lower than that of the university-educated physician in early modern Paris, in practical terms surgeons could often offer more to the sick and injured. This division between the physicians and surgeons would be reflected within the Hôtel Dieu during the sixteenth and seventeenth centuries. When Laurent Guerin was appointed to the position of surgeon of the Hôtel Dieu in 1598, his terms of service were to be at the call of the sick 'day and night', in return for which he received a salary and was given both room and board at the hospital.[68] The first men to fill this office were recruited from the ranks of the city's barber-surgeons.[69] However, the failure of the hospital surgeon to attend to the sick during the plague crisis of 1606 put the status of barber-surgeons in doubt among the directors of the hospital. From then on, all men chosen to be the hospital's chief surgeon would be selected from the master surgeons of the city.[70]

Unlike the position of hospital physician, that of master surgeon at the Hôtel Dieu was not awarded for life initially. The master surgeons of the Hôtel Dieu were offered six-year contracts, and, in order to keep the standards of medical practice as high as possible, the board developed a rigorous selection procedure for those who would hold the post. When the office fell vacant, a panel comprising two physicians from the Faculty of Medicine, two master surgeons of Paris and two barber-surgeons was convened to interview and select the best candidate in terms of medical skills

---

66   AAP HD 1438/84, 20 Mar., 1715.

67   AAP HD 1438/4, Sept., 1568. The first contract passed between the hospital and a surgeon of the city of Paris seems to have been made a few years before 1568, but by that year the surgeon was officially recognized as a member of staff by the board of directors.

68   AAP HD 1438/10, 30 Dec., 1598. The surgeons of the Hôtel Dieu were required to live in the hospital throughout the period under study. This residence marked them out as different to the more prestigious hospital physicians who baulked at the suggestion made in the early seventeenth century that their positions should involve residency as well.

69   Ibid. and AAP HD 1438/11, 19 Mar., 1603. Guerin's replacement in 1603, Pierre Corbilly, was likewise a barber-surgeon.

70   AAP HD 1438/11, 8 July, 1606. Following complaints that Corbilly had absented himself from the hospital wards during the plague of 1606, he was dismissed on the personal recommendation of the Premier Président of the Parlement of Paris. His replacement was required to swear an oath that he would provide service free of charge to the sick 'with whatever illness, even those who are contagious'. Ibid., 26 July, 1606.

and experience.[71] While the directors of the Hôtel Dieu were accustomed to exploit the hospital's financial resources as sources of patronage, the dispensing of favours to clients was not to include the offering of medical posts to the unqualified. In 1640, for example, the Premier Président of the Parlement of Paris himself recommended the appointment of a surgeon named Bernard. The latter, however, was rejected by the rest of the board because he could not prove his qualifications.[72]

The directors understood that a single surgeon was not enough to provide treatment for the sick poor at the hospital. To begin with, the hospital surgeon was expected to hire, house and feed other surgeons from his own salary to assist him in his duties.[73] Before the early seventeenth century there was no stipulation as to the numbers of surgeons hired. However, when the board decided to impose rules on the surgeons in order to prevent the hospital's reputation from suffering, the number of journeyman surgeons was fixed at five in 1629.[74] The journeymen were responsible for carrying out the majority of treatments prescribed by both the hospital's physicians and the master surgeon. They were required to visit the sick poor twice a day and to be available at the hospital throughout the day and night in case of emergency.[75] Owing to the increase in the numbers of poor received at the institution during the first half of the seventeenth century, more posts of journeyman surgeons were created, and by the 1650s, the hospital possessed nine.[76]

Similar to the hospital physicians, the lesser-ranked surgeons served the sick poor at the Hôtel Dieu because their tenure of office gave them the practical experience needed to make a name for themselves. This situation was as true for the master surgeons as it was for the journeymen. Until the 1650s, the hospital's master surgeons held their posts for the six-year term before leaving the hospital staff to build a private practice in the city.[77] After their term of office, the previous master surgeons were permitted to practise charitably at the hospital.[78]

---

71   AAP HD 1438/14, 4 June, 1625; Ibid., 18 June, 1625. After the mid seventeenth century, the role in the selection process played by barber-surgeons was ended.

72   AAP HD 1438/18, 11 Apr., 1640.

73   AAP HD 1438/10, 30 Dec., 1598.

74   AAP HD 1438/12, 18 July, 1629. The position of *compagnon chirurgien* (journeyman surgeon), which had evolved during the first decades of the seventeenth century from those assistants that the hospital surgeon was required to hire, is first mentioned in 1613. The post of journeyman surgeon was made official with the new rules in 1629. After 1629, the title of hospital surgeon was changed to that of master surgeon. The master surgeon was required to teach the journeymen the skills needed to qualify as a *garçon chirurgien*.

75   Ibid.

76   AAP HD 1438/24, 12 Jan., 1657.

77   AAP HD 1438/24, 14 Jan., 1656 and 26 Apr., 1656. Petit, the master surgeon nominated in 1654, was to remain at the hospital until the 1690s. The board, despite several serious allegations against him, seem to have allowed Petit to devote more time to his own private practice than it had for the previous master surgeons.

78   Ibid. The previous master surgeons were not only permitted to serve, they were actively encouraged to return to offer treatment. In 1656, the board asked previous master surgeons Haran (appointed in 1642) and Gouin (appointed in 1648) why they had ceased to treat the poor at the Hôtel Dieu. When the two replied that the hospital no longer possessed

Just as the master surgeons were able to build up skills through performing complicated surgical procedures on the ill and injured, the journeymen sought to increase their expertise in the lesser techniques that would allow them to earn money in the city. In 1665, the journeymen earned the right to practise basic operations such as the lancing of abscesses and drawing blood without the supervision of a master. They argued before the board that these techniques were the only means for them to secure a living after their term of service at the hospital, contrasting their limited repertoire to that of the master surgeons who were licensed to perform more complicated surgeries such as trepanning and amputations.[79] The most pressing problem facing the interests of the journeyman surgeons was to keep rival surgeons from the city from using the hospital's patient population in order to build up their experience. In this struggle, the journeymen were assisted by the board, who wished to retain absolute control over the quality of the medical care on offer. In 1655, the journeymen complained to the board that the master surgeon, Petit, had sold the right to treat the poor to surgeons of the city.[80] While the board forbade the sale of office at the hospital, the problem of outside surgeons attempting to gain illicitly the sort of experience obtained by the hospital surgeons remained largely unsolved throughout the period under study.[81]

What drew the journeyman surgeons to service in the hospital was the position of the chirurgien gagnant la maîtrise. In order to attract and reward the best men, the board ensured that the most senior would earn the title of master surgeon after six years.[82] This position allowed a young surgeon to progress to the status of master surgeon without being subject to guild restrictions or fees. By the end of the seventeenth century, the holder would rank second to the master surgeon of the hospital, being treated in all respects as a master himself.[83] Service in the hospital gave a number of the city's surgeons an alternative means to earn their masters degree. The ability to offer this benefit to one of the surgeons was not challenged by

---

suitable surgical instruments to allow them to perform their latest surgical techniques, the board offered Haran 1,000 *livres* to purchase new ones.

79   AAP HD 1438/33, 4 Sept., 1665.

80   AAP HD 1438/22, 26 Oct., 1655. The charge brought against Petit was that some of the surgeons who had bought the right to practise at the Hôtel Dieu were not properly trained and that their lack of skill endangered the health of the sick poor. The board gave its permission for a number of surgeons from the city to treat the sick poor in the hospital, providing they were approved by the medical staff and followed the institution's rules. These surgeons from the city would eventually become known as *chirurgiens externs* and obtain an official place at the Hôtel Dieu.

81   Ibid. Petit answered the charge against him that he was not the only chief surgeon to profit from selling the right to practise.

82   AAP HD 1438/22, 13 Feb., 1654. This right to grant the title of master surgeon is first mentioned in 1654, but seems to have been an accepted practice of the hospital since the sixteenth century, see Fosseyeux, 1912, p. 401.

83   AAP HD 1438/72, 16 Feb., 1703.

the community of surgeons of Paris owing to the prestigious judicial backgrounds of the members of the board.[84]

During the early seventeenth century, the board, at first, attempted to cope with the demand for the hospital's services by licensing surgeons from the city to practise in the wards under the strict supervision of the master surgeon.[85] The famine crisis of 1662 to 1663 created difficulties that required a greater commitment on the part of the directors. They hired four surgeons to live in the hospital alongside the institution's surgeons on a temporary basis; however, these temporary surgeons insisted that they be given permanent posts as hospital surgeons. Furthermore, they complained to the board that the Hôtel Dieu did not have a staff of surgeons able to cope with the demand for medical treatment from the city's lower orders.[86] Following the advice given to the board, the number of journeymen was raised to 20 for the duration of the crisis.[87]

The rise in the number of surgeons at the Hôtel Dieu during the seventeenth century reflected the board's recognition of the growing demand for medical services offered by regular practitioners among the urban population. The Parisian ruling elites capitalized on the social prestige they gained through the offering of forms of care that would be unaffordable for the greater part of the city's population; however, the hospital had to balance the gains made socially by its benefactors with the costs associated with the daily functioning of the institution. In 1666, after the patient population of the hospital had fallen following the famine years of the early part of the decade, the directors decided to retrench costs by reorganizing the surgical staff. The number of journeyman surgeons was reduced from 20 to 12, while those who lost their right to lodge at the hospital would be licensed to practise in the wards as externs.[88]

The role played by the externs became progressively more important to the hospital. The number of city surgeons allowed to practise at the Hôtel Dieu without benefit of room and board increased dramatically over the next decade and a half. In 1680, in an effort to keep a measure of quality control over those who practised surgery at the hospital and to retrench expenses, the board limited the number of externs to 45.[89] The prospect of a place to hone skills and increase one's reputation led many surgeons to ask the board of the Hôtel Dieu for a position as extern and the directors complained in 1679 that they were overwhelmed by the number of

---

84   The Hôtel Dieu in Montpellier attempted to obtain a second hospital surgeon in a similar manner, but the resulting post was the cause of a law suit brought by the city's College of Surgeons against the hospital in 1716 (the case was still unresolved in 1789). ADH HD, F37 & F39.

85   AAP HD 1438/22, 26 Oct., 1655.

86   AAP HD 1438/30, 14 June, 1662. One of the temporary surgeons cited that he was expected to perform over 400 bleedings every day.

87   Ibid. At the time there were nine journeymen.

88   AAP HD 1438/34, 12 Mar., 1666. The 12 most experienced journeymen kept their posts at the hospital. The journeyman surgeons were to be distinguished from the externs by wearing a white surcoat instead of black.

89   AAP HD 1438/48, 11 Dec., 1680.

requests to be recognized as externs.[90] The matter was made worse by the influential patrons of Parisian surgeons who attempted to use their influence with members of the hospital board. The directors emphasized that it wished to select medical candidates on the grounds of skills and experience regardless of whom they treated in their private practice.[91] The demand for the post led the board to create rules for a surgical career at the Hôtel Dieu, and from 1679 onwards, those who wished to serve in the hospital had to serve for at least two years as an extern before making the progression to a journeyman surgeon when a position fell vacant. This career path and the post of extern of the hospital were made official when the regulations governing the surgeons were rewritten in 1693.[92]

During the course of the seventeenth-century enlargement of the surgical staff, the hospital directors faced the difficulty of maintaining a high standard of service. The first step taken toward regulating the surgeon's practice at the Hôtel Dieu was to forbid apprentice surgeons from applying to hold the position of extern or journeyman.[93] A second, and more important, step was to introduce rules that defined the surgeons' daily routine from ward rounds to operation procedures.[94] The first surgical regulations of 1655 seem to have been unsatisfactory to both the board and the surgeons themselves, as the Dean of the Faculty of Medicine was asked, in 1659, to observe the hospital surgeons at work.[95] New rules based on his report were drawn up in accordance with the directors' desire to increase the survival rate of the institution. Thereafter, the physician deputed to the hospital's *salle de taillés* was required to submit a written report on all surgery carried out. Likewise, all patients who died in the care of a surgeon were to be the subject of an autopsy to determine cause of death.[96] The reports generated from operations and autopsies were used to inform the board of potential areas of improvement and to increase the surgical knowledge of practitioners at the Hôtel Dieu.

The rules for surgical practice were intended to increase the survival rate of those who sought treatment at the hospital. The regulations were designed to prevent malpractice, while being flexible enough to allow hospital surgeons to improve their skills and experiment in order to add to the number of different surgical procedures on offer at the Hôtel Dieu. While the board wanted the surgeons to improve their skills, the fear of malpractice and the misuse of the dead at the hospital undermined the educational value of the institution during the early seventeenth century. Anatomical

---

90   AAP HD 1438/47, 9 June, 1679.

91   Ibid.

92   AAP HD 1438/62, 3 June, 1693. The 1693 regulations referred to the journeymen as interns for the first time.

93   AAP HD 1438/17, 15 July, 1639.

94   AAP HD 1438/22, 14 July, 1655. The 1655 rules were drawn up by the board with assistance from the hospital physicians.

95   AAP HD 1438/26, 4 May, 1659. The observation carried out by the Dean of the Faculty, Blondel, provided the directors with an opinion of the abilities of all the surgeons.

96   Ibid., 13 June, 1659. None of the reports on operations carried out at the Hôtel Dieu during the seventeenth century have survived. The rules also required a register to be kept of all those who underwent surgical procedures and their survival rate. This register has not survived.

dissections were expressly forbidden before the middle of the seventeenth century as being contrary to both criminal and canon law. In the rules governing surgery, however, the board allowed the hospital's medical staff to circumvent this prohibition. While the directors emphasized that anatomy studies were against the rules, they did permit autopsies to be carried out at the discretion of physicians or surgeons in order to understand the cause of death. The board further stipulated that all autopsies must produce knowledge of service to the poor.[97] At every autopsy performed by the master surgeon, the journeyman surgeons were required to attend in order to further their knowledge of anatomy and surgical technique.[98]

The close proximity of a source of cadavers tempted surgeons from both the hospital staff and the city to use bodies for study without permission. Thefts from the hospital mortuary were a regular occurrence during the period under review.[99] Even living patients were occasionally at risk of winding up on an anatomist's table. In January 1681, two of the hospital surgeons were suspected of kidnapping a patient from the wards, lowering him by a rope from the Pont-au-Double to the frozen Seine below. The unfortunate patient died when the two were disturbed by the night watch, causing them to drop him from a height sufficient to cause a fatal head wound.[100] By the early eighteenth century, the hospital board sought to solve the problem of body theft by building an amphitheatre designated for the teaching of anatomy to the journeymen and externs.[101] In order to stop unauthorized surgeons from acquiring cadavers from the Hôtel Dieu, in 1706 the directors allowed the chief surgeon to conduct a course of anatomical dissection in the amphitheatre for the surgeons of both the hospital and the city.[102] The chief surgeon and the hospital's Mother Superior were ordered to consult together in order select cadavers from the mortuary, presumably choosing those who were unknown in the city and had no relatives to voice a complaint.

The desire of the hospital governors to increase the institution's ability to educate its practitioners in the second half of the seventeenth century was reflected in attempts to increase the range of procedures. The surgical technique of cutting for the stone (lithotomy) was identified as a form of operation that could increase the status of the hospital, not only among the Parisian population, but nationwide as well.[103] The board's decision in the early 1640s to hire a surgeon who could practise lithotomy on the sick poor would eventually lead to the hospital breaking the monopoly held by

---

97   AAP HD 1438/22, 1 Feb., 1655.

98   Ibid., 14 July, 1655. Although the board had forbidden dissections in February 1655, the rules governing surgery in July 1655 order the journeymen to be present at all dissections. This choice of language would suggest that the open-ended definition of an autopsy at the Hôtel Dieu was a deliberate ploy for the board to allow the master surgeon to teach the journeyman surgeons anatomy at the hospital.

99   AAP HD 1438/14, 30 Dec., 1626.

100 AAP HD 1438/49, 8 Jan., 1681. The two suspects were never brought to justice.

101 AAP HD 1438/72, 16 Feb., 1703.

102 AAP HD 1438/75, 31 Dec., 1706.

103 Lithotomy, or cutting for bladder stones, was particularly important to early modern urban society due to the large percentage of protein in the population's diet.

the influential Parisian family of empirics, the Collot.[104] The earliest forays into this form of surgery were undertaken by the chief surgeon, Jacques Haran, who had been appointed to the hospital in 1642 because of his close relationship with the Collot.[105] Haran recruited members of the family to perform the surgery charitably at the hospital. The Collot found performing the operation on the poor both a way to fulfil their own charitable obligations and a way to practise and perfect their technique.

In 1651, however, the Parisian lithotomists attempted to protect their monopoly against the threat to their livelihood presented by the potential of the Hôtel Dieu's surgeons learning the technique, by withdrawing their service and by founding their own charitable hospital.[106] In doing so, the city surgeons capitalized on the break in relations between the crown and the judges of the Paris sovereign courts during the Frondes. The board stated publicly that if lithotomy was to be offered as a charitable service to the poor, it must be practised solely at the Hôtel Dieu. The directors, unwilling to accept the competition posed by the new surgical hospital to their own monopoly over professional medical services offered to the poor, used the restoration of normal relations between the king and the city's ruling classes to gain royal assent for the closure of the Collot's hospital.[107]

Following the demise of the Collot's hospital, the directors of the Hôtel Dieu continued their efforts to make lithotomy part of the repertoire of the hospital surgeons. In 1657, they encouraged the former master surgeon, Gouin, who had learnt the skill from the Collot in the 1640s, to teach the current master surgeon, Petit.[108] The board also decided to make a deal with members of the Collot family, offering them official posts at the Hôtel Dieu to operate on the poor for free.[109] The Collot took up the positions offered, despite the requirement that they teach the hospital surgeons their techniques, because it gave them a large number of sufferers on which to gain practical experience and because the reputation of the hospital as the premier charitable institution in Paris increased their reputation in the eyes of their wealthier clients. If the Collot had hoped that they could come to an accommodation with the hospital board in order to perform surgery without revealing their secrets, they were wrong. The hospital surgeons were able to capitalize on the presence of the

---

104 The Collot family (also spelled Colot) were the heirs to Laurant Collot who had perfected adult lithotomy in the sixteenth century. The family and its allies maintained a monopoly on the technique well into the seventeenth century. Brockliss and Jones, 1997, p. 106.

105 AAP HD 1438/18, 21 Feb., 1642, 6 May, 1643; AAP HD 1438/19, 22 Apr., 1644. Haran's early experiments in lithotomy during 1643–44 were under the supervision of 'master operators of this art', which would suggest that members of the Collot family were participating in surgery at the Hôtel Dieu from this early date. The board was so excited by Haran's early success that it designated one of the newer wards to be converted to an operating room exclusively for lithotomy.

106 AAP HD 1438/21, 21 Aug., 1653. The hospital was established by the Collot and their allied surgeons, Theveyn, Girard and Ruffin.

107 Ibid. In their complaint to the crown, the directors described the Hôtel Dieu as the *hôpital des hôpitaux* for the first time.

108 AAP HD 1438/24, 26 Jan., 1657.

109 Ibid., 11 Apr., 1657; 9 May, 1657.

lithotomists and, encouraged by the directors' desire to increase the prestige of the Hôtel Dieu, to attempt innovations of their own. In late 1658, one of the journeyman surgeons, Lanier, caused controversy among the hospital staff by designing a new instrument to cut for the stone.[110] While some of the surgeons were concerned about the deaths of the earliest patients cut with the new tool, the board wanted Lanier to continue to develop it in order to perfect the technique.[111]

The fear that they would eventually lose their monopoly of the surgical technique, not only at the hospital, but, more importantly, in the Parisian medical marketplace, led the lithotomists to attempt to outflank the board's desire that they teach their skills to the hospital surgeons. The chief surgeon, Petit, colluded with them, entering into a written contract to perform the operation only in their presence, forbidding the journeymen from the operating room.[112] Although the presence of the lithotomists increased both the civic and national reputations of the Hôtel Dieu,[113] their presence at the hospital during the 1660s caused problems as well. Complaints were made to the directors that the Collot were breaking the institution's rules by billing patients for their services.[114] The Collot were accused of charging the parents of children on whom they had operated. They argued before the board that the parents should pay for their services if they could afford it.[115]

The problems of having the Collot at the Hôtel Dieu led the directors increasingly to seek ways of breaking the family's monopoly of lithotomy in the city. Under increasing pressure from the members of the board and their clients, the Collot recognized that their skills would not remain secret for much longer. In 1674, Hierome Collot attempted to secure his financial future by selling his secrets to the hospital. He offered to teach the journeyman surgeons the techniques in return for a single payment of 30,000 *livres* and a pension for life of 2,000 *livres* per year. However, by that date, the board was confident that there was no longer good reason to pay for the knowledge.[116] In late 1679, the directors ordered two of the journeymen to practise lithotomy in secret on cadavers in the hospital mortuary.[117] At the same time that the hospital board sought to develop the skills in-house, it put pressure on city surgeons who already knew the techniques to fulfil their charitable obligations by instructing

---

110 AAP HD 1438/25, 6 Sept., 1658. What Lanier's new surgical instrument was has been lost. Lanier developed his new instrument as part of an effort to replace the Collot as the sole lithotomist at the Hôtel Dieu. However, the board refused to allow him to establish his own monopoly at the hospital.

111 Ibid.

112 AAP HD 1438/25, 13 Nov., 1658. The board commented that it would not allow any monopolies to develop at the Hôtel Dieu.

113 AAP HD 1438/32, 29 Aug., 1664. A surgeon from Languedoc petitioned the board for the right to perform surgery at the hospital and to consult the Collot's opinion regarding his own technique for lithotomy.

114 AAP HD 1438/33, 14 Sept., 1665; 20 Oct., 1665.

115 Ibid.

116 AAP HD 1438/42, 30 May 1674.

117 AAP HD 1438/47, 11 Jan., 1679. The two surgeons were then examined on their skills in 1681 before being allowed to perform on living patients. AAP HD 1438/49, 7 Mar., 1681.

the hospital's surgeons.[118] The directors were successful in acquiring the teaching services of the surgeon of the Hôpital de la Charité, Morel, who agreed to instruct the journeyman surgeons in 1681.[119] By 1692, the surgeons of the Hôtel Dieu were regularly performing lithotomy. The numbers of individuals seeking this form of surgery at the hospital grew and this demanded that improvements be made to both the rules governing surgical procedures and to the fabric of the operating rooms.[120] Although the directors were satisfied with their association of the Hôtel Dieu with the practise of lithotomy, and in particular with the survival rate for a complicated invasive surgery,[121] they remained committed to improving the services offered to the poor by allowing those who had alternative techniques for the operation to experiment at the hospital.[122]

Financing medical assistance

At the start of the seventeenth century, the finances of the Hôtel Dieu, relatively unchanged in form since the Middle Ages, were dominated by the revenues derived from charitable sources. Over the course of the century the hospital found itself increasingly unable to meet its commitments during crisis years, and was forced to seek a new basis for its finances by the end of the reign.

The age of the Hôtel Dieu was an advantage to its finances. Ever since its founding it had accepted bequests of land from the wealthy, as well as using monetary gifts to purchase estates to provide an annual income. Almost 500 years of donations had allowed the hospital to build up a considerable domain of land mostly concentrated around Paris, but including farms throughout northern France. The most important lands for the finances of the hospital were those in the faubourgs of Paris. One of the hospital's largest territories was known as the *grand pressoir*, which occupied much of the area of modern-day Montparnasse. This seigneurie had been even larger before 1626, when Marie de Médicis had purchased the portion which prevented the extension of the Luxembourg gardens. In return for this land, the crown exchanged rights on its domain worth an equal amount. In theory, the Hôtel Dieu was supposed

---

118 AAP HD 1438/49, 7 Mar., 1681. The Premier Président of the Parlement of Paris himself asked the Collot to teach the journeyman surgeons of the Hôtel Dieu.

119 Ibid., 14 Mar., 1681; 19 Mar., 1681. Morel quickly found that the commitment required by the board of the Hôtel Dieu interfered with his private practice. In 1683, he pled poverty in an unsuccessful effort to break his contract with the hospital. AAP HD 1438/51, 28 Apr., 1683.

120 AAP HD 1438/61, 12 Apr., 1692.

121 AAP HD 1438/61, 20 Sept., 1692; AAP HD 1438/77, 1 Dec., 1708. Only 18 of 108 patients who underwent the procedure died in 1692 (16.7%). Ninety-seven individuals were operated on in 1708 of whom 21 died (21.6%).

122 AAP HD 1438/67, 26 Apr., 1698. The board members' desire to profit socially from the prestige of offering advanced surgical services at the Hôtel Dieu could lead them to make mistakes. In 1698, the directors authorized the empiric and fraudulent monk, Frère Jacques, to demonstrate his new lithotomy procedure in the hospital's operating room. The death rate of his new technique was 61%, which led the board to quickly forbid him from performing at the hospital. See Lister, 1967, pp. 236–9.

to live off its own estates, but this was not the case by the seventeenth century. In 1663, the rents paid on its agricultural lands accounted for 23,192 *livres* out of a total income of 360,098, and as the expenses of the hospital grew during the century, the proportion of its revenues derived from its agricultural properties decreased.[123]

The rents paid by peasants on lands owned by the Hôtel Dieu were not the greatest portion of its income, but were important enough to warrant careful monitoring by the members of the board of directors. The administrators were, by the regulations governing them, under obligation to renegotiate these rents on the best terms for the hospital. These men and their deputies spent time each year visiting the lands owned by the hospital, inspecting them to see that they were farmed to peak efficiency, ensuring that improvements or repairs made to buildings were not too expensive, and protecting its seigneurial rights.[124] The duty to take proper care with the management of lands donated to the hospital was important. The Hôtel Dieu was not allowed to sell off these bequests without the consent of the heirs of the benefactor due to the legal right and expectation of donors that their legacies would remain in place forever. There was a very strong feeling that men had donated these lands for the purpose of taking care of the sick poor and, therefore, they should be tended carefully.

Besides agricultural land, the Hôtel Dieu owned a great deal of property within the city. Wealthy residents had left a number of houses in various quarters, for example the Hôtel Blérancourt in the Place Royale which had been donated to the hospital by the comtesse de Pont-Audemer in 1672.[125] The hospital directors leased out these houses to provide an income for the institution. The collection of rents could sometimes prove a problem for the hospital, in particular with its noble tenants. The duchesse de Rohan, for example, moved out of the Hôtel Blérancourt owing a great deal of unpaid rent, provoking the hospital to seize her furniture.[126] In 1663, the revenue derived from the city houses of the hospital was 51,872 *livres*.[127]

Many benefactors left the Hôtel Dieu gifts in the form of pensions to be continued after their death. As well, cash donations to the hospital had traditionally been used to contract *rentes* on various municipal, church and crown revenues. This source of income, which should be regarded as part of the charitable legacy of the hospital, amounted to almost one-third of the total revenue in the period between 1656 and 1690.[128] During the Middle Ages, the hospital had also acquired various financial rights which it continued to exploit for its profit. One of the most important of these was the sole right to sell meat, along with a dispensation, during Lent. The hospital sold licences to selected butchers to act as its agents in this respect and employed officers to ensure that the monopoly was properly policed. More important than these medieval rights, however, were the consumption taxes placed on the sale of salt in the city of Paris in the 1630s in order to help repay loans contracted to pay for

123 AN K1024/16.

124 AAP HD 870.

125 Fosseyeux, 1912, p. 364.

126 Brièle, 1881, p. 195.

127 AN K1024/16.

128 Ibid. In 1663, for example, the total income derived from its *rentes* brought the Hôtel Dieu 117,677 *livres* out of a total of 360,098.

the construction of new wards during the early decades of the century. These taxes, which were to increase both in number and percentage of the overall income by the end of the century, amounted to 90,000 *livres* of the 360,098 total in 1663.[129]

The lands, houses and *rentes* which provided the bulk of the revenue of the Hôtel Dieu before 1690 had been the result of several centuries of charitable donations. While the hospital relied heavily on the income derived from these sources, it could not forecast the levels of new donations, and thus did not treat charity as a part of the regular accounts. The hospital adopted two strategies to cope with the unpredictability of its charitable income. The board of directors preferred to convert any cash gifts into *rentes* constituted on a reliable source; however, in years when the Hôtel Dieu borrowed heavily to cover shortages, donations were indirectly used to repay debts and to reassure creditors.

The pattern of charitable giving to the Hôtel Dieu caused the unpredictable nature of this sort of revenue. Besides the casual alms given to collection boxes in the churches of the city, which never amounted to a significant percentage of the revenues, most donations were made in the form of legacies left to the hospital after the death of the benefactor. As a result, it was impossible to forecast from year to year how much income would come from this source. The majority of gifts to the institution comprised small amounts of cash, or quite commonly the donation of movable goods to be sold to profit the hospital. For example, Ithier-François Chastelain, a canon of the cathedral chapter of Paris, left his substantial library to the Hôtel Dieu, which brought the hospital 2,149 *livres* in 1660.[130]

Large donations to the institution often did not improve its regular accounts because benefactors could direct the uses to which their money was put in the terms of their will. A significant portion of the 55,000 *livres* which Jean Bachelier left to the Hôtel Dieu was intended to be used to fund a trust to endow a yearly dowry for a girl, an apprenticeship for a boy and to pay the salaries of a priest and two Sisters of Charity to teach the children of Villeneuve Saint-Georges. Bachelier entrusted the continuing survival of the trust and the selection of worthy candidates to the directors of the hospital. The donation of Jean-Baptiste Colbert similarly specified that the board oversee 20 yearly dowries for worthy girls from his seigneuries of Chateauneuf and Lignières.[131]

The Paris Hôtel Dieu was fortunate to benefit from bequests left to it by some of the nobles who resided in the city. A list of its noble benefactors during the period included the duc d'Epernon, the duchesse d'Aiguillon and the prince d'Harcourt.[132] The majority of these donations were quite small because the pattern of giving of most nobles was to leave the bulk of their charitable donations to the residents of their lands. The legacies of Marie de Lorraine princesse de Guise, who used the directors of the Hôtel Dieu as her executors in 1688, demonstrated this trend. The princesse, who was the last of the Guise family, left her lands and the majority of her liquid wealth to her closest relatives the Harcourts. As a gift to the Hôtel

---

129 Ibid.
130 AAP HD 1068.
131 AAP HD 1037, Brièle, 1866–82, tom. I, p. 352 and Brièle, 1881, p. 260.
132 AAP HD 1414.

Dieu she donated 50,000 *livres* out of respect for her executors. Next, to fulfil her obligation to her servants, she left 150,000 *livres* and a further 15,000 *livres* worth of pensions to her domestics. She gave 150,000 *livres* to the abbey of Montmartre (in which her heart was buried) where she had spent much of her life in order to pay for dowries in the order for 20 girls from Lorraine. As the duchesse de Lorraine, she felt a duty to leave a further 100,000 *livres* to establish a seminary for impoverished 'gentilshommes d'épée' from the duchy. She ordered 10,000 *livres* to be distributed to the poor of the duchy of Lorraine, another 10,000 to the poor of her own lands and pensions for charitable schools for both boys and girls to be built on her properties. To further benefit the people of her lands, she left 2,000 *livres* of annual *rentes* to found a hospital to care for the sick poor.[133] While the testament of the princesse de Guise was exceptional in its size and complexity, it seems to have followed the pattern which less wealthy nobles would have followed.

Most donations to the hospital were given from a religious motivation. The Hôtel Dieu had an obligation to say a great amount of memorial services in its chapel in honour of individual benefactors each year, a situation which continued – although with periodic limiting of the numbers during the eighteenth century – until 1789. There was no significant diminution of individuals donating for this purpose in any decade before the Revolution.[134] The organization of masses of remembrance for its wealthier donors could prove to be a problem for the administration of the Hôtel Dieu. The princesse de Guise, whose wishes the directors of the hospital acting as the executors of her will had to arrange, left money for 10,000 masses to be said for her soul in numerous churches on her lands, above and beyond the permanent annual services to be said which were tied to other donations.

The financial history of the hospital throughout the seventeenth century was a shift from reliance on its estates and charitable bequests to taxes levied on the city. This process was not the result of a steady decline in the income of the Hôtel Dieu and a growth in its responsibilities. Instead, the pattern was long periods of stability ended by years of crisis which necessitated the implementation of new forms of revenue. The institution experienced a period of financial stability between 1651 and 1661, when it was able to complete the building of the new wards on the left bank of the Seine and propose the construction of the hôpital des Convalescents. The levels of income meant that a small surplus was common in most years. This surplus was, however, much too small to act as the capital required for expansion. As a result, the hospital had traditionally borrowed money in the form of *rentes viagères* to finance its plans. An example of this sort of loan was the *rente* contracted between the Hôtel Dieu and the architect François Mansart in 1662 for a yearly payment of 1,000 *livres* in return for a single loan of 18,000 *livres*.[135] These *rentes* were a gamble on the part of both sides. The hospital determined the rate of repayment according to the age of the contractor, lowering the percentage of payments the younger the individual. Individuals undertook these loans in order to provide a permanent source of income for themselves, hoping to live until they received a profit from their investment.

---

133 AAP HD 1108.
134 Brièle ,1866–82, tom. I, pp. 339–45.
135 Brièle ,1881, p. 157.

The hospital was able to cover its expenditure and repay its debts during normal years. When there was a period of crop failure or sickness, the increased demands placed on it forced it to look elsewhere for money. The contracting of *rentes viagères* to pay for the new wards on the left bank had not harmed the hospital financially.[136] Between 1661 and 1663 the population of the institution grew to unusually high levels, numbering between 2,400 and over 4,000.[137] These were the first years during the period under study in which the Hôtel Dieu could not cover its costs through its own revenue. In previous years it could rely on charitable contributions to meet much of its expense, deflecting the rest through retrenchment. The finances of the hospital suffered gravely from the destitution caused by the food shortages of 1662–63. The number of rural poor coming to the city in search of assistance increased dramatically and many urban poor were unable to afford food during the scarcity. In these years, the Hôtel Dieu was unable to collect much of its revenue, causing it to operate with a large deficit, which exceeded 225,000 *livres* for 1662–63 compared to a total income for the two-year period of 360,000 *livres*, much of which was not paid until after the cessation of the crisis. The response to the hardships of these years by the hospital was to petition both crown and public for aid. This was indeed the strategy which the administration undertook. It published, as it had in previous years of crisis in 1640 and 1652, a pamphlet outlining the urgent need of the institution. It claimed that:

> If the charity of wealthy Parisians continues to abandon the hospital, as it has done for the last few years, then this celebrated hospital must fall and in this failure the poor will lose whatever hope remains to them in their misery. The great charitable gifts which were sometimes given over to the hands of the hospital governors have ceased to be granted, the Hôtel Dieu's collection boxes no longer attract the amounts that they used to bring, the donations and legacies are much more rare and their sums are very modest and the universal legacies which were rather frequent in previous centuries are now unknown.[138]

The creation of the Hôpital Général was blamed as the main reason for the diminution of donations, and the administrators accused it of spreading rumours that the Hôtel Dieu was concealing its wealth.[139] This is an interesting example of a dispute between partisans of the two institutions which, in theory, complemented each other. The tension between the two hospitals was never to be successfully resolved, despite the 1690 reform of their administrations, continuing into the eighteenth century. Besides the Hôpital Général, the Hôtel Dieu's directors came into conflict with those religious organizations which raised money for use outside the kingdom. They identified in particular the frères hospitaliers de la Charité, whom they accused of sending 'some considerable amount of money to Italy' and turning 'to the care of foreigners those sums which should be employed for the poor of this kingdom'.[140] In 1662, with its own finances undergoing a reform, the central government was reluctant to authorize

---

136 AN K 1024/4. Jean Bachelier's accounts for 1660 show a surplus of 62,131 *livres*.
137 Brièle, 1881, pp. 150–52.
138 AAP HD 879.
139 Ibid.
140 Brièle, 1881, p. 160.

new taxes which might diminish its own revenues. Instead, in the Edict of 1662, the crown agreed to demands to force towns and villages to care for their own poor in the hope that this would reduce the number of refugees from the provinces coming to the city. With the crown unwilling to help further, the administration of the hospital had to solve its financial crisis by appealing for increased donations and agreeing to convert its debts into *rentes* constituted on future income. The evidence for how the Hôtel Dieu overcame its deficit are scanty, but it seems that the appeal for more charity, coupled with the temporary cessation of payments to those holding *rentes* (although new ones were soon contracted to continue to purchase buildings needed for the construction of the hôpital des Convalescents), was enough.[141]

The Hôtel Dieu was trapped by its legal obligation to the descendants of Mazarin to build the hôpital des Convalescents. Much of the area to be redeveloped remained in private hands and it proved necessary to contract many new *rentes viagères* to purchase houses which occupied the site of the planned wards. The increased burden of payments brought the institution into financial problems in the 1670s and 1680s when the hospital ceased making repayments of the *rentes* which it owed. In these years the administrators followed a pattern of raising revenues which was to prove successful throughout the rest of the reign. First, the hospital appealed to the central government and the public for extraordinary alms. The amount of money granted to the Hôtel Dieu by the crown, even in periods of crisis, was generally given to inspire other private donations rather than to bail it out of trouble. This was the case in 1686 when the king gave 6,000 *livres* to the hospital, which was certainly not enough to cover the debts owed, but showed the interest the crown took in the survival of the institution.[142] The second tactic of the board of directors was to threaten to sell off much of its lands and houses, as happened in April 1690 when the administration:

> decided to have *letters patentes* registered as soon as possible that will bring permission for the hospital to sell some of its lands and possessions. The Hôtel Dieu will sell off its goods up to the value of 1,200,000 *livres* and the hôpital des Incurables will do so to the value of 800,000 *livres* in order to pay arrearages of *rentes viagères* owed by both.[143]

This judgement was accompanied by the announcement that the gardens of the hôpital Saint-Louis and the organs of the Hôtel Dieu were going to be sold, but there is no record of a liquidation of the lands or houses owned by the hospital. It is more likely that this decision was made to emphasize its poverty to the populace in order to smooth over any discontent there might have been in regard to the new tax on wine entering the city, which would benefit the hospital and calm the fears of existing creditors. The third tactic taken by the administration was to appeal to both the civic elites and the government to allow new local taxes to be raised to prevent bankruptcy. In January 1690 the Hôtel Dieu received permission to collect a tax of '30 sols par muid de vin' entering the city of Paris.[144] Consumption taxes on the entry of goods into Paris were a major part of the Hôtel Dieu's income already by 1656,

---

141 Fosseyeux, 1912, p. 403.
142 Brièle, 1881, p. 229.
143 Ibid., p. 238.
144 AAP HG 26 and Brièle, 1881, p. 236.

but after 1690 they were to proliferate. The income from the tax on wine was granted to the Hôtel Dieu, but the right to collect it was sold to tax farmers. This new tax brought in slightly less than 150,000 *livres* per year, effectively doubling the total income of the hospital and enabling it to escape a financial calamity and to continue its obligation to repay its debts.[145]

The Hôtel Dieu returned to its familiar strategy of retrenchment coupled with appeals for assistance during the crisis of the winter of 1709 when the number of sick at the Hôtel Dieu rose above 4,500. The board requested the assistance of the archbishop of Paris, now himself a governor, in soliciting charitable donations from the city's churches.[146] By September 1709, the hospital had ceased to make its payments on its debts, and asked for permission once again from the crown to sell off part of its domaine to meet its commitments. This request seems, as well, to have been a bargaining ploy to secure the crown's help through raising new taxes on the city. In October, the board had received the right to levy an extraordinary tax on Parisian landlords. In November, a lottery, in effect a voluntary tax, was granted to raise 400,000 *livres* for the hospital.[147] As with the taxes raised on the city earlier in the century, the lottery was renewed each year, shifting the balance of the hospital's finances more towards reliance on local taxes rather than its own estates. When the crisis subsided in the following year, the Hôtel Dieu was able to begin to make payments on the *rentes* it owed. By 1714, its revenues were in firm enough state to begin the construction of new wards on the left bank of the Seine, completing the link between the Pont-au-Double and the Petit Châtelet.

By the time of the death of Louis XIV, the ruling elites of Paris, whose interests were represented by the board of directors of the Hôtel Dieu, had transformed the hospital from a shelter for the sick staffed by amateur practitioners into an institution where the poor of the city could seek charitable treatment from physicians and surgeons. This fact should not diminish the important clinical changes made during the French Revolution, but the development of the medical staff of the Paris Hôtel Dieu points out an important, if sometimes under-researched, aspect of the history of medicine. The elites in France, from the nobility on their estates to office-holders and bourgeois in urban centres, had begun to recognize the social importance of medicine as early as the sixteenth century. Ambitious families sought to further their own social aspirations through the provision of medical charity.[148] Likewise, both physicians and surgeons used their service at the Hôtel Dieu as a means to advance their own careers. In Paris, this convergence of ambitions helped to establish a staff of medical men in the Hôtel Dieu. Medical charity, the offering of services well beyond the means of most Parisians, was a participatory means for the urban elites to negotiate for social and political dominance in the city. The Hôtel Dieu functioned, in part, as

---

145 Brièle, 1881, pp. 237–9, AAP HD 868 and AN K1024/16. The total income of the hospital for the two-year period of 1662–63 had been 360,098 *livres*.

146 Brièle, 1881, pp. 262–3.

147 Ibid., pp. 264.

148 Albert, 1658. Luynes outlines the duties of nobility, an important part of which was the provision of medical services to the poor on a seigneur's estate.

a form of social control, but not an authoritarian one. The hospital offered a place of shelter and healing to the lower orders, who deferred to their social superiors in return. If the Parisian ruling elites recognized that the services of physicians and surgeons could be turned to their own social profit, this fact must point to the desire of the lower orders to acquire those services. The increased demand for the services of the institution's staff attests to the fact that hospital medicine during the period assisted in popularizing learned medicine amongst the urban population.

Late eighteenth-century attacks on the quality of care at the Paris Hôtel Dieu should not lead historians to judge the hospital's early modern history in a negative light. Jacques Tenon's criticisms of the institution were informed by new standards of hygiene and hospital construction that had been developed during the Enlightenment.[149] The fire that badly damaged the wards in 1772 also reduced the quality of care offered by the hospital. Although Tenon argued for revolutionary change, insisting that the only way to improve care for the city's population was to demolish the centrally located Hôtel Dieu and replace it with a series of smaller suburban hospices, the hospital remained largely unchanged until it was rebuilt on a site on the opposite side of the Ile-de-la-Cité in the mid nineteenth century. While Tenon's arguments were based on Enlightenment ideas, he was equally influenced by the developments of the early modern period. During the sixteenth and seventeenth centuries the patrons and directors of the Hôtel Dieu led the way towards creating an institution where both professional and amateur medical practitioners sought to treat and cure the sick.

---

149 Tenon, 1788.

Chapter Four

The Reform of Poor Relief in Paris

During the medieval and early modern period Paris attracted the able-bodied poor from the countryside in both good times and bad. Many of the newly arrived immigrants did not have established kin networks with enough resources to assist in periods of unemployment Likewise, the city's sixteenth-century relief system benefited mostly those who had ties in the city, were known in their parishes and had a lengthy residence there. The unskilled, particularly the young and the old, who had no formal relationship, such as an apprenticeship, to their employers, found employment often temporary or seasonal. Often the underemployed were forced to turn to begging in order to supplement their income.

The 1656 reorganization of Paris's poor relief system in the form of the Hôpital Général was designed to cope with those sorts of the worthy poor not granted assistance elsewhere. It was designed to retrain the young and to shelter the old in order to monitor expenses and to direct services away from those perceived as the undeserving poor. By the eighteenth century the importance placed on this reorganization is witnessed in the crown's claim to have been the guiding hand behind it. One of the series of medallions commissioned to celebrate the events of Louis XIV's reign commemorated the 1656 foundation of the Hôpital Général of Paris and linked its origin to the king's wish to eradicate the problem of vagrancy.[1] The Parisian reform of poor relief for the able-bodied poor has come, in the eyes of many historians, to be symbolized by this grand institution.[2]

The urban elites of Paris, the *noblesse de robe* and the bourgeois who aspired to that rank, oversaw the creation, the administration and the finances of the Hôpital Général of Paris. The hospital directors and their allies in the sovereign courts were a major force in putting pressure on the crown to develop a policy toward the poor in order to protect their Hôpital Général. While the hospital never succeeded fully in its stated aim to eliminate public begging, the reform of poor relief in the city from a system offering out-of-doors assistance to one that confined the poor was important for the Parisian elites. In the Hôpital Général, they exercised their religious obligations, displayed their civic leadership by retraining the poor and demonstrated their social worth through providing assistance in an urban context similar to the charitable obligation of the old nobility on their rural estates.

---

1 *Médailles sur les principaux évenements du regne de Louis le Grand*, 1702, p. 42.

2 See, for example: Lallemand, 1909–12; Paultre, 1906; Foucault, 1961; Imbert, 1993; Hickey, 1997.

The foundation of the Paris Hôpital Général

Paris in the sixteenth and seventeenth centuries grew in both physical size and population. The city as a place of opportunity for those who had little to hold them in the countryside proved irresistible for many. Indeed the city could not have survived and grown without a constant influx of outsiders to make up for the discrepancy between birth rates and death rates. The presence of a large number of religious houses also tempted those facing poverty in rural parishes to come to the capital in search of charity from the church. Waves of crop failures, food shortages and epidemics in the Paris basin during the sixteenth and seventeenth centuries could put large numbers of the rural poor on the road to seek shelter and assistance in the city. While the poor could overwhelm Paris during crises, it was the perceived increase in numbers during the first half of the sixteenth century that created a fear of the potential for disorder caused by beggars. Prior to the sixteenth century, Paris had lacked any formal poor relief system. Besides the customary handouts and shelter offered by some of the religious houses in and around the city, the poor of medieval Paris could turn only to kinship and occupational networks of assistance, if that was possible, or to whatever charitable funds the parish of their residence might have to offer. Impoverished newcomers would have found it difficult to find enough help to prevent them from turning to begging for casual alms to survive.

The presence of individuals who had little or no formal connection to society was feared in as strict a hierarchy as early modern France. The city took action against vagabonds in 1532 by ordering all able-bodied poor caught begging within the city walls to be put to labour on public works. The city government then took action to restrict assistance to only the worthy poor. In 1544 it reorganized municipal poor relief under the Grand Bureau des Pauvres. This organization was administered by a board composed of *échevins* of the Hôtel de Ville until 1577 when the judges of the sovereign courts flexed their muscles and took over control.[3] The Grand Bureau was responsible for distributing funds levied from a direct tax on the householders of Paris to the worthy poor. The poor received assistance in their own homes, a method found to be inexpensive and flexible. The poor were provided with food, clothing and some access to medical treatment, if necessary, providing the officers of the Grand Bureau judged that they were eligible for relief. As much of the population of Paris existed in a working environment where even a minor injury or sickness could cause destitution, the outdoor relief was popular among the city's lower orders. It allowed those artisans who were unable to work temporarily a certain amount of relief to stave off long-term poverty. In function, the Grand Bureau des Pauvres protected artisans below the level of master. Journeymen who relied on their labour to put food in their mouths and a roof over their heads could be confident that a temporary period of unemployment would not result in utter destitution. Men and women who were known as being worthy to the Bureau or to their parish curés were those most often assisted.

The Grand Bureau helped established workers and their families, but it failed to address the Parisian elites' most pressing concern regarding poverty: that of the

---

3   Imbert, 1993, pp. 29–35.

newly-arrived poor who turned often to begging and who were perceived as a threat to public order. As well, hand outs were made to the poor with no control as to how they spent the money. For the devout of Paris, this was a second and more significant problem posed by the sort of poor relief embodied by the Grand Bureau. The Grand Bureau lacked any mechanism to tie assistance to religious instruction. During the early decades of the seventeenth century, with the spread of Catholic Reform ideas, outdoor relief was discredited because of concerns on the part of some authors about the value of supporting the poor outside the walls of an institution.

The creation in 1612 of the Hôpital de la Pitié was the earliest attempt to put the confinement of the poor into practice in Paris. This hospital was organized by a number of the city's bourgeois under the patronage of Marie de Médicis, but it was not intended that the institution would replace the Grand Bureau des Pauvres. The hospital did not offer assistance to adults who were deemed physically capable of earning a living. In theory, the hospital would help to exterminate begging and idleness by removing from the streets the deserving poor, confining the young to be instructed, the old to receive relief and religious succor. Workers made idle would still be given assistance by the Grand Bureau if they were judged worthy. While it was recognized that this policy would be expensive, the directors of the Pitié hoped that by restricting relief to the deserving poor, the idle poor would receive no income from begging and would return to work. However, by 1620, the plans to imprison all of the deserving poor in the city within the institution had come undone due to a lack of financial support, leaving it limited to offering relief only to young girls. The Hôpital de la Pitié failed as a hospital of confinement because a majority of the urban elites before the 1650s remained unconvinced of the need to support such a costly policy.

A change in attitude among the city elites came during the decades of the mid seventeenth century. Influenced by humanist writers on economic matters and inspired by the zeal of theologians such as François de Sales, the policy of confining the poor, or *enfermement*, became the cornerstone of the Compagnie du Saint-Sacrement's plan to reform the moral and religious nature of France. The Paris chapter of the Compagnie was founded in 1629 by the duc de Ventadour. The main goals of the secret society was to continue during peacetime the armed conflict against Protestantism in France that had ended with the Catholic victory over the Huguenots at La Rochelle and the defeat of the duc de Rohan's Protestant army in Languedoc.[4] In Paris, this group, who, over the decades, grew in number to include many of the senior members of the Parisian sovereign courts, as well as a broad selection of the social elites of the capital, both lay and ecclesiastic, worked to spread its ideas throughout the 1630s and 1640s. The growth of this and of other confraternities inspired by similar Catholic Reformation beliefs was of paramount importance for the foundation of the Hôpital Général. The Compagnie petitioned influential men to bring about moral reform amongst the population of the city.

---

4   Poujol, 1982, p. 10. Poujol reprints transcripts of the minutes (now lost) of the first three meetings of the Hôpital Général's board of directors, cf. Elmore, 1975. The full importance of the *dévot* movement to the founding of the Hôpital Général is explored in Depauw, 1999.

Devout members of the sovereign courts and city government concluded that the Grand Bureau had failed to reduce the number of the city's poor because it had lacked a religious motivation.[5] In the seventeenth century, a concurrence of ideas between religious and secular authors developed that the best method to reform the morality of the poor and to reshape them into productive subjects was by means of supervised religious instruction within confinement hospitals. The fear common among the devout that the poor could die lacking salvation because of their ignorance was a great motivation for action.[6]

During the 1630s and 40s the Compagnie recruited members from the judges of the Parisian sovereign courts. Among its membership plans were developed to fully put the theory of confining the poor into effect. For the Compagnie, the logic of the plan to end idleness by making sure that only the deserving poor received assistance was unassailable. Most important for the members was the fact that confinement would allow the hospital to teach the poor proper religion and to monitor their progress. *Enfermement* had sprung from the desire of the urban elites to reform the poor in both mind and soul. Poverty was blamed on the religious ignorance of the poor. The Edict of 1656 that established the Paris Hôpital Général listed 'that many of them [the poor] of both sexes live together without marriage, many of their children are not baptized and almost all live wholly ignorant of religion'.[7] It was for this reason that they had to be taught proper Christian behaviour. Most theorists on the subject of charity and poor relief identified a lack of proper understanding of Christian principles with poverty and criminal behaviour. The devout groups, such as the Compagnie du Saint-Sacrement, argued that there was little point in offering support to the poor in their own home, as the Grand Bureau provided, if it was unlikely to effect changes in their character. Change, it was believed by these individuals, could only be accomplished by religious instruction, hard work to keep idle hands busy, and constant supervision to prevent backsliding.

During the decades after the founding of the Compagnie du Saint-Sacrement in 1629 until the establishment of the Hôpital Général in 1656, the membership of the Compagnie worked to spread the concept of *enfermement* as the predominant theory of poor relief and charitable policy among the Parisian elites. In 1640, the judges of the sovereign courts discussed the possibility of creating a new confinement hospital in Paris, but no action was taken.[8] The events of the years that followed seem to have convinced many of the magistrates of the city that the ideas urged on them by the Compagnie du Saint-Sacrement needed to be implemented. In the late 1640s, poor harvests caused the income from agricultural lands owned by Parisian charitable institutions, such as the Hôtel Dieu and the Hôpital de la Pitié, to fall while expenditure rose as the rural poor came to the city to seek assistance.[9] In 1648 the judges of the Parlement entered into direct opposition with the policies of the first minister,

---

5   Ibid.
6   *L'Hospital General de Paris*, 1676, p. 2.
7   AAP HG 2.
8   Poujol, 1982, p. 30.
9   AAP HD 868. The Hôtel Dieu suffered a deficit of 67,311 *livres* in 1651, provoking a public appeal for charitable donations by its administration.

Mazarin. The situation for Paris turned from bad to worse when *parlementaire* obstructionism escalated to civil war. These political matters only served to make the problems facing poor relief in the city worse, causing the disruption of the Grand Bureau's ability to function, and meetings were held in 1649–51 during the upheaval of the Frondes by senior members of the sovereign courts to discuss the idea of utilizing the munitions works known as La Salpêtrière to confine all of the city's poor in a single place.[10] The number of homeless in the city reached its peak in 1652, when famine and fighting caused the worst disruption of the seventeenth century in the region around Paris.[11] In 1653, the Premier Président of the Parlement, Pomponne de Bellièvre proposed that a major reform of poor relief be undertaken. Providing assistance to the poor of the city would allow the judges of the sovereign courts to reassert their leadership and social control over the lower orders. Doing so was seen to be especially important after the reputation of the Parlement and its allies was damaged during the Frondes. Bellièvre argued against the need for an entirely new institution and requested an investigation into the viability of reforming municipal poor relief by uniting those charitable establishments which already existed, such as the Hôpital de la Pitié, into a new general hospital of confinement under a single direction led by members of the sovereign courts:

> The previously mentioned seigneur [Bellièvre] stated that it was impractical to build new hospitals in the city and that it would be better to reform those which were already established, he asked M du Plessis to conduct an investigation of these hospitals. Then a meeting was held ... where it was decided that the goal was possible, that there was only a question of making its outcome seem achievable and that the matter should be placed in the hands of God. Three days later a meeting was held with Bellièvre, he first warned of the difficulty of achieving the foundation but was finally persuaded that it could be accomplished.[12]

It was very important that a senior figure in the Parlement such as the Premier Président should be seen to lead the foundation. His presence lent credibility to the new institution:

> One of the most illustrious magistrates that we have had in our time embraced this plan with a signal affection. This magistrate was M de Bellièvre the Premier Président of the Parlement. God had inspired within him all of the sentiments on the subject of poverty that one could desire in a person of his rank. The hospital to which he gave the name of Hôpital Général is obliged to have and eternal respect for his memory and must never cease to recognize the good service that it received from him.[13]

His support could command the attention of others, bringing with it both the administrative and monetary support of those who wished to ingratiate themselves with him. Once the decision to found the Hôpital Général was made, Bellièvre took

---

10 Poujol, 1982, p. 30.

11 J. Dupâquier, 'Demographic crises and subsistence crises in France, 1650–1725', in Walter and Schofield, 1989, p. 192.

12 Poujol, 1982, p. 31.

13 *L'Hospital*, 1676, p. 3.

control of the plans, appointing a committee made up of men selected from the sovereign courts, to write the rules by which the hospital and its board of directors would work.[14] With the inclusion of Bellièvre, who was not only influential with the wealthy of the capital, but who also had an important relationship with the crown, the hospital was more secure in the knowledge that it could command the resources required for its survival.

While the city's elites might have been convinced by the increase of beggars on the streets that the policy of *enfermement* was necessary, the central government seemed to be indifferent. Members of the ministry left the implementation of poor relief up to the Parisian elites, a situation which had been traditional. It was prepared to offer some support to the Hôpital Général because this was a way for the crown to co-operate and demonstrate its usefulness to important citizens of the capital. The crown approved the assumption of responsibility for poor relief in Paris by Bellièvre's committee. It did not, however, wish to be responsible for the success or failure of the institution, particularly during a difficult period for Mazarin following his disastrous relations with the judges of the Parlement during the Frondes:

> and by the good service that M de Bellièvre had rendered, all of the royal ministers swore to assist with the goals of the hospital, but the ministers did not want to be charged with making something succeed about which they still had doubts.[15]

Following the death of Bellièvre in 1656, the board of directors of the Hôpital Général:

> asked Messieurs the royal ministers to give their orders for the confinement of the poor, they returned the authority for the execution of the confinement to the judges and M de Nesmond who then presided over the Parlement began this great work with much zeal and with all of the ability that we could desire from him.[16]

There was a contemporary belief that the Hôpital Général would be successful thanks to the new 'concours' of the interests of the established Parisian elites, judicial office-holders and bourgeois of the city, and the crown.[17] It is clear here that the crown meant to provide what immaterial assistance it could to aid the Parisian elites, but not to direct the administration itself or be responsible for the financial survival of the hospital. For the central government, this assistance was a good way of showing that it could help the influential citizens in the capital, and could repair relationships badly damaged during the Frondes by upholding the traditional right of the locality to manage poor relief.

---

14 Poujol, 1982, p. 31.
15 *L'Hospital*, 1676, p. 4.
16 Ibid., p. 5.
17 Ibid.

Governing the hospital

By the terms of the edict of April 1656 members of the Parisian elites formed the administration of the Hôpital Général. At the head of the hospital's board of directors the edict named, as *chefs-nés,* the holders of the offices of Premier Président of the Parlement of Paris and Procureur Général du Roi.[18] At the time of the foundation of the hospital these posts were held by Pomponne II de Bellièvre, who was influential in its creation, and Nicolas Fouquet, not only a person with ties to Mazarin, but also a member of the Compagnie du Saint-Sacrement.[19] It was vital for the sovereign courts, who felt that they had a right to oversee poor relief in the capital, to have senior representatives on the board in order to act as a check on any unnecessary expenditure which might be requested by other members. While these two directors had a great deal of influence in shaping the course which the Hôpital Général was to take, the day-to-day operation of the hospital was taken by the lower-ranking members.

The *chefs-nés* of the hospital board scrutinized the decisions taken by the rest, but did not take an active part in the administration of the daily operations of the various parts of the hospital. The greater part of the board (26 of the 28 individuals named) was composed of a combination of lesser figures of the sovereign courts and members of the bourgeoisie of Paris and represented a cross section of the urban elites.[20] These men held their positions in the administration for life, being replaced on their death by individuals elected by the board of directors.[21] It was these men who managed most of the administrative tasks of the hospital. Their responsibilities required them to make regular inspections of the hospital buildings, to serve in rotation as the director in charge of receiving new admissions and to carry out the administration of the institution's finances. Many of these administrators were clients of the senior men and regarded service in the hospital as a stage in their *cursus honorum* toward attaining higher offices. While many board members would have felt the need to defer to the wishes of the Premier Président and the Procureur Général on many of the issues raised in discussion due to their senior positions and social rank, each member had an equal say in the operation of the hospital.

The entire membership, including the *chefs-nés* or their deputies, met twice a week in a general meeting, where the business which concerned the Hôpital Général as a whole would be discussed. To look after the affairs of each of the component houses of the hospital, the board divided itself into various commissions,

---

18 AAP HG 2. Both offices were part of the Gens du Roi of the Parlement, but once in place, those who held these posts acted with great autonomy.

19 The membership of the Compagnie du Saint-Sacrement was a closely guarded secret. If Fouquet was not an official member of the society, he certainly knew its members and strongly approved of its aims. Dessert, 1987, pp. 189–94.

20 Ibid. The Edict of 1656 named, besides the Premier Président and the Procureur Général: nine members of the sovereign courts – the Parlement, Chambre des Comptes, and Cour des Aides; three seigneurs of lands in the immediate vicinity of Paris (who might also have been members of the sovereign courts or the bourgeoisie); eight 'ancien consuls;' and six 'bourgeois de Paris'.

21 AAP HG 2 and AN K1024/45*bis.*

each reporting to the general meeting. Besides these committees, members were deputed to independent commissions to oversee various aspects of the operation of the Hôpital Général. The most important of these was the eight-man committee established to manage the finances of the hospital. There are no surviving records of who besides the Premier Président of the Parlement sat on this committee; but, as its duties included the collection of income, repayment of debts, and the prosecution and defence of the hospital's civil suits, it is likely that it was composed mostly of men from the sovereign courts who would have had skill in conducting such matters.[22] For individual problems faced by the Hôpital Général, temporary committees were set up to discuss them if the business merited a deeper consideration. All matters discussed in these committees would be submitted to an executive board, which was held every Thursday in the residence of the Premier Président, for a final recommendation.[23] In these meetings, in his own residence, the Premier Président would have been able to ensure that the hospital's affairs would be settled to his liking, presenting final decisions for approval by the general assembly of the board of directors.

For an institution which placed such an emphasis on religion, it is surprising that the church should have been denied representation in its administration in 1656. The Hôpital Général relied a great deal on the support of devout Parisians, many of whom were members of the secular and regular clergy, who saw in it an outlet for Christian charity. Since its inception, the hospital had collected donations via boxes placed for this purpose in all of the city's churches. In 1673, an edict was issued to bring the archbishop of Paris on to the board of directors. The inclusion of the archbishop has been interpreted as the interference of a more devout Louis XIV forcing a new religiosity into the crown's social policy.[24] Robert Poujol argues that this was a turn away from the 'modernism' of the original charter of the Hôpital Général (which, in his opinion, saw a combined effort between central and local government looking after social welfare) and a return to a 'medieval' church-dominated charity.[25] This idea is mistaken. The Royal Edict of 29 April 1673, which changed the composition of the administration, shows that the decision had been petitioned from the board itself, stating that the directors of the Hôpital Général had remonstrated with the government that the hospital had been founded at a time when the diocese of Paris was empty (in fact the office was claimed by the Cardinal de Retz), preventing the appointment of the archbishop to head the board as had been originally planned.[26] In 1673, the directors asked to have the archbishop appointed in order to inspire zeal and to raise charitable funds for the hospital among the devout of the capital. A 1722 report written for the cathedral chapter about the finances of the Hôpital Général believed that the change had been inspired by the Procureur Général, Achille III de Harlay, to bring his relative François de Harlay, then the Archbishop of Paris, into the administration as head of the board in order to lessen the prestige of the Premier

---

22 *L'Hospital*, 1676, p. 11.
23 Ibid., pp. 10–11.
24 Poujol, 1982, p. 23 and Imbert, 1993, pp. 211–16.
25 Ibid.
26 AAP HG 6.

Président, Guillaume de Lamoignon, his rival.[27] Whatever the reason for the reform, the report stressed the good that it, and the administrative change later in 1690, had achieved for the finances and management of the hospital.[28]

In January 1690, at the same time as a reform of the administration of the Hôtel Dieu, which was suffering from financial difficulties, a further change in the composition of the board of the Hôpital Général was carried out by royal edict. The amendment was brought about as the hospital was suffering a great deal from its inability to make payments on its outstanding debts.[29] The directors of the hospital asked for a reform in its administration, bringing other senior officials of the courts and the city on to the board. A royal edict was granted to enlarge the board to include as new *chefs-nés* the Premiers Présidents of the Chambre des Comptes and the Cour des Aides, the Lieutenant Général de Police and the Prévôt des Marchands. The new members were put on the board to aid in the administration and facilitate relations between the hospital and the police and judicial bodies of the city:

> We [the king] have judged it appropriate to join some of the principal magistrates of our city of Paris to those who we have already charged with the administration of the hospital at the time of its foundation. This is done not only to increase the assistance that we desire it should have with the rules of law in all of our courts where its business could be brought, but also to better the necessary relations that this hospital has with the police and the good order of our fine city of Paris.[30]

The reform provided all of the sovereign courts as well as the Hôtel de Ville and those charged with the city's police with representation on the board, giving them a stake in the hospital's survival. Royal edicts were required in both 1673 and 1690 in order to change the terms of the original Royal Edict of 1656 which had established the form the hospital board would take. Of course the positioning on the board of a royal appointee such as the Archbishop of Paris and of so many influential office-holders gave the crown a greater ability to keep an eye on the hospital's finances; however, the new members seem to have acted more as supporters of the institution than as royal spies or operatives during the reign of Louis XIV.

Confining the poor in Paris

The 1656 reform of poor relief in Paris that created the Hôpital Général was intended to separate the able-bodied poor from the rest of society following the precepts of the theory of *enfermement*. The hospital has often been regarded as a prison for the able-bodied poor. However, at the beginning it was planned to confine only those too young and too old to earn a living. Separate laws forbidding casual alms-giving in Paris would be put into effect, compelling anyone capable to return to work. The hospital's backers believed that confinement was a logical approach to put public

27 AN K1024/45*bis*.

28 Ibid.

29 AAP HG 26. The royal edict sanctioning a new tax on wine in 1690 stated that both hospitals were required to spend the new income to repay the debts which they owed.

30 AAP HG 6.

begging to an end. Inside the Hôpital Général the able-bodied poor who deserved relief were to be taught a skill and morally retrained. During the second half of the seventeenth century the concept of *enfermement* continued to evolve, as the deserving poor were categorized and more individuals would come to fit its definition.

When its doors were opened in March 1657, the goal of the Hôpital Genéral was:

> to end begging and idleness and to prevent all of the disorders which derive from these two sources and to establish manufactures. It is to bring the poor to the fear of God and to a better regulated life, to make them into good artisans, into good citizens and into good Christians. It is to give an ample opportunity to all persons of piety to undertake works of mercy in these charitable spaces and to assist them to work for their own sanctity while helping win salvation for the poor.[31]

It was an ambitious venture, requiring resources, not only to feed and house the poor, but also to reform their work habits and personal morality. It is typical of contemporary beliefs about the poor that the founders of the Hôpital Général felt that those in their charge could earn their living simply through improving their character, giving little or no thought to economic and demographic causes of poverty.

The original foundation was not an entirely new hospital, but a reorganization of several charitable institutions under a single administration.[32] In 1656, the buildings of the newly united Hôpital Général required renovation to accommodate the expected number of the deserving poor. This enlargement of the hospital, especially the wards of La Salpêtrière, continued sporadically throughout the late seventeenth and early eighteenth centuries. The hospital's renovation allowed its wealthiest benefactors to display their devotion and social worthiness in a very public setting.[33] Benefactors made sure their names were associated with the hospital and their donations were made known to the public, such as the donations made by the duchesse de Guise in 1686.[34] Those families who chose not to build or to donate furnishings could still play a participatory role in the assistance of the poor through organized visits and public ceremonies involving chosen inmates of the hospital. Missionary activity in the wards was organized by the Jesuits and devout members of the elites were invited to participate.[35] Milestones in the hospital's history were celebrated first in the chapel at La Pitié and then, after 1670, in the chapel at La Salpêtrière. These important masses involved both the institution's benefactors and the poor, such as the mass said to commemorate the hospital's opening in 1657.[36] The crown, too, made the effort to associate itself with the institution, demonstrating the king's devotion through occasional gifts. Selected poor girls suffering from scrofula were brought

---

31 Ibid.

32 *L'Hospital*, 1676, p. 1.

33 Brièle, 1888, p. 237. Brièle reprints the register of deliberations of the board members deputed to manage La Salpêtrière from 1677–87.

34 Ibid., p. 252.

35 Ibid., pp. 239–40.

36 AAP HG 23. Many of these masses were advertised in advance by the printing and distribution of broadsheets.

each year from the hospital to be healed by the king's touch during the court's Easter celebrations.[37]

The Hôpital Général replaced the outdoor relief granted by the Grand Bureau des Pauvres with aid directed to the worthy poor inside the walls of the institution. Following the reform, the poor would be categorized and processed by the hospital staff; their freedom to move outside the walls of the institution was limited. Once the hospital opened its doors in March 1657, the able-bodied poor were expected to make their own way to the main reception courtyard at La Pitié in order to claim assistance. There, the member of the hospital board assigned to the task for that day would assess each individual and send him or her to the appropriate house and ward of the hospital. The poor would each be given tickets allowing them to travel to their destination unmolested in the streets by the various police bodies of the city.[38] The hospital was granted a troop of archers of the poor who were required to make regular patrols of the streets and to post guards at the city gates to detain those who did not present themselves to be confined. Individuals of both sexes caught in this manner were also sent to La Pitié and then escorted to the house to which the director sent them.[39] The hospital was not intended to imprison all of the city's poor; only those considered deserving of relief were given shelter. The able-bodied poor caught by the archers who were judged to have no physical impediment to work, and who were judged to be unemployed from laziness and willful idleness, were classified as vagabonds and ordered to be banished from Paris in accordance with the previous laws of the city.[40]

Contemporary social and religious attitudes helped to shape how the policy of *enfermement* developed. At first the Hôpital Général was intended to confine only the unmarried poor of both sexes. A pamphlet, published in 1657, overstated the case that the hospital would provide aid to all of the able-bodied poor.[41] In fact, it was not planned to receive married couples at first, as it was deemed contrary to the sanctity of the sacrament of marriage to separate them. They would be given outdoor relief;[42] however, the children of such couples were taken into the wards to be given food, shelter and instruction. This separation was harsh, but the administration saw it not only as vital to ensure that children were properly taught, but also as a way to help those poor who found their family resources being overburdened by a large family. In the absence of useful methods of birth control, the Hôpital Général acted as a shelter for children whose parents were unable to afford them.

The provision of outdoor relief to married couples had proved a problem for the administration by 1661. In order to receive their dole, couples were required to present themselves daily at La Salpêtrière where they could be given some religious

---

37 Brièle, 1888, p. 253. In 1686, 84 girls were brought to Versailles. The king gave each girl a gift of 15 *sols* (which was subsequently taken from them by the hospital directors as a donation to the institution by the king).

38 AAP HG 14.

39 AAP HG 11.

40 Ibid.

41 AN K1024/35.

42 AAP HG 2.

and moral instruction. During the period of famine of the early 1660s, however, it was no longer considered acceptable to permit any individuals or married couples to remain at large where they might supplement their charitable assistance by begging. Robert Poujol claims that it was the wish of the king himself to see the success of the policy of *enfermement* which changed the original rules of the hospital and allowed the confinement of married couples in the hospital.[43] It is true that an *Edit du Roi* had initiated the change, but royal legislation, requested by the directors of the hospital, had been needed to change the original *lettres patentes* of 1656, which had forbidden the housing of married couples.[44] The hospital board had concerns that couples who received alms from the Hôpital Général would continue to beg in the streets, therefore undermining the theory of *enfermement* which was under severe pressure in 1661 to 1663. There was also a fear that these couples, who were not subject to the continuous religious atmosphere of daily life in the hospital, would revert to a sinful life more easily outside the hospital.[45] The policy change to force married couples into the hospital was the first of many the administration faced due to the unforeseen difficulties in putting the theory of confinement into practice.

The poor within the Hôpital Général were segregated from each other according to type. Each house of the hospital dealt with different categories. The largest, the Maison de Saint-Denys la Salpêtrière, was responsible for the confinement of children of both sexes up to the age of four, but the greater part of the house was devoted to women who were categorized as incapable of work. In effect it came to house a large population of young and very elderly women along with the blind, the mad, the handicapped and a large number of epileptics.[46] Young women were taught the tenets of Catholicism and, if they were deemed able, were instructed in skills such as spinning thread and weaving cloth. A few girls of a suitable age were chosen each year to receive one of the few dowries placed charitably at the disposal of the directors to ensure that the poor could marry a respectable man. The house also had rooms for boys between the ages of four to six, who were segregated from the women and taught to read, to write and to learn the catechism.[47] From the age of six or seven, the boys learned lacemaking or were instructed in the petit Seminaire, where the best suited were taught how to sing and were sent to serve as altar and choir boys in some of the city's churches.[48] At 12 years old, the boys would be sent to the men's house at Bicêtre to be taught new skills by master artisans paid by the directors.[49] After 1661, in the three *grands dortoirs* of La Salpêtrière, which were subdivided into 250 small

---

43 Poujol, 1982, p. 17.
44 AAP HG 11.
45 Ibid.
46 *L'Hospital*, 1676, p. 8.
47 Ibid.
48 Ibid.
49 Ibid. The boys were 'pour estre employez à des métiers ou manufactures, selon leurs inclinations et talens; y ayant pour cet effert outre le tricot des Maistres Fileurs de laines Drapiers, Tisserands, Lacetiers, Tissutiers, Cordonniers, Charrons, Serruriers Cordiers, et de toutes autres professions et mestiers'.

rooms, the hospital housed elderly married men, segregated from their wives, who were no longer able to earn their living by work.[50]

After its inclusion in the Hôpital Général, the building of La Pitié continued to confine young girls. From ages four to six, these girls were taught to say prayers and the precepts of Catholicism as authorized by the board and by the cathedral chapter of Paris. At six the girls were divided according to the assessment of the nuns. The nuns taught the rudiments of reading and writing and the catechism to those who were deemed to be both intelligent and worthy. When they were physically able, the girls were taught the techniques of lacemaking, sewing and needlepoint so that they could eventually find employment and earn a living.[51] La Pitié also contained a subdivision of up to 100 boys aged 12 and 13 which was known as the Petit Pitié. Here, the boys were under the control of two masters who taught them to become gravediggers for the communal graveyards of the city.[52]

The Maison de Saint Jean-Baptiste de Bicêtre, located south of the city, was the place of confinement for adult men. It was not an accident that this house was located the farthest away from the city of all the components of the Hôpital Général, as these poor were considered to represent the gravest risk of social disorder for the capital.[53] Here the younger inmates were put to work at a variety of tasks similar to the work performed by the women at La Salpêtrière, learning various skills in the textile trade which would hopefully enable them to seek employment. As well, men were taught skills in the trades considered to be more appropriate for their sex than for women, such as locksmithing and barrel-making.[54] As at La Salpêtrière, the house was mostly populated by elderly and crippled men who could not work. A Maison de Force, in effect a prison, was established in the building in 1680 in order to confine able-bodied men deemed to be incorrigible idlers and sent by the archers of the poor or by *lettres de cachet*. These men were sheltered for a month and subjected to the rigours of life within the institution, given religious instruction and training, before being released to seek work.

The showpiece of the attempt of the Hôpital Général to retrain the poor into productive subjects was, at first, intended to be the carpet manufacture at La Savonnerie located in Chaillot. This facility was converted in 1664 into a luxury manufactory of 'tapis de turque' in an effort to teach a highly skilled trade to selected young poor boys. However, this project was one of the first of the hospital board to fail, being described as a 'very heavy burden for the Hôpital Général'.[55] The hospital found it very expensive to pay, not only for their food, clothing and education, but also the apprenticeship fees of the boys. At the request of the board, La Savonnerie was separated from the rest of the hospital and privatized by leasing it directly to a

---

50   Ibid.

51   Ibid., p. 7.

52   Ibid., pp. 7–8.

53   The Hôpital de Bicêtre is the only part of the original Hôpital Général which is still located outside of the official city borders of Paris.

54   AAP HG 14.

55   Ibid.

master carpet-maker in 1673.[56] Other manufactures did exist in the various houses of the Hôpital Général, but most were involved in the production of items needed by the hospital itself. The directors themselves commented that it was difficult to establish a skilled manufacture because of the need to placate the worries of city workers.[57] Artisans feared that the poor would undercut their prices and be used as a subsidized workforce by unscrupulous employers. Despite the promises made by mercantilist economists that such hospitals of confinement would eventually become profitable, the directors of the Hôpital Général understood that the hospital could not establish a profitable manufacture without threatening the level of employment in the city.

The final house of the hospital was the Maison de Scipion. It had already existed as a charitable institution prior to 1656, and following the foundation of the Hôpital Général it was renovated in order to provide a variety of services. The only inmate population was composed of pregnant women who would be attended to twice per week by the resident physician of the hospital. These women would be cared for by the hospital, doing whatever small tasks were required of them, until their ninth month when they would be transferred to the maternity ward of the Hôtel Dieu. The house also served as the site of the butchery and bakery of the hospital.[58]

The plans in 1656 had called for the Hôpital Général to offer shelter, food, clothing and training for 3,000 people. This figure was greatly exceeded early on in the hospital's history. By 1660, it was caring for over 6,000 on a regular basis, and after 1680 it commonly held between 8,000 and 10,000. The greater part of the hospital population was composed of the young between 18 months to 16 years old, the elderly over 65 and those considered unable to work (such as the blind, the deaf, the handicapped, epileptics and those suffering from mental disorders). There was always a much larger number of women than men, and the poor who were being detained against their will were in the minority. For example, in June 1701 the hospital had a total population in its various buildings of 8,910, of whom 411 were staff of various sorts. Of the 8,499 poor in the wards, 1,240 were men and only 985 (505 women and 480 men) were being held in confinement as vagabonds or by *lettre de cachet*.[59]

The emphasis placed on the daily life of the poor of the hospital was on work as a good Christian trait. At the outset, the failure of previous attempts to eliminate vagrancy in Paris was blamed on a lack of religious motivation. In 1656, du Plessis-Montbard had urged his fellow directors that the objective of the new hospital board must be:

> the goal of all pious companies, and its duty must be to work by every means possible for the elimination of vagrancy and idleness. We have been working at this task in Paris for 120 years but we have not succeeded. God has given us the time. But we can say that the greater part of those engaged in previous attempts [the Grand Bureau des Pauvres]

56 Ibid.
57 Ibid.
58 Ibid.
59 AN K1024/43.

acted from a concern to police the city not from compassion alone and almost never from charity and for the love of Jesus Christ.[60]

The Catholic Reform sentiments of the hospital's founders were enshrined in the institution's *lettres patentes* that dedicated the hospital to the glory of God and to the good of the public.[61] A number of the administration were members of the reform-minded Compagnie du Saint-Sacrement, which was concerned that a proper understanding of Catholic doctrine and ritual be spread to all members of society.

The teaching of approved Post-Tridentine Catholicism by the nuns in each of the dormitories of the hospital was considered to be as important as the manual work performed by the inmates. Prayers were said in common, in each of the houses, both morning and evening and before and after meals. The able-bodied poor heard mass daily in the hospital churches of Saint-Denys and Saint-Louis, while those considered to be a potential disturbance to the services, notably the poor with epilepsy or mental health problems, would hear it in a secure and separate chapel known as the Ange Gardien, and the bedridden and otherwise invalid would hear it at the chapel at the head of their dormitories.[62] The poor said prayers for the souls of the hospital benefactors, allowing ambitious families to associate themselves publicly with the institution. A large chapel at La Salpêtrière, begun in 1670, with sections that segregated the poor from wealthy patrons, was built in order both to encourage the elites to donate after witnessing the hospital's work at first hand as well as to allow benefactors to be seen by their peers. It was in these circumstances, or in the many public expressions of faith organized by the directors, that the elites of Paris who chose to participate in the financing or administration of the hospital demonstrated their worth of themselves and their families.

Although official documents were often filled with pious notions about the poor, the directors of the Hôpital Général did not regard all of their charges in an uncritical light, viewing them often with a large amount of distrust. While they often referred to the poor as living representations of Christ, they seem to have genuinely felt that any good work done in reforming their character would go astray if not constantly monitored.[63] Supervision was provided by the nuns who lived alongside the poor in the hospital. They were responsible for correcting the behaviour of the poor through a variety of means approved by the board. This ranged from simple admonishments for bad behaviour to corporal punishment, as happened to Marie Panyer in 1678. At the time of her whipping in the courtyard of La Salpêtrière, Panyer, who was a 22-year-old married native of Orléans, had been brought to the Hôpital Général six times previously for being caught begging. Her record as a repeat offender, which legally should have seen her branded and exiled from the city, weighed less in the sentence of the hospital board than the fact that she had broken one of the hospital's windows during the period of her last detention. Although her case merited a corporal

---

60 Poujol, 1982, p. 28.

61 AAP HG 2.

62 *L'Hospital*, 1676, p. 8.

63 AAP HG 2. The Edict of 1656 states that a good Christian should regard 'les pauvres mendiants comme membres vivantes de Jésus Christ'. At the same time it lists a number of crimes and disorders committed by them.

punishment as an example for the other inmates, the directors usually seem to have been more lenient towards poor women than to men.[64]

From its opening, able-bodied men and women of legal age with no obvious hindrance to employment were confined in the Hôpital Général for short periods of time (normally a month), in order to provide some training and religious education alongside the food and shelter desired by the poor before being put back on the street. This confinement seems to have been used by some as a means to overcome seasonal unemployment, as, soon after the hospital opened, directors sent to visit the wards discovered that many of the inmates were repeat offenders. The Edict of 1656 restated the previous laws forbidding vagabonds from entering the city. As well, it provided the hospital with the right to punish individuals arrested as repeat offenders. Men caught begging in Paris a second time could be punished by a whipping and those apprehended a third time could be sent to the galleys. Women taken were at risk of the slightly lesser punishment of a branding and banishment from the city.[65] These rules were intended to discourage rural poor from seeking their living in Paris rather than laws to be enforced for every repeat offender. Laws forbidding anyone from begging were continually reissued for the capital throughout the period, with little success in achieving their goal.

Following the dearth of 1662–63, which saw great numbers flocking to Paris seeking relief, edicts were issued increasing the variety of the poor who were to be housed in the hospital in order to assist clearing the streets of vagrants. At the outset, the Hôpital Général had planned to confine only the very young and the elderly for long periods of time, while offering temporary relief to adult men and women when the need arose. The administration soon realized the necessity of confining different types of poor to stop them from begging. The insane, the blind, sufferers of venereal diseases (who were not accepted at the Hôtel Dieu), the handicapped and epileptics were granted space in the wards in the years between 1663 and 1715. After 1684, prostitutes sent by order of the Lieutenant General de Police were to be imprisoned in the Maison de Force of the hospital. The sons and daughters of the bourgeoisie deemed to be living a 'vie scandaleuse' could be confined after 1690. The Hôpital Général was unable to reduce the number of the invalid poor, such as *insensés* and *paralytiques*, because their infirmities prevented them from earning a living through work. Harsher penalties, such as the sentence of life imprisonment for being caught as a vagrant a second time, which were imposed for limited periods in 1669, 1685 and 1699 before falling into abeyance, only served to make overcrowding worse. This posed a problem for the administration which had to deal with the increased number of poor staying for longer periods of time. The directors often found it easier to ignore the terms of the royal edicts they themselves had requested which imposed this punishment and release beggars in the hope that they would find employment or leave the capital.

---

64   Brièle, 1888, p. 241. Panyer was sentenced, on the suggestion of the Superieure of la Salpêtrière to the commissaires deputed by the board of the Hôpital Général, to ten lashes of the whip in one of the house's courtyards and six in the other.

65   AAP HG 2.

As overcrowding was such a problem for the Hôpital Général, it is not surprising that the directors felt the easiest and least expensive solution should be to prevent the poor from other localities coming to Paris. This sort of legislation secured on behalf of the hospital represents a continuation of anti-vagrancy laws which dated back into the Middle Ages. The board approached the crown in 1669 to change the terms of the 1656 edict governing the hospital's rights over the poor. New terms for the stay of the able-bodied poor dictated that vagrants caught begging a second time were ordered, in theory, to be held for life instead of for 30 days as had been the punishment previously. Due to the problems of overcrowding and the lack of space to confine the worthy poor for long periods of time, this punishment was soon changed so that women would be branded and banished from the city, while men would be condemned to serve in the galleys. The hospital used the new rules as a threat to dissuade the poor from living off the donations of almsgivers and as a mechanism to hold the able-bodied poor for as long as was deemed necessary for their retraining. The directors were left with the option to release these inmates when they could earn their living and pay at some time before their release the costs of their stay at the hospital.[66] The hospital used the most extreme punishments only on those deemed to be troublemakers. And, as the crown never sent an agent to examine the operation of the hospital, these rules could easily be ignored by the administration when it chose.

The policy of *enfermement* required that individuals ceased giving casual alms in order to stop whatever incentive there was for the poor to beg. In 1657 the Parlement forbade giving alms to beggars in the streets on penalty of four *livres*.[67] From then on, the only legal way for Parisians to grant casual charity was via the collection boxes set up in all of the city's churches. Likewise, it was prohibited for landlords to lodge, shelter or rent accommodation to anyone living from begging for fear that they would encourage such behaviour in order to profit from alms given to their tenants. One such case was prosecuted at the request of the directors of the Hôpital Général in 1660 against Nicolas Bolen, a *drapier* who was fined 100 *livres* for providing shelter for a group of vagabonds in his house.[68] As with the anti-vagrancy laws of previous periods, none of these laws seems to have had the desired effect, and the problem of beggars in the capital was never solved.

Relations with the working population of Paris

If the Hôpital Général was an institution created by members of the Parisian elites, it remains to be asked how it was received by the shopkeepers and artisans of the city. While the Hôtel Dieu was intended to assist journeymen and others who could not afford a period of sickness, few members of the Parisian artisinat expected to seek shelter in the Hôpital Général. However, the perceived problem of vagabondage and public begging was as much of a problem for them as for the judges and lawyers of the sovereign courts. In the early reports made by the archers of the poor in 1657, it

---

66 AAP HG 11.
67 Ibid.
68 Ibid.

was clearly shown that the hospital had created a tense reaction amongst the citizens. Although it is true that the greater part of the population of Paris worried about the disorder created by the poor, it was also apprehensive about the implementation of the policy of *enfermement*. The life of many Parisians was separated from that of the destitute only by a thin thread. They feared being made poor and being forced into the Hôpital Général rather than being assisted in their own homes, as would have been done previously by the Grand Bureau des Pauvres. The introduction of the archers of the poor with powers to detain those whom they felt ought to be confined proved to be a strong grievance. Artisans and shopkeepers, in particular, felt that their children, who provided a source of revenue for many artisan households, could be subject to being declared idlers and confined in the hospital. An example of the fear inspired by the introduction of involuntary confinement occurred on 14 June 1657. Jacques Poillon, the *bailli des pauvres*, on patrol in the Marais with 14 archers of the poor, encountered:

> a little man dressed in linen carrying crochet hooks over his shoulder. After he had hailed us he humbly asked us several times with tears in his eyes to take pity on him. He asked us to arrest a youth aged around thirteen who he held by the arm and who he said was his son who had taken to begging in public for the last six or seven months or thereabouts. He said that his son swore often and took the Lord's name in vain. He said that he was dying from regret for seeing his son abandoned in the company of some thieves and cutpurses … we spoke with him and told him … that the hospital would not be burdened with such cutpurses or thieves, that this place was only destined for the shelter of the able-bodied poor … but around such a public conversation curiosity brought many people close by to listen in. Several women, being gathered together, who, after having heard a part of the above conversation, happened to tell us that we would never throw the boy into the hospital. They said that the crowd would attack the father and that the archers would not get out of the mob's clutches or even out of the neighbourhood. They advised us that we would do better to save ourselves as quickly as possible for there was nothing there for us except a beating.[69]

By this time the number of onlookers had grown very large (more than 500 in their estimate) and several individuals among them were becoming violent. The greater part of the crowd seems to have been under control but remained opposed to the archers carrying out their duties. When the archers attempted to arrest a man in the crowd who had made threatening gestures towards them with a knife, a grocer named Fontaine intervened along with a group of other shopkeepers to prevent them. While members of this group escorted the man to safety, the leader, Fontaine, warned the archers that their best course of action would be to retreat.[70]

A similar occurrence took place on the very next day. This event happened when the archers were interviewing an inmate of Bicêtre who had been released to seek work in the city. A worker who witnessed the archers attacked them shouting that they were not the real archers of the poor, but criminals bent on robbing passers-by. His cry brought the rest of the neighbourhood into the street. Violence was prevented

---

69   AAP HG 12.
70   Ibid.

on this occasion only by the intervention of an individual described as 'un homme de condition' who verified their identity to the crowd.[71]

The problem posed by bad feeling towards the archers of the poor never really resolved itself. Occasional riots directed against them continued throughout the period. Matters were only made worse when the policy of deporting some inmates of the hospital to overseas colonies was implemented in 1663. Rumours spread that the archers were part of a conspiracy to populate Canada with children kidnapped from Paris. Rioting on 17 April 1663 left one archer dead, and the Parlement issued a declaration forbidding the kidnapping and forced deportation of individuals to the colonies in an effort to placate the fears of the crowds.[72] Although some of the population believed in the truth of such rumours, it is likely that many individuals invented these tales in order to justify their attacks on the archers to the authorities.

The soldiers of the city garrisons proved to be one of the worst dangers for the archers. Troops continually interfered with the arrest of the poor, in particular with the imprisonment of young women. During the seventeenth century there were several occasions when soldiers broke into the wards of La Salpêtrière to free individual girls. The repeated issuing of orders forbidding soldiers from clashing with the archers seems to have done little to prevent this situation.[73] The general population of Paris was not as enthusiastic as the city's elites in its support for the Hôpital Général. In part this was due to misunderstandings about the purposes of the institution; many were willing to use the institution to lighten their family's burden through placing costly members in the hospital, but at the same time some Parisians resented the arbitrary powers of the archers of the poor which could lead to imprisonment and those who existed close to the poverty line had genuine fears that if their economic situation got worse, they would be confined in the hospital.

The hospital's finances and the crown

The finances of the Hôpital Général were based on a mixture of charitable endowments and local taxes. It possessed estates of farmland in the region surrounding Paris and houses in the city itself. These it had inherited from the different hospitals which had been united together by the terms of the Edict of 1656. The hospital suffered from the disadvantage of being a new foundation compared to medieval hospitals such as the Hôtel Dieu. Unlike that institution, which had received legacies in the form of property and pensions since the twelfth century, the majority of the lands which the Hôpital Général possessed were inherited from those donated to the Hôpital de la Pitié since 1612, and therefore the revenue from its estates was much lower. More important than the income derived from leases of rural and urban properties was the local tax on the entry of wine into Paris, which had passed from the Hôpital de la Pitié and the Grand Bureau des Pauvres to the Hôpital Général in 1656 and was subsequently increased in value. Of the initial income of the hospital of 300,000

---

71 Ibid.
72 Ibid.
73 AAP HG 11 and 12.

livres in 1656, 200,000 *livres* were derived from this source.[74] From its origins throughout the period, the Hôpital Général was to remain reliant on local taxation for most of its revenues, with the percentage of income received from such levies actually increasing.

According to mercantilist writers, a hospital of confinement ought to have been able to contribute to its own finances from the goods produced by the poor being trained. The directors of the Hôpital Général, however, never believed that the labour of the inmates could do more than lessen the expense of their stay. At the outset the governors and patrons of the hospital felt that the poor confined in the wards were incapable of doing enough work of sufficient quality to support themselves:

> The Hôpital Général is the common refuge for all of the poor: the elderly, the incurably sick, the handicapped, artisans who can no longer earn a living, workers who have no work, young children who must be educated and who are all, or the majority, from Parisian families.[75]

The financial situation of the hospital began to deteriorate as soon as it opened its doors to the poor in 1657. The founders of the Hôpital Général had made a grave error by seriously underestimating the number of poor which it would have to shelter. As early as 1658, a year after the opening of the hospital, the board had already petitioned for the right to collect a new tax in order to defray the expenses incurred when the numbers of poor cared for in the first year of operation dramatically exceeded earlier predictions. This new levy was a second entry tax on wine which was sold to the General Farm for a further fee of 200,000 *livres* per year.[76] The new income, large though it was, did little but reduce the size of the deficit, not eliminate it altogether.

Between 1657 and 1661, the income of the Hôpital Général fell short of its expenditure by as much as 42,000 *livres* each year even after the increase in the amount of local taxation granted to support it.[77] These years had seen no food shortages in the region, causing fear among the administration about what should happen when a crisis occurred. Turning to the crown for help, new incomes to reduce the deficit were petitioned for and received in late 1661. A local monopoly on the manufacture of cards, tarot decks,and dice was granted, worth 35,000 *livres* per year.[78] Following the lead of the Hôtel Dieu, the directors published pamphlets warning its benefactors of the seriousness of the situation, not being above scaremongering to solicit more donations and support. They advised that if nothing was done 'the poor who are just beginning to earn a living … will very soon be in the streets, in the churches and in all public places, in front of houses, and in merchants' shops in order to beg for their bread.'[79] However, such pleas for public support only brought in small sums that the hospital could use to cover its immediate expenses.

---

74   AN K1024/35, AAP HG 21 and 23.
75   AAP HG 14.
76   AAP HG 24.
77   AN K1024/35.
78   AAP HG 27.
79   AAP HG 14.

Although a part of the deficit had been addressed in late 1661, the crisis deepened in early 1662 when spring crops in the Ile-de-France failed and the poor, in greater numbers than before, sought to gain entry to the Hôpital Général. The famine seems to have caused significantly more dislocation in rural parishes of the Paris basin than the worst years of the Frondes when support was first raised for the reform of the city's poor relief system.[80] In 1662 the daily expenditure of the hospital increased so much that it doubled the debt it had owed from the previous five years of operating at a loss. Faced with feeding between 8,000 and 10,000 poor at the cost of 5 *sol* 5 *deniers* per day, the administration of the Hôpital Général found itself forced to retrench hospital expenses.[81] The amount of meat and vegetables doled out to the inmates was cut back to all but the oldest. The board authorized the hospital to cease making payments on the *rentes* which it owed. Most importantly, the directors began to accuse provincial hospitals of not providing for their own poor. These accusations led to the issuing of the Royal Edict of 1662.[82]

The numbers of poor at the Hôpital Général who came from the area surrounding Paris sparked fears that the capital would soon have to provide material relief for all of the region as smaller cities and towns lessened their expenditures by encouraging those made destitute in the famine to seek succor elsewhere.[83] Along with the directors of the city's other main hospital, the Hôtel Dieu, the administration asked the crown's assistance in preventing the rural poor from overloading its stretched resources by ordering smaller localities to live up to their traditional commitment to provide relief. The board was particularly worried about a widely spread rumour among the rural poor that the hospital was about to change its constitution and allow its inmates to roam freely in the city by day to beg.[84] The Royal Edict of 1662 issued in December was an attempt to force towns close to Paris to comply with already existing laws and traditions to care for their native poor. It commanded the creation of new hôpitaux généraux in all towns and cities of the kingdom and ordered those which already had institutions of confinement to ensure that the local poor were assisted there and not allowed (or indeed encouraged) to travel to the capital. It was granted in the form of a royal edict because it would carry more weight with local administrations and because it had become accepted practice since the sixteenth century that the creation of new hospitals required the consent of the crown.

To accompany the edict for the entire kingdom provided by the crown, the Parlement of Paris issued a tough law in 1662 for the court's area of jurisdiction in order to continue the struggle to save the hospital. It concurred with the royal edict that localities ought to provide for their own poor, and commanded that all beggars not native to the capital be banished from the city. Vagrants were to leave the city on pain of punishments stipulated in decisions of the Parlement of 1617, 1618, 1624, and 1626. Those native to Paris were ordered to present themselves to the Hôpital

---

80 Walter and Schofield, 1989, p. 192.

81 AN K1024/36.

82 AAP HG 4, AAP HG 14, AN K1024/36 and *Code de l'Hôpital Général de Paris*, 1786, pp. 423–4.

83 *Code de l'Hôpital Général*, 1786, pp. 423–4.

84 Ibid.

Général within one day of the proclamation of the decision, after which the various police bodies of the city (the lieutenant-criminel de robe-court, the prévôt de l'Isle and the chevalier du Guet) could seize and deport them for service in the galleys 'sans forme ni figure de procès'.[85] This new law, however, was little more than an attempt to frighten the poor back to their place of birth, a tactic already familiar to the municipal authorities. The different civic authorities seem to have limited themselves to ordering the archers of the poor to escort the homeless who could not prove that they were residents outside the city limits with a stern warning not to return.

In February 1663, the Parlement reiterated the responsibilities of other towns and regions of the kingdom to prevent beggars from coming to Paris:

> On what has been advised by the Procureur-Général du Roi that even though there is an order for the provision of charity and justice that every town and province should nourish its own poor and that the assistance which has been given in the Hôpital Général of this city of Paris to the poor from several provinces who flock to it has only been given in the current pressing necessity ... it is ordered that the poor will be returned to their own localities.[86]

The court also turned its attention to individuals who assisted vagrants along their journey to the city. The hospital directors complained to the Parlement that 'messagers, voituriers, et les conducteurs des coches' flaunted the law by providing transportation for the poor seeking shelter in Paris. The court issued new laws ordering corporal punishment and a fine of 1,000 *livres* to anyone caught bringing vagrants into the city.[87]

The members of the sovereign courts on the hospital board proved their worth by securing more concrete financial support in 1662. The Parlement issued a warning in April of that year to 'all secular and regular communities (of both sexes) ... all lay organizations, the councils of parish churches, chapels et confraternities, and others, even the corps des métiers, that if they did not contribute willingly to the Hôpital Général, they would be taxed.[88] The court asked the various religious groups of the city to pay, according to their revenues, a voluntary levy of 100,000 *livres* for that year only. To accompany this payment, the Parlement ordered an extraordinary tax:

> All owners who occupy their houses and the principal landlords who keep lodging houses in this city and its suburbs will be taxed to pay for the subsistence of this hospital during the current year ... a sum equal to what they are currently taxed for the cleaning of the roads will be paid.[89]

To combat the problem of the provincial poor, the *arrêt* ordered senior magistrates and ecclesiastical figures in towns in the jurisdiction of the Parlement of Paris to

---

85 *Code de l'Hôpital Général*, 1786, pp. 424–5.
86 Ibid., pp. 425–6.
87 Ibid.
88 Ibid., p. 59.
89 Ibid., p. 60.

impose taxes on the notables of their localities for the subsistence of 'the poor of each of the cities and large towns'.[90]

The taxes imposed by the court on Paris proved very difficult to collect during the famine, but the hospital used the promise of this future revenue to bolster its credit and to secure new loans to permit it to survive. The Parlement, following inaction by the church in the city, reissued its decision, changing the voluntary nature of the contribution into a direct tax on religious property worth at first 50,000 *livres* in June 1662, and later raised it to a total of 100,000 *livres* in September.[91] Despite the best efforts of the Parlement, the taxes levied on the city were still unpaid early in 1663, and the situation for the hospital was dire. The court decided to dispense with the use of commissioners to assess taxes on both religious houses and secular landlords as long as they paid something. The Parlement declared that this situation was extraordinary due to the financial need of the hospital:

> being of the sort that if we are obliged to follow the order of assessments and to make a regular appeal in order to oblige landlords to make their affirmation and to claim their rents and quittances it is without doubt that this will take up a considerable amount of time and be totally prejudicial to the care of the poor who are waiting for help without which they cannot survive.[92]

The publication of the results of the inquiry made into the financial situation of the hospital by two councillors of the Parlement, Pajot and Doujat (both of whom were directors of the Hôpital Général), and the plea made to an assembly of notables of the city held at the Hôtel de Ville in March 1663, seems to have finally convinced the majority of taxpayers to contribute.[93] Although it took several years for the taxes to be collected in their entirety, they had been enough to ensure the survival of the hospital during the famine by allowing it to continue to borrow and contract new *rentes* on the potential income.

Enforcing the theory of *enfermement* harmed the long-term financial situation of the hospital in the years after 1663. The policy required all of the deserving poor to be cleared from the streets to remove the need for the giving of casual alms. The basic flaw in this policy was that a single beggar left free to find his living on the streets could encourage others to do the same. During this period, when the hospital was expanding its authority to confine more categories of the deserving poor and to imprison more incorrigibles as a way to force them into a productive life, the board of directors, paradoxically, had to find ways to reduce the number of inmates at the hospital for financial reasons. The permanently poor, such as the insane, the elderly and the crippled, could not be let out to fend for themselves, unlike the able-bodied who were released when overcrowding occurred in the hope that they could find work. The administration tried to develop strategies to cope with overcrowding. Some poor were sent to overseas colonies, but the numbers were very small as it

---

90 Ibid.
91 Ibid., pp. 61–2.
92 Ibid., pp. 68–9.
93 AN K1024/36 and *Code de l'Hôpital Général*, 1786, pp. 62–8, 70.

was an expensive process, and they could only send certain categories of poor.[94] They had to be able-bodied, young and fairly willing to go. Similarly, the directors sought to deal with the problem by allowing the army to conscript young men from the men's wards at Bicêtre.[95] Often the directors sought to keep numbers down by requesting the archers of the poor to escort the vagrants they caught to the gates of the city rather than to the hospital.[96] But none of these solutions coped with the problem of those who were incapable of caring for themselves.

During the 1670s the central government was willing to offer immaterial support to the Parisian elites in the form of circular letters sent to the bishops and Intendants of the kingdom in 1671 and 1676, encouraging the foundation of new hospitals through local charity. It also gave its patronage in 1673 to a committee composed of board members of the Hôpital Général that corresponded with concerned elites of other localities in an effort promote the policy of *enfermement*.[97] The lack of any significant crown assistance to enforce the policy throughout the kingdom during the reign of Louis XIV, with the exception of its patronage of the Jesuit missionaries Calloet-Querbrat, Chaurand and Guévarre in the 1670s, proved to be a sore point for the administration of the hospital. As late as 1688, after a number of provincial hospitals had been established through the efforts of the Jesuits during the 1670s, the directors of the Paris hospital continued to complain that the crown was ignoring the terms of the Edict of 1662 by discouraging localities from creating new institutions for fear of losing revenue and diminishing its rights, and as a consequence the central government was harming the financial health of the Hôpital Général.[98]

The hospital faced serious financial difficulties from the late 1680s onwards due to the number of inmates and to its level of indebtedness. The administrative reform of 1690 which gave greater representation from the sovereign courts of Paris allowed the hospital more success in petitioning for new revenues. The Hôpital Général took a share in a new tax on wine entering Paris granted to the Hôtel Dieu in 1690.[99] In 1693, to increase revenues further, the Premier Président of the Cour des Aides made his presence felt by securing the approval for an imposition of 12 *livres* on all *lettres patentes* registered in the court.[100] As a result of the harsh famine year of 1694, the numbers of inmates and the expenses of the hospital increased, and it was once again unable to make payments on its debts. This perilous financial situation continued

---

94 AN Marine B7/50 and Brièle, 1888, p. 244. Young men and women, following their selection by the nuns of the hospital, were sent overseas to the colonies in the Americas once per year. The number never surpassed 150 of either sex. Although he was initially an advocate of populating Canada with poor taken from the hospital, Colbert seems to have preferred to send peasants rather than paupers because of the former's proven capacity for hard work. Colbert, 1861–73, t. III, p. 476.

95 AAP HG 11. Male inmates of the Hôpital Général were officially subject to conscription after April 1675, but no records exist of the number (if any) who were taken by the army.

96 Brièle, 1888, p. 249.

97 Boislisle, 1881, pp. 415–17.

98 Ibid.

99 AAP HG 26.

100 AAP HG 14.

until the end of the decade. Crown assistance with the operation of poor relief in Paris in 1699 proved to be a miscalculation for it, allowing the hospital directors to take advantage. Following the years of famine, members of the central government feared that a great number of the poor, who had fled to Paris to seek relief, had not quit the city when the situation improved. The perceived dearth of rural labour created the fear of an occurrence of a second famine caused by an inability to harvest the new crops. On 10 February 1699, the crown issued a declaration intended to frighten beggars off the streets of the capital and back to the parishes of their birth. The rural poor were ordered to leave Paris within three days of the proclamation of the edict or face severe punishment, 15 days imprisonment on bread and water in the Hôpital Général for the first offense of both men and women, and for the second offense a life sentence in the galleys for men or a whipping and exile from the city for women.[101] This first edict was unsuccessful and the crown needed to reissue its terms in a second declaration in July 1700, in which beggars were ordered to return to their place of residence by the shortest route possible and local authorities were required to provide food and lodging on their journey. It also offered the poor a financial incentive to return to the countryside:

> And in order to convince the poor to follow those who have already left the idle life and to go work in the fields in the country and to take up a lasting and permanent residence there, we allow them to take possession of lands worth up to thirty *livres* of revenue without paying the *taille* on them.[102]

The directors of the Hôpital Général had requested and approved these measures designed to scare the poor away from the city, and they used the new government regulations on the imprisonment of the poor in the hospital in order to justify their calls to raise more money through local taxation. They argued that the new laws had required the hospital to confine many more inmates for a longer period of time, burdening the institution and harming the care of the worthy poor unless the crown allowed new local taxes to be collected. The directors followed their familiar tactic of publishing the state of the hospital's finances and inmate population, claiming that the institution was again on the verge of collapse.[103] To placate the governors of the hospital and those who held *rentes* on its revenues, the crown allowed the Parisian sovereign courts to impose a series of indirect taxes. A new tax of a *sixième* on tickets to the Opéra and Comédie was organized in 1699.[104] In January 1700, the hospital began raising money by means of a kingdom-wide lottery, in effect an optional tax, which by 1704 generated an income of more than 300,000 *livres* per year.[105] After 1700 the hospital, thanks to the support given to the institution from influential members of the sovereign courts, was able to raise more consumption taxes on the city to cover its deficit. A further tax on wine was added in 1702 which

---

101 *Code de l'Hôpital Général*, 1786, pp. 436–8.
102 Ibid., p. 440.
103 AN K1024/43.
104 Déthan, 1990, p. 367.
105 AN K1024/40.

was followed by others on olive and nut oil and on hay brought into Paris.[106] The corps des Marchands Épiciers denounced the tax on oils as unfair, believing that it would be evaded by the robe and bourgeoisie who could buy their supplies outside the city. The Parlement subsequently reduced it to a quarter of its original value and suppressed it outright in 1713.[107]

New sources of income were granted, but the Hôpital Général remained weak in the face of the sorts of pressures exerted on it by the crop failures that occurred with regularity during the reign of Louis XIV. The after-effects of the harsh winter of 1709 almost caused the closure of the Hôpital Général and provoked a flurry of activity. The finances were in a state perilous enough to warrant royal action on calls for assistance from the Parisian elites. Resorting to a method used previously in the crisis years of 1662–63, religious communities in the city were ordered to tax themselves for the year in order to support the hospital. The directors took the step of requesting the help of the crown in authorizing this extraordinary levy because it was felt that royal edicts would ensure better compliance than the various *arrêts* of the Parlement of 1662–63 had done. In order to prevent the flood of refugees that had poured into the city in previous crises, each parish in the kingdom was ordered to convoke a special assembly of local notables to provide out-of-doors relief for those made destitute. Finally, following the precedent set in 1662, an extraordinary tax was imposed on landlords in the capital, giving the hospital a secured source of revenue on which to acquire loans in order to overcome the crisis. As a result of the new impositions granted during the period, by 1715 the finances of the Hôpital Général were more deeply rooted in local taxes levied on Paris than ever.[108]

By the end of Louis XIV's reign, the government claimed that the king himself had been the founder of the Hôpital Général of Paris. However, the crown had little direct involvement in the foundation, administration or financing of the hospital beyond facilitating, when it chose to do so, decisions taken by the board of directors. Under Louis XIV, there was no attempt by the crown to extend its prerogatives to include the management of Parisian social welfare under its auspices. The desire of devout members of the Parisian *noblesse de robe* after the Frondes to ensure that the city streets were rid of beggars led to the reorganization of poor relief and the creation of the Hôpital Général in 1656. A combination of individuals from the sovereign courts and the bourgeoisie managed the hospital and secured charitable donations and local taxes to finance it. For its part, royal policy towards the poor, as reflected in the Edict of 1662, was dictated by the concerns of these important citizens of the capital. The central government only implemented royal edicts as a means to assist the Hôpital Général overcome difficulties during crisis years. Local matters outside the royal prerogative were not areas with which the king chose to interfere unless asked to resolve a situation between competing interests. This was what happened when the central government issued the Edict of 1662 at the request of the directors of the Hôpital Général and Hôtel Dieu of Paris in an attempt to force other communities to live up to their commitments during a crisis.

---

106 AAP HG 25, 28, 29 and AN K1024/44.
107 AAP HG 29.
108 *Code de l'Hôpital Général*, 1786, pp. 78–86, 443–6.

The indirect support offered to the Hôpital Général during the reign demonstrates both one of the limitations and one of the strengths of Louis XIV's monarchy. The success of the regime rested on its manipulation of the traditional bonds that tied the elites of the country to the crown. The hospital's history demonstrates, in a small but clear way, how the absolute monarchy worked in the second half of the seventeenth century to ensure stability within the state. Showing support for the concerns of the important elites of the capital was a way for the crown to manifest the effectiveness of its leadership.

For the city fathers who managed the Hôpital Général, by the middle decades of the century, it was no longer acceptable to grant assistance without tying support to the moral and religious reform of the individual himself. From then on, the perceived roots of long-term poverty, ignorance of both work and religious practice, were to be combated within the walls of institutions. Religion was important, but the church hierarchy did not gain any significant control over poor relief. The archbishop came to sit on the board, but the rest of the hospital board remained secular (although most probably devout). The secular elites of the city reformed poor relief and maintained their authority over the new institution because their social prestige was increased through association with the hospital. The Parlement and the other sovereign courts increased their roles in the governance of Paris by effectively taking over the administering of poor relief. The motivation of directors and benefactors was a complex mixture of pious charity, economic and social theory. Individuals seem to have had little problem with strengthening their city's economic position, improving their family's social status and fulfilling their religious obligations. Although the hospital did not succeed in its aim of fully eliminating begging from the streets, it became the most important social welfare institution in the kingdom, one that would affect the reform of poor relief in other cities and towns.

Chapter Five

Social Welfare in a Developing Provincial Capital: Montpellier

Located in the south of the kingdom in Languedoc, Montpellier faced economic setbacks during the century, but grew in both size and in political importance during the second half of the seventeenth century as the capital of the province. The city shifted from Protestant to Catholic control in the early seventeenth century. A large and powerful Catholic religious community entered the city in an effort to convert its Protestant population in the years following the siege of 1622. Most important among these religious figures was the bishop who, as the successor to the see of Maguelone, was the fourth highest-ranking in the province after the archbishops of Narbonne, Toulouse and Albi.[1] The bishopric was held by a series of reform-minded men in the years after the siege, who took their leadership role in the government of the city very seriously as it provided them with the means to make sure of the conversion of the population.[2] In secular affairs, the city came to be the political focus of the province, becoming the official residence of the Governor of Languedoc, and the preferred site for the meetings of the Provincial Estates after mid century. These sessions brought members of the provincial nobility, the church and the representatives of the towns of Languedoc to the city. As well, the important officers of the Estates, its secretaries and treasurers, were permanent residents of the city. The meetings of the Estates created a vibrant elite culture in the city which induced the substantial nobility of the region to build aristocratic townhouses similar to those of their peers in the Marais of Paris. As with the aristocracy in Paris, members of the provincial nobility in Montpellier did not consider themselves as citizens of the city, but they felt themselves to be residents, concerned with the quality of life there, but unwilling to take an active part in the administration. Below the level of the aristocracy, the city developed a substantial robe presence. While the provincial Parlement held its meetings in Toulouse, a prestigious sovereign court, the unified Cour des Comptes, Aides et Finances, was established in the city. It was also the site of Présidial and Sénéchal courts, and a bureau of the Trésoriers de France.[3] After 1661, the intendants of both Haute- and Bas-Languedoc had permanent residences in the city, providing it with access to the most important crown officials in Languedoc.[4] The municipal

---

1   Jones, 1982, p. 19.
2   Cholvy, 1984, pp. 188–90.
3   Ibid., pp. 139, 178.
4   Although Languedoc possessed two official posts of intendant during the period, they were often held by the same person. For example, both Daguesseau and his successor Bâville had authority for the whole province.

administration, responsible for assessing the tax burden on the citizens and for managing the revenues, debts and loans of the city, was headed by consuls elected for a year from the various recognized orders of the city. The consuls acted as local magistrates through their exercise of the office of the *viguier.*

The social composition of Montpellier underwent a change in the middle decades of the seventeenth century. The judges of the sovereign courts and the permanent officers of the Provincial Estates and the royal finances came to form a new patrician elite at the top of urban society. The city government, however, still reflected its medieval origins. It did not represent the shift which had taken place in the division of wealth and power in the city during the seventeenth century. Of the six members of the consulate, the first three offices were filled from the ranks of the bourgeois or wealthy merchants of the city and the last three represented members of the class of artisans and small shopkeepers.[5] In the sixteenth and seventeenth centuries, the merchants of Montpellier, of whom those who had made their fortune in the trade in wool, medicines and dyes were the most important, had grown much richer compared to the tradesmen who were elected to the fourth, fifth and sixth consular offices. Nor did the government of the city, which at the time was responsible for poor relief, include members of the sovereign courts, who claimed to have a stake in police matters. This division had direct effects on the history of charitable hospitals in the city.

The religious history of Montpellier had a significant impact on its charitable institutions. During the sixteenth century, the city had been the site of violent conflict between Catholic and Protestant factions. Control had passed from one side to the other several times between 1560 and 1622. Despite short periods of stability, this situation had not ended until the capitulation of the city to a royalist army in 1622. Following this event, the crown and Catholic Church made significant efforts to ensure the loyalty of the population. A citadel garrisoned by royal troops was built to prevent violence from recurring. In order to begin the task of reconverting the citizens to Catholicism, a series of reforming bishops was appointed to the see. To assist them, the bishops had invited members of reforming regular orders to establish houses in the city. By 1656, these included the Capuchins, Dominicans, Carmelites, Sisters of the Visitation, Ursulines, Jesuits and Fathers of the Mission.[6] The effort had an effect in changing opinion. The city was mostly free of civil and religious disorder throughout the period after the siege. While there continued to be a Protestant community in the city, its size and power quickly diminished due to a combination of conversions and emigration, allowing the Catholic elites to ignore its claims to share power by the 1650s.[7]

The history of charity and poor relief in Montpellier was affected by three things: the previous history of religious conflict in the city and the subsequent reforming bishops appointed to the diocese; the shift in the status of groups within

---

5   Most of those who claimed the status of bourgeois in Montpellier were merchants (or their descendants) who had left their trade to live off investments or active merchants who were wealthy enough and who possessed enough land to claim to live a 'noble' life.

6   Cholvy, 1984, p. 190.

7   Baumel, 1976, pp. 230–31.

the urban elites with the diminution of the importance of the consuls (the artisanal representatives in the consulate in particular) and rise of the robe and wealthy bourgeois; and its economic history, as the city attracted a flow of immigrants throughout the seventeenth century while the economy of the rural regions of Bas-Languedoc diminished. These factors affected the local response to the poor. There was no crown interference in the organization and provision of poor relief during the period, as the central government preferred to support the efforts of the urban elites than to meddle with the tradition of the kingdom. The occasional crown edicts which dealt with matters of poor relief were ignored except where they could be used to support the interests of the elites of Montpellier.

Reforming charitable health care in Montpellier

Set within the city walls, the Hôpital Saint-Eloi (after 1663 the Hôtel Dieu) of Montpellier was the sole survivor of the many medieval hospitals which had been founded in and around the city for a variety of reasons: to relieve the sick poor, to shelter pilgrims on their way to Santiago de Compostela and to isolate lepers. By the beginning of the seventeenth century, it had assumed control over all of these institutions and functioned only to treat the sick poor of the diocese. The increase in the civic power and social prestige of certain elite groups, most notably from the sovereign courts and finance, and the relative decline of others, namely the members of the lesser trades and professions, over the course of the seventeenth century marked the history of the hospital. Religion also played a vital role in reforming the provision for the sick poor in a city which had witnessed tremendous conflict between Catholic and Protestant factions during the previous 100 years.

The Hôtel Dieu of Montpellier had existed in one form or another since the twelfth century. Its own account of its history, written in the eighteenth century, attributed its origin to a hospital founded to aid the sick poor in 1183.[8] This original hospital (named the Hôpital Saint-Eloi in 1328, but in its early years it seems to have been known simply as the hospital of Montpellier) had been founded outside the city walls, and seems to have been part of a movement throughout the kingdom which had witnessed the creation of similar institutions from the twelfth to the fourteenth centuries to provide care and shelter both for pilgrims who fell sick on the route to Santiago and residents alike.[9] These other hospitals founded in the Middle Ages were all built outside of the town: the Hôpital Saint Jacques in 1220, the Hôpital des Pauvres Malades in 1369, the Hôpital de la Miséricorde in 1310, and the hospital founded by Guillaume de Tournefort (the so-called Hôpital Guillaume) in 1403.[10] Although the original hospital had been founded in 1183 outside the city, it was moved during the Middle Ages within the walls. It was enlarged considerably in 1228 by donations of lands around Montpellier by Rostang Pocher, which were to form the basis of the hospital's domain until the Revolution. Before 1328, when

---

8   ADH HD E16.

9   Ibid.

10   Ibid. The Hôpital Guillaume was given the title of Hôtel Dieu in its charter of 1444, but the name seems to have never been used by the population of Montpellier.

it was rededicated to St Eloi, it seems to have lacked a patron saint. The hospital was not given its official title of Hôtel Dieu de Montpellier until 1663 when it was confirmed by the prince de Conti (the governor of Languedoc) and the marquis de Castries (the governor of Montpellier) as the primary charitable institution of the city.[11] During the fifteenth century, the hospital was transferred by the city consuls (who were already its administrators) to the rue de l'Aguillerie and then, in 1599, to the rue de la Blanquerie.

The medieval hospitals of Montpellier continued to exist in some form or other until the sixteenth century. There was a trend throughout the century for some of these to shut down or merge with another, in particular those which had acted as leper houses. In Montpellier the closure and unification of the small hospitals into the Hôtel Dieu was carried out at the request of its administration by the city consulate during the sixteenth century. Some of the hospitals which had been built outside the city walls had effectively ceased to function by the outbreak of the Wars of Religion in 1560. While many were undoubtedly physically affected by the various conflicts and movements of troops through the area during the period, and unable to survive the disruption of their revenues (mostly based on collecting rents on agricultural lands) caused by the fighting, some had ceased to function as the incidence of leprosy in the kingdom declined. The eighteenth-century administration of the Hôtel Dieu judged that:

> The civil wars and the religious troubles, of which the Languedoc was the bloody theatre for several centuries, brought about the ruin of the hospitals of Montpellier ... and the disappearance of the largest share of their goods and sources of revenue, and thus it was without doubt only with the signal protection of Divine Providence that the Hôtel Dieu Saint Eloi alone escaped the furor of the soldiers.[12]

While in many other localities small hospitals were suppressed in favour of larger ones only during the course of the seventeenth century,[13] the administration of the Hôtel Dieu of Montpellier had already completed the suppression of the other medieval hospitals of the city and had seized their properties long before the royal edicts at the end of the seventeenth century. At the outbreak of civil war, the hospital board, which by 1477 was already a secular institution composed solely of the consuls of the city, had begun to transfer all of the goods, titles and privileges of defunct hospitals to the Saint Eloi. Much of this activity took place quite early during the Wars of Religion between 1562 and 1565. The reason for this activity was both because the hospitals had been greatly affected by events in the early 1560s, and the result of a changing attitude toward poor relief when Protestants dominated the consulate.[14] The fact that the Hôtel Dieu acquired the lands of the older hospitals during a period of unrest was also likely to have been a result of the Protestant consuls taking advantage of troubled times in order to rationalize the public welfare system provided by the city and to redistribute the lands of closed hospitals.

---

11   Ibid. The title of Hôtel Dieu was generally used to refer to the hospital after 1663.
12   Ibid.
13   Hickey, 1997.
14   ADH HD E16.

The history of changes made to the hospital board reflected the evolution in the composition of Montpellier's elites during the seventeenth century. Before 1693, the Hôtel Dieu was managed by the first four consuls of the city.[15] Six consuls formed the municipal government, administering the business of the merchants and tradesmen of the city, policing local laws through their possession of the office of the city *viguier*, collecting local taxes and managing municipal loans and debts.[16] The operation of the hospital fell under the authority of the consuls as part of their legal responsibility to protect the citizens from unsanitary conditions. The consuls (and therefore the governors of the Hôtel Dieu) were chosen on a yearly basis by a complicated election procedure. Each year a list of 35 suitable candidates was compiled by the seven *échelles* (the name of the occupational groupings of the city) who each submitted five of their own members. One candidate from each of the *échelles* was drawn by lot to sit in committee with the six serving consuls of that year. This committee then chose a list of 18 men, three from each of the six *échelles* eligible to serve as consuls. From this list, the six consuls for the next year were drawn by lot. The composition of the consulate reflected the civic elites of medieval Montpellier. The first consul was selected from the ranks of the 'gentlemen' of the city, being not from a true noble family but from a family which had given up commerce to live off its investments. The second consul was elected from the ranks of the city's wholesale merchants. The third was generally chosen from a group of professionals such as notaries or lawyers (although sometimes this post was filled instead by a bourgeois acting in the place of a professional). The fourth, fifth and sixth consuls were drawn from artisans working in a number of the trades of the city.[17]

The consuls as members of the hospital bureau were responsible for both the daily operation of the Hôtel Dieu and for ensuring its future. The Montpellier board members divided the task of overseeing the functioning of the institution among themselves. By tradition, the position of receiver of the hospital, who was responsible for its finances, was left to the fourth consul, one of the representatives of the artisans of the city. He received the funds generated by the pensions left to the hospital by charitable bequests, negotiated the terms of new *rentes* made on the city and oversaw the collection of the civic tax. The first three consuls took an active part in the operation of the hospital; deciding on actions to be taken should problems arise in the institution, hiring new staff and ratifying the accounts held by the fourth consul.

The constitution of the administration of the Hôtel Dieu came under scrutiny in the 1680s as part of a general dispute between the consuls and the other office-holders in the city. The management of the hospital by the consulate had not been criticized in the decades before 1684, with the exception of Protestant complaints about the exclusion of their poor. In 1684, however, the bishop and intendant were petitioned by the city's notables to ask the permission of the crown to investigate claims of financial mismanagement at the hospital.[18] The period after the siege of

---

15 ADH HD B1.
16 Beik, 1985, p. 71.
17 Ibid., pp. 68–70.
18 ADH HD A1.

1622 had witnessed a diminution of the authority of the consulate. Much of the impetus behind the demand for change was a result of the overshadowing of the groups which provided the membership of the consulate by newer, more prestigious residents of the city, such as the officers of the Estates and the judges and lawyers of the sovereign courts. In the middle decades of the seventeenth century, the changes made to the services offered by the hospital, the hiring of the nursing order and the contracting of the surgeon and physician had been petitioned for by individuals from these groups as well as devout members of the provincial aristocracy. From the mid seventeenth century, the hospital's most influential charitable benefactors also came from these elites. A concern was raised about the ability of those who were elected as consul to manage the affairs of the hospital, and as such to manage the legacies of members of these elites, in the wake of several scandals involving them. The election of consuls had caused rioting on several occasions following 1643 and had resulted in the suspension of elections during the 1650s. In 1662, the intendant had been forced to oversee the repayment of civic debts on the behalf of the consuls. He had again been forced to protect the consulate from the creditors of the city in 1683 by confiscating all of its fiscal records from 1673.[19] It was during this crisis of confidence in the abilities of the consuls that the reform of the administration of the Hôtel Dieu was begun.

The problem which caused most concern was the unpredictable nature of who was elected as consul and therefore as a governor of the hospital. As the consuls served for only one year, so too did the Hôtel Dieu's directors. The system of a yearly rotation of the board of directors had been acceptable in the past, but ideas about the operation of hospitals in the seventeenth century could no longer support this situation. Those who donated to the hospital, for example the judiciary, nobility and bourgeoisie, would be upset at their family donations going astray through carelessness or incompetence. A board with permanent members would be better able to ensure that money was properly collected and spent in accordance with the terms of bequests. The claims of mismanagement of the hospital finances made in the early 1680s were directed against the transitory nature of the board. In particular, because so many of the donations on which the hospital relied were given by members of the nobility, judiciary or bourgeoisie, complaints focused on the person responsible for handling the institution's income and expenses, the fourth consul. It was felt that it was no longer acceptable that the representative of the trades of the city (the fourth consul) should be responsible for the administration of its finances. All of these elite social groups in the city could be placated by reforming the board to include lifetime appointments filled by more prestigious – and therefore considered by contemporaries to be more responsible – citizens. By the 1680s, the hospital risked losing favour with the groups who had, in effect, become the city's patriciate if it failed to address these complaints.

The Bishop of Montpellier, Charles Pradel, took action to solve the problems facing the Hôtel Dieu. He was one of a series of bishops appointed to the see because of their commitment to Catholic reform, and their abilities in carrying it out.[20] Pradel

---

19 Beik, 1985, pp. 68–9.
20 Cholvy, 1984, pp. 188–90.

was named in 1676 to continue the work of his predecessor Bosquet, in particular the training of the rural poor and the conversion of the Protestants in the diocese.[21] Pradel, like many others, recognized the usefulness of such an institution both as a tool to convert Protestants and to instruct ignorant Catholics. Before turning his interest towards the reform of the administration of the Hôtel Dieu, he had already presided over the transformation of the Maison de Charité into the Hôpital Général and had shown his commitment to raising charitable donations from the ranks of the social elites of Montpellier.[22] He had been involved in the establishment of a company of the Catholic-Reformation confrérie de la propagation de la foi in 1679 and had invited missionaries, including the Jesuit Louis Bourdaloue, to attempt the conversion of Protestants at the time of the Revocation.[23]

The bishop was able to carry out the administrative change because he possessed the requisite presence and authority in the area of charity. He had been appointed because he was associated with the ideas of the Catholic Reformation and he seems to have believed in the claim of the Catholic Church during the Council of Trent to have authority over the hospitals of the diocese. He took this responsibility seriously. From 1684, when he undertook the audit of the operation and finances of the hospital, Pradel saw the problem which was inherent in the system: the lack of representation of the true social elites of Montpellier on the board of directors. He had been very active in the reform of relief for the able-bodied poor and the foundation of Montpellier's Hôpital Général, whose board more accurately reflected the city's social hierarchy and provided stability in its governance.

Pradel worked throughout the 1680s to convince the city government of the need for reform. The complaints made in 1684 about the financial situation gave the bishop the excuse to exercise his right to oversee the operation of the hospital. The main charge levelled against the board of directors was the mismanagement of the funds granted to the Hôtel Dieu when the smaller hospitals of the city had been disbanded during sixteenth century.[24] This dispute took place at a time when the institution was having difficulty raising enough revenue to pay its costs. Pradel took the situation seriously enough to approach the intendant for government assistance in reforming the board. He requested help from Bâville, not because he considered the hospital to be under the direct authority of the crown, but because he wished to resolve the situation in a manner which would be final. This assistance from the intendant was a way to secure enough support among both the urban elites and the representative of the central government, so that once the change was made, there would be no legal objection left to prevent it. The bishop presented his concerns to representatives of all the city's elites, including the consuls, in a meeting held in concert with the intendant. The sorry state of the hospital was blamed officially on the inefficiency of the board created by the lack of continuity.[25] The meeting concluded with an

---

21 Ibid., p. 192.
22 Ibid.
23 Baumel, 1976, p. 232.
24 ADH HD E16.
25 Ibid.

agreement to allow the bishop to undertake the reform of the structure of the board of directors to improve the efficiency of the hospital administration.

The bishop was quite successful in his tactics. The consuls were outmanoeuvred because they had agreed to the change and could do little more than make attempts to obstruct the election of new members of the administration in order to protest about their lost authority. In 1693, Pradel publicly attacked the consuls for their lax approach to the government of the hospital. He appealed to the civic pride of the elites by pointing out that similar institutions in other cities were run in a much more efficient manner.[26] Bâville, most likely in complete agreement, acted as a conduit through which the bishop lobbied the crown for its support.[27] This co-ordinated action between the bishop and intendant on behalf of the interests of the city demonstrates both a way in which the urban elites invited the government to aid them, and the manner by which the crown could elicit support for itself from these same elites. The use of the intendant in this matter was an inexpensive and easy way for the central government to demonstrate that it upheld the position of the elites.

While the bishop, intendant and members of the sovereign courts agreed about the necessity of reform, there was the potential problem of the disagreement among members of those elite groups who had always been eligible to hold the post of consul. Some bourgeois and merchants were certainly in favour of a change in the nature of the administration. Those who did not agree with the diminution of the role of the consulate probably felt unable to protest because of the demonstrated unity of their social superiors in the city, the church and the crown. Many of them seem to have acquiesced with the changes after 1693 because it removed the element of chance from the direction of the Hôtel Dieu, and it dislodged the fourth consul – one of the three artisanal representatives – from holding the purse strings, while opening up more positions of authority on the board which would in future be held by them.

The changes made to the board of directors, confirmed by royal statute on 14 October 1694, considerably reduced the role of the consuls in the administration and increased the ability of other members of the urban elites to participate. Unlike Paris, where all directors held their post either because of the office they possessed or because they were elected for life by the membership, the reformed board of the Montpellier Hôtel Dieu was a combination of permanent and temporary positions. In theory the consuls remained, but in a reduced capacity, possessing only a single vote as a corporate body over matters such as the elections of the newly created positions of syndic and intendant of the hospital. The power in the new board of directors lay in the lifetime posts held by the bishop and a new group of administrative officers, the four syndics. These positions were filled for life from members of the sovereign courts and bourgeois of the city. There was little chance that these posts would be filled by inappropriate men because they were elected by the membership itself. The syndics oversaw the operation of the hospital with a special responsibility for checking the yearly accounts of the receiver appointed by the board and the daily expenses submitted by the *soeur oeconome*. To assist the syndics in carrying out their administrative functions, four hospital intendants were chosen. Two were

26   ADH HD E1.
27   ADH HD A1.

chosen each year to hold the office for a two-year term in order to ensure that there was an overlap of experienced men. These posts were filled from members of the urban elites, being taken from the judges and lawyers of the sovereign courts and bourgeois of the city.[28] The post of intendant served as a recruiting ground for the more distinguished posts of syndic, giving men who would later fill the senior posts the chance to experience the actual operation of the hospital and to demonstrate their capacities to the permanent members of the board. The receiver of the Hôtel Dieu was always chosen from one of the intendants in their second year.[29]

The reform solved two problems faced by the hospital. Firstly, it provided stability and continuity in the bureau by making the bishop and syndics lifelong members. Secondly, it gave the elites of late-seventeenth-century Montpellier, members of the sovereign courts, the wealthy merchants and bourgeois, a greater stake in the hospital. This was accomplished by ensuring that all of the permanent and temporary offices of the administration were held by them and not by artisans of the city. It also created a pool of men among the elites who understood the problems faced by the hospital, and who could be relied on to convince their peers to support the institution if the need arose.

The men who filled the new posts of the board of directors in 1694 were representative of those who would serve the Hôtel Dieu throughout the remainder of the period. The four syndics who were elected were a trésorier de France and three bourgeois of the city. Maire, one of the newly elected bourgeois syndics, had been on the hospital board in 1693 which had agreed to the reform, suggesting that the bourgeois who were eligible to sit in the consulate had approved of the need for change. The intendants appointed in 1694 were a Président of the Cour des Comptes, Aides and Finances (who subsequently was elected to a free post as a syndic), and three merchant drapers. The original intendants included one of the merchants from the influential Colondres family, of whom one had been on the board the previous year and an earlier relative, Jean-Paul Girard de Colondres, had been sent on the behalf of the hospital in 1662 to recruit a new *soeur oeconome*, suggesting that in Montpellier as in Paris there were families which had a tradition of service to the institution.[30]

Although the consuls of 1693 had originally agreed that there was a need to reform the hospital board, a rift between the new administration and the consulate immediately occurred over the changes. From the election of new intendants in 1694, the consuls always refused to take part in proceedings.[31] While some of the consuls were from the same group of bourgeois eligible to become intendants or syndics, those elected as consuls protested against the diminution of the traditional authority of the office rather than the reform of the hospital administration as such. The point of dispute was the removal of the individual votes of the consuls on the board of directors replaced by a single vote as a corporate body. Each new consul elected from 1694 until the Revolution refused to take part in the administration. This dispute

---

28   ADH HD E16.
29   ADH HD E34–40.
30   ADH HD E1, E22, and Jones, 1989, p. 124.
31   ADH HD E1–3.

quickly began to take a ceremonial form, with the hospital administration dispatching a member every year to request the presence of the consuls at the elections of new intendants. The reply of the consulate was always to ignore the messenger.[32]

Throughout the period, the Hôtel Dieu Saint-Eloi performed a similar function for Montpellier as the Hôtel Dieu in Paris, namely offering a place of refuge for the sick poor present in the city and the surrounding region. As in Paris, there was a concern among prominent citizens that some form of welfare be offered to those who should fall sick without the ability to care for themselves. Both cities were wealthy and attracted numbers of poor, who came to seek employment. It was these newly arrived immigrants, along with seasonal labourers and travellers, who could not rely on their families to care for them during an illness that the hospital existed to serve.

The control of the Hôtel Dieu passed to the Catholics of the city in 1622 along with the consulate. According to the hospital's statutes, it was to care for all of the sick poor who presented themselves regardless of faith or place of residence.[33] While the terms of the Edict of Nantes had stated that care ought to be extended towards Protestants as well, this was generally not the case. The hospital proved to be a source of tension between the Catholic and Protestant factions of the city in the years before the Revocation in 1685.[34] After the siege of 1622 had confirmed the superiority of the Catholic community, Protestant civic rights were gradually undermined. A garrison of royal troops was established in the citadel built outside the city to ensure that the new peace was maintained. Protestants were repeatedly excluded from the consulate after the Catholic reconquest despite royal edicts confirming their right to hold the office.[35]

Without representation on the hospital board, the delegates of the Protestant community soon found themselves kept out of the wards as well, which meant that their sick poor were effectively isolated and subject to conversion attempts by the Catholic staff.[36] Complaints were continually made that ministers were prevented from attending Protestants in the hospital, while Catholic priests freely visited the wards. In the 1650s, the Catholic consuls responded to these complaints directly to the crown, claiming that the Protestants wished simply to use the hospital wards as places to convert the Catholic poor. They argued that the spiritual direction of similar institutions throughout the kingdom was led by the bishop of the locality because of the necessity to provide the three sacraments of penitence, Eucharist and extreme unction to the sick and dying which required the presence of priests in the hospital.[37] It was the Catholic belief in the patient's need for these sacraments which provided an excuse to bar Huguenot ministers from the hospital:

32 Ibid.
33 ADH HD A1.
34 Isambert, 1821–33, tom. XV, p. 178.
35 AN TT256B/133. A royal order was made in 1652 to split the consulate in Montpellier between Catholics and Protestants but was ignored by the Catholic government of the city.
36 AN TT431/6.
37 AN TT256B/130.

the sick poor of both the Catholic faith and those of the Protestants were received these without distinction, and from this situation the Protestants should have been satisfied without feeling that it was necessary to summon their ministers to the hospital. As well, it is prohibited by their faith to bring Holy Communion to the sick and so there was no other function for their ministers to exercise in the wards. For in order for them to preach to the Protestant sick each minister was able to all of them including the Catholics. And it is not necessary for them to preach to those who are already persuaded by their Protestant beliefs that they are already infallibly saved.[38]

The consuls argued that not only were Protestants unlikely to be converted on their sickbed because of their faith in their elect status, but also that they were likely to prove a threat to the faith of the Catholic poor. At the same time they underlined to sympathetic members of the central government the role the hospital could play in converting Protestants:

> on what has been alleged that there is a danger for the conscience of the sick and because there are so many of them in a single bed lying side by side, when the Catholic patient is preached at by a priest, the equally sick Protestant one is forced to hear this discourse. We could reply that this is the privilege not only of the true faith but also that of the king and the kingdom to enjoy all of the freedoms of the state.[39]

As a result of the administration's desire to exclude Protestant ministers from the hospital, efforts between 1622 and 1685 to use it as a tool of conversion were of limited success. In Montpellier, the Huguenot community tended to provide support for its own poor in private houses, which were kept secret to avoid legal persecution. Granting assistance to the sick in their own homes protected established members of the Protestant faith in the city, allowing artisans to recover from a sickness without entering the hospital, but vulnerable newcomers and those with limited ties to the community did not have that option.

Although much smaller than the Hôtel Dieu of Paris, the Montpellier hospital was large by provincial standards. With the exception of some periods of dearth, the numbers of patients in the hospital generally ranged between 150 and 250. The hospital governors began to reform the services on offer and to improve their efficiency from the 1640s onwards. By the mid seventeenth century the building was reorganized in a manner similar to other hôtels dieu of the period, being divided into different wards: those of the sick and injured, segregated by sex and symptoms, and a large ward for children of both sexes.[40] This segregation reflected what was becoming the prevailing belief throughout the kingdom during the period about the best way to treat the sick poor, that men and women should be separated to prevent them from corrupting each other morally.

The hospital's population always contained more male patients than female, demonstrating that it mostly served the needs of journeymen from the city's pool of labour for whom a period of sickness that prevented them from working could lead to utter destitution. Women, even those who worked in the textile trade, were

---

38   Ibid.
39   Ibid.
40   ADH HD E1.

more likely to be married, or otherwise have a male guardian or employer to pay for their treatment or to provide shelter during a sickness. The hospital also treated a large number of petty merchants travelling through the city and casual labourers from the nearby countryside who sought seasonal employment. For example, in September 1707 there were 72 adult men in the wards compared to 50 women.[41] This gender discrepancy could be increased even further when troops passed by or through the city and during the yearly migration of workers between the Cévennes and the coastal plain, as had happened in May 1707 when the ratio was 154 men to only 26 women.[42] Because the hospital was also responsible for the care of orphaned and abandoned infants in the city, a large number of children were always present in the wards. Traditionally, the Hôtel Dieu had paid for rural wet nurses to care for newborn children, but after 1680 the hospital was given the task of providing aid only after their return from the wet nurses until they were considered old enough to be received at the newly founded Hôpital Général. The number of sick children in the wards was always high, normally representing around 30 per cent of the patient population.[43]

While under Protestant control, the hospital had simply granted a bed and food for the sick poor. The change to Catholic control offered the opportunity for the elites of that faith to use the hospital as a way to demonstrate their civic leadership. The transformation of the Hôtel Dieu in Montpellier from an institution that simply offered shelter to one that sought to treat curable patients, however, took much of the seventeenth century to develop. The board created a post for a hospital surgeon to provide daily visits to the sick in the wards soon after 1622, but often his practice in the city interfered with his duties. This arrangement was changed during the 1640s when a single surgeon of the city was hired by the administration to provide care for both the poor in the hospital and those to whom the Hôtel Dieu provided medical treatment in their own homes.[44] The surgeon was still able to provide treatment to others, but the board monitored his work and expected him to be present when directors and benefactors made visits to inspect the hospital.

Montpellier in the middle decades was able to bring about further reform of the hospital, creating in the city an institution that could provide medical services in order to heal and to rehabilitate sick workers. The changes made to the hospital between 1661 and 1715 were designed as well to demonstrate the civic leadership, the piety and the social worthiness of its directors and benefactors. As the city developed into an administrative and cultural capital, the benefactors of the hospital pressed for the sorts of reforms in personnel and services that were underway in other cities and towns of the kingdom, most notably Paris and Lyon The introduction of a nursing order of nuns to the wards in 1668 continued the transformation of the hospital into an institution that sought to cure the sick. Religion and care were closely linked in the hospital. The arrival of the Soeurs de Charité transformed the hospital, allowing

---

41 ADH HD F17.

42 Ibid.

43 ADH HD F13. For example, the hospital population on 6 September 1693 was composed of 65 children of both sexes compared to 112 men and 54 women.

44 ADH HD F39.

it to better care for the sick poor.[45] The number of nuns, originally three and increased to seven later in the period, served in the wards as hospital managers, as nurses and as amateur medical practitioners. Besides assisting the contracted surgeon and physician, they received and treated the sick themselves as well, providing remedies prepared by one of their order in the hospital's pharmacy.[46] The nuns performed a major role in the daily management of the hospital as well. The *soeur oeconome* was responsible for the daily purchases of the institution, reporting to the board of directors and the receiver to account for her budget.[47] A second nun acted as the apothecary of the Hôtel Dieu, preparing drugs and remedies prescribed by the visiting physician for the patients.[48] Because the number of nuns in the hospital was so few and their duties so many, the role its priest played in instructing the poor became more important. He was required to say mass each day, to hold a daily prayer in both the men's and women's wards, to make two daily rounds of the wards to console and instruct the sick, to say last rites for the dying, and to say daily prayers for the benefactors of the hospital.[49]

The hospital could not afford to pay the salary and living costs of a physician and instead in 1661 it acquired the consent of Montpellier's College of Medicine to provide one who would visit the hospital weekly free of charge.[50] While contracting these men was not the most advantageous arrangement for the interests of the patients, several of the physicians provided did seem to take an interest in improving the care given at the hospital. This situation was particularly true of the years following the reform of the administration in 1694 when the Bishop of Montpellier paid greater attention to the daily operation of the institution because he was the chancellor of the university as well as the chair of the hospital board.[51] The bishop and the administration set rules in 1694 which required the physician provided by the college to make a daily round of the wards accompanied by the hospital surgeon as part of their commitment to improve the hospital.[52]

To complement the services provided by the nuns and to carry out the treatments prescribed by the hospital physician, the post of hospital surgeon became more permanent in 1678 when the holder of the post was given a furnished lodging in the hospital. In 1694 a request was made by the hospital surgeon to create a second permanent post to deal with the large number of patients caused by the famine of that year. The surgeon was particularly worried by the increased number of soldiers from the city garrison in the wards. The board of directors responded to this request by asking for more money from the military, but another permanent surgical post was created only in 1716 when a 'garçon chirurgien gagnant maîtrise' was also given

---

45 ADH HD F34.

46 ADH HD E1. The seventh place for a Sister of Charity was founded in March 1699 by the comtesse de Ganges.

47 Ibid. and ADH HD F34.

48 ADH HD E1.

49 ADH HD E2.

50 ADH HD B2 and F37.

51 ADH HD E1 and F37.

52 ADH HD E1.

rooms, as well as the right to pass as a master surgeon after six years of service.[53] The creation of the post caused a rupture between the College of Surgeons and the hospital board over the right to confer the title of master surgeon which would last unresolved until the Revolution. The college resented the right claimed by the board to confirm the master's degree on its own authority. During the eighteenth century the matter was taken before both the Parlement of Toulouse and the Provincial Estates several times with the losing side always ignoring the result.[54]

Surgery at the Montpellier Hôtel Dieu was not as varied as at the Paris institution. The hospital surgeon seems to have been limited to carrying out simple procedures such as setting broken bones and performing routine body maintenance. The hospital, like other provincial hôtels dieu, saw its role as an institution that healed, and as a result it restricted access to the sick who could be cured so that precious resources would not be spent on hopeless cases. The sick poor who suffered from diseases which required more complex surgery were forbidden entry to the hospital. In July 1710 the board of directors noted that the rules of the institution prevented the entry of 'the sick poor who suffer from bladder stones and because of this these poor have often been allowed to suffer to the point of death without having any recourse to assistance'.[55] The board seems to have found the inability of the hospital to perform this form of surgery unacceptable and it began a search for a surgeon who could rectify the situation. The hiring of the surgeon Laperonnie, who had learnt the technique of cutting for the stone at the Hôtel Dieu in Paris, allowed the board to accept the poor afflicted with bladder stones.[56] Here, as in Paris, the new procedure allowed the directors to heal more of the city's sick as well as to profit socially from providing services beyond the means of most.

The Hôtel Dieu provided service for not only the sick who came to the hospital for care, but also for the city's respectable poor in their own homes. The hospital was responsible for purchasing drugs and medicines prepared by the apothecaries of Montpellier for the city Hôpital Général following its foundation in 1678.[57] The institution also provided medicine and paid for occasional visits from a physician or a surgeon if the family was known to be in need, to be native (or at least have a long history of residence in the city) and to be of a respectable quality. Relief was reserved for the families of workers who were unable to work due to sickness or injury and were unable to afford to pay for medical care.[58]

---

53 ADH HD F37.

54 Ibid. and ADH HD F39. The Montpellier College of Surgeons possessed the right to examine all who wished to practise the skill of surgery in the city from a statute of 1528. The position of a surgeon earning his master's degree at a charity hospital was a common way for boards to defray some of the costs involved in hiring a qualified candidate. The post was very popular and the hospital archives contain large number of applications for the few posts which became available during the eighteenth century. The reason for this popularity was the expense and difficulty for individuals in passing the requirements of the college for the degree.

55 ADH HD E3.

56 Ibid.

57 ADH HD E2.

58 ADH HD F13.

Outside the hospital wards, the Hôtel Dieu provided relief for a number of orphans and foundlings of the city. In Montpellier, the Hôtel Dieu took care of orphans and abandoned children by arranging their placement with wet nurses in the countryside around the city. As the costs of keeping children fed and clothed until they were old enough to be put to an apprenticeship (or into the care of the Hôpital Général after 1679) were quite high, the board of directors of the Hôtel Dieu sought to lower the expenses of the hospital. In 1695, it ceased to feed children below the age of seven in the hospital, choosing instead to send them to relatives or 'bons artisans' (if they were 'anciens catholiques et de bonne vie et moeurs') in the hope that they would be adopted by their guardians.[59]

The commitment of the Hôtel Dieu to outdoor relief performed a valuable service for the city workforce. The hospital fed a number of sick heads of families in their own homes in an effort to keep costs down. For example, in September 1693 it paid for bread and meat for 136 men outside the hospital compared to 112 in the wards.[60] Men assisted in this manner benefited because it prevented them from contracting more serious illnesses from other patients in the wards and it spared them the shame of receiving help publicly by being admitted to the Hôtel Dieu. It furthered the interests of those native to Montpellier and temporarily unable to work without forcing them into the Hôpital Général.

To pay for the services, the Hôtel Dieu received income from a variety of sources. It obtained a small amount of revenue from direct sources of charity. For example, in 1694 the revenue from collection boxes in the city churches amounted to only 68 *livres*, to which was added 160 *livres* from legacies made to the poor.[61] Past charitable donations which had been invested in the form of *rentes* constituted on city and provincial sources of revenue amounted to a greater portion of hospital income than casual alms and small donations, bringing in 4,462 *livres* in 1694.[62] While charitable sources helped to finance the institution, it was more reliant on taxes on the city for its survival.

Throughout the seventeenth century, the revenue derived from both direct and indirect taxes formed the greater part of the income of the Hôtel Dieu. Prior to the 1694 reform of the administration, the hospital had received 4,500 *livres* from a direct tax imposed on the city to support the institution. The new board of directors proved its worth in 1694 by securing the increase of this tax to 10,500 *livres* per year in order to make up previous shortfalls in revenue.[63] A second direct tax which had been levied earlier in the century for the maintenance of the poor brought in 3,375 *livres*.[64] Added to these impositions there was a further direct tax of 1,200 *livres* to pay for medicine used by the hospital both for the patients in the wards and those treated at home.[65] A large indirect tax on meat sold in the city complemented the

---

59 ADH HD E1.
60 ADH HD F13.
61 ADH HD E34.
62 Ibid.
63 ADH HD E22.
64 ADH HD E34.
65 Ibid.

direct taxes. While the value of this levy could vary from year to year, it was worth a considerable amount to the hospital, bringing in 5,260 *livres* in 1694.[66] In that year, the total receipt of taxes amounted to 20,335 *livres* which compared to a total hospital income of 28,428 *livres*.

The Hôtel Dieu possessed a very small amount of property when compared to the estates of the Paris hospitals. It was composed of a small number of plots of land in the area around the city which the institution leased out on a yearly basis and, after 1685, rights on the former Protestant cemetery. As well, benefactors had left various rights to the hospital, such as the revenue from seigneurial mills and ovens. The worth of this source of revenue was never more than a small portion of the total income of the hospital. In 1694, for example, the total value of the leases on lands and seigneurial dues was only 791 *livres*.[67]

The hospital board took the step of selling off some items owned by the Hôtel Dieu in 1694 in order to repay its creditors. This liquidation of hospital assets brought in 2,545 *livres* for that year.[68] The efforts made to increase the revenues of the institution enabled it to improve its situation. The hospital income surpassed its expenses in 1694 by almost 200 *livres*. By 1697, the board of directors was able to reduce the amount of direct taxation supporting the hospital to 11,700 *livres* by retrenching its expenses.[69]

The finances of the Hôtel Dieu stabilized between 1694 and 1709, during which period the hospital was able to repay many of its debts. In 1709, when crops failed due to the extreme winter, expenses rose dramatically. The board was able to reduce costs by reducing the amount of food available to the poor and by buying as much rice as possible instead of grain.[70] Fortunately, the revenue was increased by the legacy of 13,500 *livres* paid by the heirs of the trésorier de France Durbec which allowed the hospital to absorb the majority of the losses of that year; however, the institution still suffered a deficit of 4,725 *livres*.[71] The repayment of debts over the next few years forced the hospital to operate at a loss until 1714, when its financial situation once again improved.[72]

Providing for the able-bodied poor

As in other towns, Montpellier's Hôtel Dieu provided assistance only to the sick poor during the seventeenth century. Despite the issuing of periodic Royal Edicts regarding hospitals, the history of the reform of poor relief for the able-bodied owed more to the religious and economic circumstances of the city during the seventeenth

---

66 Ibid.

67 Ibid.

68 Ibid.

69 ADH HD E36. The total income of the hospital in 1697 was 21,310 *livres*, making the income derived from impositions on the city 55 per cent.

70 ADH HD E48. In 1709, the Hôtel Dieu spent 9,024 *livres* on grain compared to 5,543 in 1710. ADH HD E49.

71 ADH HD E48.

72 ADH HD E53. The hospital showed a profit of 1,103 *livres* in 1714.

century than to central government policy. With the increasing frequency of hosting the meetings of the Estates coupled with the permanent residence of its officers, the city was becoming an aristocratic capital, witnessing the creation of a noble quarter centred on the parish of Notre Dame des Tables. Although this attracted a number of merchants and tradesmen eager to capitalize on the increase of the luxury market, much of the economy of the city in the first half of the century still remained tied to its traditional industries, the largest of which was the manufacture of woollen goods. It was expected of workers in this type of skilled manufacture to provide for themselves and their families in times of economic hardship. Those who entered the industry as apprentices, learned a skill and were able to function at the high end of the enterprise, could fulfill this expectation. Those who did not gain employment through the traditional route, but instead worked at unskilled jobs on the fringes of the trades and industries of the city, could not. It was this sector of the populace, the underclass of new arrivals without any support network, which was at risk of utter destitution. The economy of the region around Montpellier had a long history of transient labour. There was the yearly migration from the summer pastures in the Cévennes to the coastal plains. It was also common for rural labourers to seek seasonal employment in the city, providing heavy labour during periods of the agricultural calendar when little was done. This sort of employment provided subsistence for the labourer, not leaving much for him to put aside for an unforeseen accident.[73]

At the end of the sixteenth century, relief for the unemployed of the city was reorganized under the control of a board of six bourgeois and merchants, which was responsible for the distribution of funds throughout the city. This group co-ordinated the allocation of relief in the city's parishes, providing a bread dole and small payments to individuals. Following the 1622 siege, this board came under the control of Montpellier's Catholic community. In accordance with ideas developed in the early seventeenth century about the form poor relief should take, this board established a new hospital, the Maison de Charité, in 1646. The Charité was part of the movement inspired by both mercantilist ideas about poverty and religious concerns to convert the poor which had led to the creation of the Hôpital de la Pitié in Paris and the Hôpital de Charité in Lyon. These institutions had been intended to end the problem of begging by centralizing donations given to the true poor (the elderly, the infirm and the very young) to prevent the need to give casual alms in the streets. As in Paris, the stated goal was to confine all of the deserving poor and correct their idle habits through work, but, owing to its limited finances, the Charité hospital in Montpellier could provide little more than a place for a handful of orphans and elderly women who had no resources of their own.[74] While the economy of both the city and its hinterland continued to be strong during the 1650s, there were not too many immigrants for the city to absorb, and therefore few believed there was a need to expand the Charité.

The elites of Montpellier had not seen the need to increase the amount of poor relief provided when the Edict of 1662 was registered in the province, leaving the

---

73   Jones, 1982, p. 14.
74   Béral, 1899, pp. 2–17.

city's welfare provision up to the governors of the Charité. The city witnessed an increase in the number of beggars in its streets during the late 1660s and the 1670s.[75] The general economic decline of Montpellier's rural hinterland in the years after 1665 caused the swell of the number of people coming to the city to seek a living. After a long period of population growth, the Bas-Languedoc had reached a peak in the middle of the seventeenth century. Province-wide profits in agriculture declined after 1670, although Montpellier and Nîmes were sheltered from the worst of the decline in incomes during that decade because of the continued buoyancy of the wool and silk industries. The economic success of the city had a significant drawback. It encouraged the immigration of the poor seeking employment. While the rural areas of the province underwent what Emmanuel Le Roy Ladurie has called 'the retreat of the gross product' in the years between 1675 and 1720, which could only be solved by a decrease in population, Montpellier continued to grow.[76] The size of the city increased dramatically when seasonal labourers who came to the city stayed on for extended periods of time during crisis years such as in 1709. Despite laws granting permission to the guards at the city gates to prevent the rural poor from entering, the number of beggars in the city continued to grow during the 1660s and 1670s. By 1666, the directors of the Maison de Charité, unable to finance assistance to greater numbers than planned, were forced to limit aid.[77] The economic problems facing the province combined with a new Catholic vigour to create a desire among Montpellier's elites for action.

The reform of municipal poor relief to adapt to the new situation began in 1676 with the arrival of the reformist bishop, Charles Pradel. Prior to his arrival the city had taken the sole responsibility to care for its own poor, as had been legislated for in the sixteenth and early seventeenth centuries, but there had been no calls to enlarge the Maison de Charité. The city responded to the Edict of 1662 that an Hôpital Général, by another name, was already in existence.[78] In 1671, the Provincial Estates, at the request of Cardinal de Bonzi, had discussed the 1670 letter from the crown, which had authorized the creation of hôpitaux généraux by local elites as long as they were supported from charitable sources without recourse to finance from government revenues, but the Estates had refused to contribute for the foundation of a new hospital in Montpellier.[79] Even the Bishop of Montpellier, Bosquet, who had an important role in the selection of the governors of the Maison de Charité, did not act on the suggestion of the central government to build a new hospital. In 1676, after the arrival of the new bishop, Pradel, eager to improve the religious standing

75   ADH HG G13. The governors of the Maison de Charité had requested an ordonnance preventing beggars from entering the city from the Sénéchal of Montpellier in 1666. This order was reissued just four years later, testifying to the concern about the numbers of poor entering the city and the Charité's inability to cope with the increased pressure.

76   Le Roy Ladurie, 1974, pp. 232–43. Le Roy Ladurie points out the slowdown of the Languedoc economy after 1665, and argues that Montpellier was shielded from this thanks to its own strong economy. The population of the city continued to grow until the mid eighteenth century because of the increased immigration from rural parishes.

77   ADH HG G13.
78   ADH HG A1.
79   Ibid.

of his diocese, used his authority as bishop to convince a broad section of the city's elites to finance an enlargement of the Maison de Charité.[80]

Following his appointment to the diocese, Pradel functioned as an advocate among the urban elites for the cause of furthering the reform of the Catholic faith according to the guidelines established by the Council of Trent. During his episcopate, he demonstrated that he was earnest in his charge to instruct the poor and to teach the ignorant of his diocese. On taking up his episcopal office, he stated his belief that 'the duties to assist the poor in their need and to console them in their sorrows are indispensably part of the office of a bishop.'[81] He was fortunate to be appointed to Montpellier in the 1670s, a decade which witnessed a revival of interest in missionary work throughout the kingdom.[82] The city itself had already been involved in restricting the civic rights of Protestants by prohibiting them from holding municipal office and by destroying the Petit Temple in 1670.[83]

The appointment of the new bishop in 1676 created an opportunity for the expansion of the Maison de Charité. Pradel received the circular letters of 1676 from the crown granting its support for the building of a new hospital in the city. His desire to build the new institution was seconded by the intendant. The patronage of the crown, however, did not include promises of economic support. In fact, the letter which Pradel received specifically admitted that the crown had no revenues to give and would not grant permission to levy new local taxes, which altered significantly the terms of the Edict of 1662. If the city was going to build a new hospital, it would have to pay from its own revenues.[84] In these circumstances, the stated desire of the crown to see every major town in the kingdom serviced by an hôpital général was not enough to secure compliance from local elites. Pradel found that the easiest and least expensive option for Montpellier was to change the name of the Maison de Charité and enlarge it to confine more types of the able-bodied poor. The approval for change among the civic elites was publicly demonstrated at a meeting at the Hôtel de Ville on 2 April 1677. The assembly was a conference of the elites of the city chaired by François de Mirman, the juge-mage of the Présidial court, and attended by the Trésoriers de France, the consuls and senior members of the Sénéchaussée, the Cour des Comptes, Aides et Finances, the bourgeoisie and the various mercantile corps of the city. There seems to have been general agreement that the problem of the increased number of poor needed to be addressed. In an effort to suppress any dissent over the plan which would remove control of the Charité from the city merchants and bourgeois, the first consul, Grefeuille, emphasized that by paying for an enlargement of the hospital, Montpellier would be following the royal will.[85] Once agreement was reached, matters moved quickly. The city requested new

---

80   ADH HG E2. At its first meeting, the board of the new hospital gave Pradel the credit for recognizing the problem of poverty facing the city and for the idea to enlarge the Charité into the Hôpital Général.

81   ADH HG A1.

82   Châtellier, 1997, pp. 49–55.

83   Cholvy, 1984, p. 190.

84   ADH HG A1.

85   Ibid.

lettres patentes from the crown to enable the transformation of the Charité, which it received in early 1679.

The reform of the Charité into a general hospital was carried out because the social composition of Montpellier's elites had changed in the middle decades of the century as it developed into the provincial capital. The price charged for the enlargement of the Charité was the participation in its governance by those men who had come to replace the city's medieval consulate as the social elite. The reorganization of poor relief allowed the institution to properly reflect the new realities of Montpellier's social hierarchy. The administration of the Hôpital Général was designed to be a balanced model of permanent and temporary members recruited not only from the elites of Montpellier, but also from lesser-ranked, although respectable, legal and mercantile figures. The form of the board bound representatives of the social hierarchy of the city together, confirming the leadership of the elites and encouraging the middling orders to support the hospital. The reform of 1679 eliminated the Charité's board of merchants and bourgeois and replaced it with one divided into three levels: a senior rank of four permanent syndics, a temporary group of four intendants and a larger body of 12 recteurs to carry out various tasks. The bishop sat as the chair of the board assisted by the four syndics, who acted as the hospital executive formed from senior figures selected from the urban elites.[86] The office of syndic was open to election from any member of the elites, without the need for a rotation through the various elite groups, on a two-thirds vote by the board. The service of these men created a continuity in the administration of the hospital, allowing the Hôpital Général to be assured of its long-term governance. The position of syndic gave the urban elites the opportunity to give those whom they felt were responsible and pious enough a permanent say in the administration.

Many of the hospital's daily affairs were managed by the posts of intendant, which were filled by rotation through the elite corporate bodies of the city. These posts were held in turn by officers from the Cour des Comptes, Aides et Finances, from the Trésoriers de France, from the Présidial court and from the cathedral chapter, selected by the members of the board of the previous year.[87] It is unclear exactly how these men were chosen, but most likely a list of suitable men was drawn up by the corporate body for that year and presented to the hospital for its approval.

To assist the syndics and intendants in carrying out many of the daily chores, a third administrative office was created: the recteurs. Like the office of intendant, the 12 posts of recteur were filled by a rotation of personnel from various groups in the city. Each year six new officers would be selected to serve a term of two years. They were taken from a rotation of the different corps of the city: from the lawyers of the sovereign courts, from the College of Medicine, from the apothecaries, from the notaries and from the bourgeois of the city.[88] These men served to help the syndics and intendants carry out various tasks for the hospital as well as to offer it their own expertise. Similar to the rotation of the holders of the posts of intendant of the hospital, the offices of recteur changed hands in order to create a number

---

86   ADH HG A1.

87   Ibid.

88   Ibid.

of members from different organizations of the city who not only were trained to serve the hospital, but who would also understand the problems facing it and would champion its interests.

The elites of Montpellier supported the new Hôpital Général because they believed the enlarged hospital would provide a worthy service for the city. Their individual motives would have varied from a deep religious concern to provide charity to the representatives of Christ on earth to a desire to see the streets of the city swept clean of beggars. These two motives could have been accomplished by banishing beggars from the city and providing alms to the worthy poor in their own homes, but the more expensive option of confining the poor was taken. It would have been easier to prevent the rural poor from entering the city at the gates, and some certainly were.[89] However, the littoral plain around Montpellier needed large numbers of seasonal workers to help with the harvest and to act as casual labour in the city during the winter.[90] Those who came during the autumn, and could not subsist on the income of their labour or could not find work, often turned to begging in the streets to find a living until they returned to their own plots of land.[91] Providing assistance for these workers in the context of the Hôpital Général was a compromise between the fulfilment of its benefactors' religious obligations, the economic needs of the city and the desire to see the streets properly policed. The Hôpital Général gave a sense of security to those who came to seek work in the city and were not able to gain assistance from a guild, family or parish, while reducing the visible presence of poverty which so troubled the urban elites.

Religious and economic motivations did not clash with the urban elites' desire to profit socially from the hospital. The ceremony which initiated the construction of the new buildings of the Hôpital Général in 1680 allowed both members of the urban elites and the religious orders of the city to demonstrate their civic leadership through their association with the hospital. The celebration was marred, however, by a dispute over precedence between the Trésoriers de France and the Cour des Comptes, Aides et Finances:

the first stone of the Hôpital Général was placed with great ceremony: the city's secular clergy alongside all of the regular communities processed as is the custom, each according to its rank. After them came Messieurs the chapter of the Trinity, that of Saint-Savan, and that of Sainte-Anne, followed by a band playing violins, after them came the priests of the cathedral choir with their own music, the cathedral canons followed after preceded by their verger in his surplus and cap carrying the cathedral's silver. The bishop followed them clothed in his gown assisted by two dignitaries who were M Solas the senior archdeacon and M Gervais the archdeacon of Castries. Then followed the deputies of the Cour des Comptes, Aides et Finances, and after them the judges of the Présidial court. The Trésoriers de France were absent from the procession because, it is said, that they would not follow the judges of the Cour des Comptes, Aides et Finances if they were only represented by deputies, thus after the Présidial judges marched the consuls, who were

89 ADH HG G13.
90 Hufton, 1974, p. 79.
91 Ibid. pp. 106–107.

named there on the inscription on the foundation stone, all robed in their civic gowns. They were followed by an infinite number of the people of Montpellier.[92]

Montpellier's elites continued to show their support for the new hospital publicly throughout the seventeenth and eighteenth centuries by participating in the annual procession of the hospital directors and the poor on the feast day of Saint Joseph.[93] It was through events like this, such as regular visits by donors to the hospital wards or the attendance of memorial masses sung in the hospital chapel, that elite families negotiated social space and secured political deference from the lower orders of the city, proving their value to urban society through the management of poor relief.

The stated goal of the Hôpital Général was the same as that of the Maison de Charité: to eliminate begging in the city. The regulations which governed the hospital established that, to accomplish this goal, it was necessary to confine suitable categories of the able-bodied poor in greater numbers than before and to give them food, clothing, shelter and religious instruction.[94] Owing to the need for space to house the expected increase in numbers, the first decision taken by the directors in 1679 was to abandon the old buildings of the Charité in favour of a larger new hospital to be built outside the city walls.[95] After the move, the institution was able to enlarge its capacity to confine up to 500 inmates, although in cramped conditions in the harshest years. As in Paris, the intention was to offer assistance only to those categories of the poor which the governors felt to be deserving, but often the rules were ignored when times were harsh and assistance had to be granted to those considered otherwise capable of work. Lists of ineligible types of poor were compiled, including those who received a pension, the poor cared for by religious confraternities and married couples. The greater part of the population of the hospital tended to be composed of the very old and very young, which would suggest that in most years mature men and women were able to find a living through a combination of employment, out-of-doors relief and casual charity which, despite laws forbidding it, the population of the city continued to give.[96]

The hospital was intended to grant relief only to the poor of the city and diocese. By its original statutes the hospital could only receive those who possessed proof that they had been baptized in the diocese, but the difficulty caused by defining who constituted the local poor caused problems throughout the period. Although the administration did not wish the Hôpital Général to act as a beacon, attracting by its presence more vagrants to come to Montpellier to seek relief, the directors understood the reality that much of the workforce of the city, especially the seasonal labour who came to the littoral plain, had not been born in the diocese. When the rules of the Maison de Charité were changed, overzealous members of the hospital's serving community of nuns had tried to force out some of the inmates who had been born in different dioceses.[97] The directors understood the necessity to provide some

---

92   Délort, 1876, pp. 273–6.
93   ADH HG E2.
94   ADH HG E37.
95   ADH HG E2.
96   ADH HG E37 and F10.
97   ADH HG E2.

form of welfare to those from outside the locality who might have lived and worked in Montpellier for many years, and could not support this action. They quickly revised the rules in 1679 to grant relief to those who could claim a right of residence. The new rules stated that the poor could be accepted if they could furnish proof of residence, submitted by their parish curé and confirmed by the hospital director responsible for the neighbourhood in which they lived.[98]

Inside the hospital, the poor were subject to a strict daily regime designed to keep them busy and supervised at all times. This regulation of life in the wards was felt to be important in order to prevent the inmates from becoming subject to their 'native' wicked and irreligious moral state through idleness. The daily life of inmates remained unchanged from 1679 throughout the eighteenth century. The inmates were woken by the nuns at an early hour each day, during the spring and summer at five o'clock and at six o'clock for the other six months. They then dressed and cleaned their ward under the watch of the sister in charge. Segregated by sex, they then were conducted to the hospital chapel where they said public prayers. Following this, both sexes together would hear mass. After the service, the poor would be led to the refectory for their first meal, again being conducted by their ward sisters. For two and a half hours, from breakfast until lunch, they would be divided and sent to their assigned work directed by the masters of those trades. The religious teaching of the inmates continued at the noon meal, when they would be given the Benediction, and then they listened to the life of the saint of that day while they ate lunch, followed by the reading of a selected pious book. After this meal, they were given a period of observed recreation in the hospital courtyard. From Mondays to Saturday, the adults were returned to their work, while the children were sent to be schooled by one of the nuns and the priest. On Sundays, the poor spent their afternoons in the chapel, being instructed in proper Catholic doctrine by the priest in the vernacular. Following a supervised dinner and early evening recreation period, they were returned to their wards for the night.[99]

The hospital directors believed the constant supervision of every action of the inmates to be essential to ensure that the poor learned the self-discipline which they were deemed to lack and which prevented them from earning their living. The second and perhaps more important objective of the daily routine was to teach a proper understanding of Catholic doctrine and morality. The daily attendance at prayers and mass, the constant readings of moral tracts and the weekly religious instruction were all part of the plan to convert the poor to a proper form of post-Tridentine Catholicism. The young were taught the catechism as part of their transformation from useless to useful subjects. This reflected the belief that moral and religious ignorance led directly to economic poverty. The poor of the Hôpital Général were constantly monitored to prevent any moral transgressions, and the sexes were kept apart to stop the temptation of regression. The religious training and daily labour were considered especially important among the aged population of the hospital, who were subject to the same rules as the young, although allowances were made for those too feeble to do manual tasks. While the directors did not believe that the

---

98   ADH HG E37.
99   ADH HG E2 and E37.

elderly in their care were being taught a trade in order to support themselves, they thought that the elderly were required to lead a moral life in their last years to give them a good chance of salvation.

In the Bas-Languedoc, economic necessity meant that a very different form of *enfermement* from that of Paris developed. Outdoor relief was granted by the hospital, particularly to adult males who were the heads of families. This important economic role for the institution provided help for labourers of the city who were temporarily unemployed. This aid was meant to complement the Hôtel Dieu's provision of medical help and medicines to workers in their own homes. The Hôpital Général was responsible primarily for keeping the able-bodied poor from begging in the streets. It was in this capacity that the hospital provided relief for adult men and married couples who were otherwise excluded from the wards. To enable the administration to distribute this form of relief, the city was divided into six areas or *sixains*. The distribution of aid in each *sixain* was left up to the directors deputed for that purpose, which increased their social power over the populations of those neighbourhoods.

Providing assistance to the unemployed in their own homes was less expensive than confining a large number of poor. Members of the labouring classes who had no other source of support looked to the Hôpital Général as a means to supplement their income.[100] In 1685, following the revocation of the Edict of Nantes, there was an increase in the number of poor reported in the city. The board blamed the overall number of poor, both inside and outside the hospital, on the poverty caused as a consequence of the Revocation, and it accused wealthy new converts of ignoring their duty to give charitably to institutions which were now burdened with caring for former Protestants who had become unemployed.[101] This sudden increase was unexpected and was particularly troublesome for the budget of the hospital, which increased with the number of able-bodied poor claiming relief. Despite the amount of money which the directors were forced to pay (often out of their own pockets), the board did not hesitate to defend the granting of outdoor relief as the least expensive alternative.[102] Not only did the hospital save itself the problem of feeding, clothing and housing adult men and women who might only need help for a short amount of time, but it also freed the recipients from being subject to the stigma of entering the institution.

Initially the Hôpital Général gave outdoor relief in the form of a weekly cash allowance to supplement the income of the workers of the city. The direct distribution of money to the poor came under criticism in the early 1690s when the policy was likened to sanctioned begging. The urban elites grew concerned that men who received money would spend it on drink and gambling rather than use it to support their families.[103] Abuses of the privilege were reported and the policy was changed

---

100 This is true of other cities in the kingdom: see Fairchilds, 1976 on such trends in Aix-en-Provence.

101 ADH HG E4.

102 Ibid.

103 ADH HG E37. See also Chapter 2 pp. 49 015053 on the ideas of Boulainvilliers. This attitude of paternalist mistrust of the ability of the poor to care for themselves was widespread

in 1694 following the issue of new *lettres patentes*. Thereafter, outdoor relief was granted in the form of a weekly bread dole. [104] This action seems to have been taken exclusively from a judgement about the moral character of the unemployed, rather than from financial concerns. Supplying bread as a surplus to poor families in the city dramatically increased the amount of grain the Hôpital Général needed to buy. This new expense proved to be a serious problem in years of scarcity, the very years when the numbers on the bread dole reached their maximum. Although the city was shielded from the worst price fluctuations by its ability to secure grain imports from other Mediterranean countries, the budgets of the hospital were very sensitive to the slightest increase.[105] Following the troubled winter of the 1709, for example, the purchase of grain amounted to 33,135 *livres*, 10,000 *livres* more than had been spent in the previous year, representing one-third of the total expense of the hospital.[106]

The Hôpital Général shared a responsibility for wet-nursing children with the Hôtel Dieu. The hospital provided a greater service, not only granting assistance to orphans and foundlings, but it also took in children from large families who had difficulties in feeding them. Following 1701, when the rules governing the placement of children with rural wet nurses were changed, legitimate children would be accepted for relief:

> on the loss of the mother's milk, recognized and attested to by Messieurs the Directors of the *sixain,* and on the inability of the family to supplement this lack of milk by paying for the services of a wet nurse. In this case, the children must be given milk wholly at the expense of the hospital.[107]

The hospital also provided men with a way to dispose of illegitimate offspring who could be given to the Hôpital Général in return for a cash payment for their support.[108]

Prior to the foundation of the hospital, the consulate had the responsibility to pay for the *pauvres passans,* or those poor who were granted relief while on their journey back to the parish of their birth. Starting in 1680, the directors of the Hôpital Général of Montpellier granted the poor, who could provide a letter from a civic official and a priest from the last locality visited providing the name of their destination, food and lodging for the night.[109] The number of this type of poor who were assisted could vary greatly, but it was usual for the hospital to grant the *passade* to between 15 and 65 individuals per month.[110]

The hospital was supported financially by a combination of charitable income and local taxation. The new buildings of the Hôpital Général were paid for by an extraordinary donation by the diocese which amounted to 20,000 *livres* paid over

---

among the elites of the whole kingdom.

104 ADH HG A1.
105 Wolff, 1969, pp. 250–51.
106 ADH HG E71 and E72.
107 ADH HG E36.
108 ADH HG E37.
109 ADH HG F11.
110 Ibid.

a four year period.[111] The operating costs of the institution were supported from other sources of income. As with other hospitals in the kingdom, the Hôpital Général invested donations given to it in the forms of *rentes*. The Montpellier Hôpital Général contracted its *rentes* on various sources including the revenues of the province, the income of the cathedral chapter and the direct tax levied for the benefit of the Hôtel Dieu. The money generated from this source of revenue made up the lesser part of the hospital income, representing only 5,955 *livres* (14%) in 1700.[112]

The finances of the Hôpital Général were similar to those of the Hôtel Dieu because they too originated primarily from the direct and indirect taxes levied on the city to support the poor. Montpellier paid several direct taxes to underwrite the costs of the hospital. A 4,000 *livres* imposition for the maintenance of orphans and exposed children was inherited from the finances of the Maison de Charité.[113] To this tax a second imposition of 4,000 *livres* was added in 1680 to pay for the increased costs of the new institution.[114] Besides these direct taxes levied on the city, the population of Montpellier paid for the hospital through indirect taxes placed on the sale of a variety of products. Like the Hôtel Dieu, the Hôpital Général was given the right to collect a tax of one and a half *deniers* on each pound of meat sold by the city butchers. In 1714, for instance, the income from this source was 12,260 *livres*.[115] It received a percentage of the price of the sale of live pigs in the city, a tax worth 5,530 *livres* in 1700.[116] A third indirect tax was placed on the sale of tripe and offal in the city, which brought in 2,225 *livres* in 1700. The total percentage of revenue raised from taxes on the city was high in the period before 1701, when it made up the greater part of the income. For example, in 1700 the total sum collected by taxation was 23,468 *livres* out of a total income of the hospital of 42,783 *livres*, representing 55 per cent of the budget.

Between the origin of the hospital and 1700, its finances were dominated by local taxation, but the needs of the hospital were underestimated and it ran deficits throughout the period. For example, in 1700 – a year with no agricultural crisis in the region – the Hôpital Général operated at a loss of 2,701 *livres*. During this period the hospital already collected more than half of its income from local taxes, and the directors were unwilling or unable to raise the level of taxation much. After 1700, the board sought to increase its revenues through other means. As the hospital already collected a significant portion of its finances from taxes, it turned to increasing the level derived from *rentes*. In order to provide the capital needed to contract new *rentes*, the board received permission in 1700 to hold a yearly lottery.[117] The lottery was worth in total 500,000 *livres* of which the hospital received 15 per cent (70,000 *livres*) to provide capital with the remainder being paid to winners.[118] To support such

---

111 ADH HG E41.
112 ADH HG E61.
113 Ibid.
114 Ibid.
115 ADH HG E75.
116 ADH HG E61.
117 ADH HG E369.
118 Ibid.

a large endeavour, tickets were sold throughout the kingdom.[119] The capital raised by the lottery was in turn contracted in the form of *rentes* on various sources of crown, provincial, church and city revenues, which increased the total collected from this source to 20,343 *livres* in 1714 (compared to 5,955 *livres* in 1700).[120] However, the funds raised from the new *rentes* did little but reduce the deficit. In 1709, the harsh winter created a great increase in the demand placed on the hospital. The hospital struggled to repay its debts caused mostly by the dramatic increase in the cost of grain and the increased number of mouths it had to feed, as the seasonal labourers who came to Montpellier from the Cévennes remained in the city to seek relief. It was forced to borrow 17,200 *livres* from members of the urban elites of Montpellier in 1710 to buy grain for the poor.[121] Unlike similar debts in other hospitals, this one was not converted into *rentes* to be repaid over time, but was repaid in full out of the revenues of the next year. Why the directors were unwilling to convert the debt of the hospital into *rentes* is unclear, but the hospital continued to do this, which only served to make matters worse. In 1711, revenues fell behind expenses by 20,113 *livres*.[122] This debt increased to 37,653 *livres* in 1715.[123] The problem of the hospital debt was not solved until later in the eighteenth century when more revenues were secured for the institution.

The reforms of poor relief and charitable health care provision in seventeenth-century Montpellier reflected the social, economic and religious changes experienced by the city. The coalescence of a new patriciate composed of elite groups who did not have representation in the municipal government, and thus, on the boards that controlled poor relief, led to the reform of the administration of the Hôtel Dieu on the one hand and the transformation of the Maison de Charité into the larger Hôpital Général on the other. By the second half of the seventeenth century, the benefactors of the city's charitable institutions no longer felt it was acceptable for the lesser-ranked consulate to control distribution of assistance. The history of these charitable institutions demonstrates the forging of the alliance of various civic elite groups which was the cornerstone of the ancien régime. Members of the robe, the church, the bourgeoisie and the wealthy mercantile classes proclaimed their superiority over the rest of the population of Montpellier by removing the representation of the artisanal ranks from the governing body of the Hôtel Dieu and by not including them in the board of the new Hôpital Général.

Charity and poor relief in Montpellier remained the responsibilities of the locality during seventeenth century throughout the reign of Louis XIV. The crown did not wish to interfere with the right of local elites as long as they dealt with the problem of the poor. While the foundation of the Hôpital Général and the changes made to the administration of the Hôtel Dieu were initiated by a single individual, the bishop

---

119 Ibid. Of the 6,400 tickets printed for the lottery of 1700, 600 were sent to Lyon to be sold, 600 to Paris, 300 each to Nîmes, Marseille, Toulouse and Carcassonne, and smaller numbers to Perpignan, Béziers, Uzès, and Narbonne among others.

120 ADH HG E76.

121 ADH HG E71.

122 ADH HG E72.

123 ADH HG E76.

Charles Pradel, this fact does not support an argument that either the church or the crown assumed control over poor relief in the city. The bishop was a keen advocate of the conversion of both the Protestants and those ignorant of the proper tenets of Catholicism in his diocese. He wished to use the city's charitable hospitals to assist in this aim. Pradel's actions were approved by the local elites, who profited socially from the changes made. Without the financial and administrative support of the urban elites, these endeavours would have undoubtedly failed.

Chapter Six

Reforming Social Welfare in a Divided Town: Nîmes

By the beginning of the seventeenth century Nîmes had become the most important manufacturing centre in Languedoc and a significant Protestant city. The Reformed faith had made significant gains among the people of the city, converting the greater part of the urban population. Louis XIV's Edict of Fontainbleau, issued in 1685, ended the guarantee of civil rights to the Protestant population of France under the terms of the 1598 Edict of Nantes and restored the official monopoly of faith in the kingdom to Catholicism. However, for over 50 years prior to that, after periods of unrest culminating in the siege of La Rochelle and the Peace of Alès, the confessional peace had lasted from 1629 to 1685. The effects of the Revocation are well known, but the problem of how the Reformed and Catholic congregations interacted during the years when the terms of the Edict of Nantes were in effect has been studied to a lesser extent.[1] That the middle decades of the seventeenth century marked a time when tensions and hostilities between the two faiths remained but went underground has long been assumed.[2] Those interested in finding points of intolerance and conflict within the kingdom are able to list devout organizations, angry publications, isolated riots and disturbances to confirm a long-held view that the two religions inhabited separate spaces.[3] Some, however, have dug deeper into the relationships between communities to search out similarities and toleration. Elisabeth Labrousse argues that, in terms of daily life in the localities, there was no great controversy over coexistence between Catholic and Protestant. In fact, she has found that in many parts of France, it was difficult for the two faiths to stay separate for reasons of family, neighbourhood and professional ties.[4] Gregory Hanlon has argued convincingly that the seventeenth-century definition of toleration included a deep-seated hostility toward the other religion that recognized the inability to destroy

---

1   Most notably Hanlon, 1993; Labrousse, 1985; Benedict, 2001; and Benedict, 1991. The general history of seventeenth-century Catholicism in France is covered in: Delumeau, 1971; Lebrun, 1980; and Taveneaux, 1980. Hoffman, 1984 and Durand, 1985 are important studies of individual regions. Nîmes itself is studied in Sauzet, 1979, although little of the city's poor relief history is covered. The relationship between the Protestant community and the Catholic community in La Rochelle, where the Catholic elites were able to undermine the terms of the Edict of Nantes after the reconquest of the city, is studied in Robbins, 1995.

2   For example, Pugh, 1974, p. 350; Pugh, 1980, p. 503, who argues that the political and religious life of Nîmes during the seventeenth century was dominated by the struggle between Catholic and Protestant to control poor relief.

3   Ligou, 1968; Garrisson, 1985; Martin, 2000.

4   Labrousse, 1985, pp. 81–9.

it without causing unacceptable damage to society. As he has found in Aquitaine, after 1629 communities with sizable minorities, fearing the return of violence, chose often uneasy coexistence as an alternative to war.[5] It is not surprising that closely knit urban populations should seek compromise in order to heal wounds rent open by the Wars of Religion.

Following the triumph of Catholic forces at the siege of La Rochelle (1627–29), Nîmes, located in the Bas-Languedoc, became the heart of French Calvinism until 1685. The city had a population of approximately 15,000[6] dependent mostly on the manufacture of textiles for employment. A four-man consulate composed of two Protestants and two Catholics (selected strictly from the wealthy citizens of the town) formed the civic government. After the city suffered setbacks caused by the Wars of Religion, it enjoyed economic growth during the seventeenth-century peace. Although the period under study witnessed the decline of the cloth trade in the city, a more lucrative manufacture of silk replaced it.[7] During the sixteenth century Calvinism had become the dominant faith in Nîmes, and despite an influx of mostly Catholic rural immigrants during the mid-seventeenth-century boom, Protestants still held a majority in the diocese in 1685 with approximately two-thirds of the population.[8] After 1629 two groups composed the city's ruling classes: wealthy Protestants who had made their fortune in the various industries of the city and Catholic members of the judiciary in the Présidial court. Despite the religious and occupational differences between them, the city's rulers were fairly homogeneous in terms of wealth, attitude, aspirations and concerns. As Nîmes did not possess a senior sovereign court, there was little social difference between a wealthy Protestant bourgeois and a Catholic judicial figure. While the presence of a Calvinist majority naturally pushed the Catholic minority toward toleration, there was also a significant pull toward intolerance during the period. Being the de facto capital of Protestant France after 1629, it attracted numerous Catholic partisans who wished to prove the strength of their faith by entering into dispute with the Protestants, making the city a site where religious tensions potentially could erupt into conflict.

This chapter examines the important roles played by religion and economics in the history of social welfare in Nîmes. In a city otherwise divided along confessional lines, poor relief provision was a significant point of interaction between Catholics and Protestants particularly from 1629 to 1685, but also behind the scenes after the Revocation of the Edict of Nantes.[9] This interaction between faiths over poor relief often came against the wishes of the crown, particularly in the years after 1685. The history of charity in such a city sheds light on the relationship between confessions, since, from the earliest days of the Reformation, both Catholics and Protestants used

---

5   Hanlon, 1993, pp. 1–7.

6   Sauzet, 1979, pp. 359–60. Sauzet's estimate that there were 8,000 Catholic inhabitants and 12,000 Protestant inhabitants reflects the city's population in 1685.

7   Ibid.

8   Ibid.

9   The history of charity has been successfully used to study the relationships between various groups in society in early modern Europe. See Jones, 1982; Jones, 1989; Cavallo, 1995; Gutton, 1970; Fairchilds, 1976; Norberg, 1985. The most recent assessment of hospital administration and organization in seventeenth-century France is in Hickey, 1997.

their approach toward charity as a way to define their faiths.[10] The divide over the role good works played in an individual's salvation obscures the fact that both saw charitable giving to the deserving poor as part of every Christian's duty toward God. Charity was a way to profess the strength of the faith,[11] especially for those Catholic religious who came to the city in order to combat Protestantism. The devout of both faiths viewed charity as a means to prevent the poor (a group perceived to succumb more easily to conversion due to its ignorance of proper religious practices) from switching religion. This was important particularly to the Catholic minority of Nîmes since its population was the most likely to convert in the years before 1679.[12] For laymen and for secular authorities, poor relief was essential for the maintenance of civic order.[13] In this respect, the study of charitable institutions highlights the value placed by the city's ruling classes on their relationships with the poorer elements of society.[14] In Nîmes, with its mixed population, there was great potential for issues surrounding municipal poor relief to devolve into conflict.

The restoration of Catholicism in the city in 1629 was a significant turning point for the laymen of Nîmes. Despite the possibility of civil strife in the divided city, order was maintained after 1629. With peace, came a determination to prevent a return of civil disorder and bloodshed in the future. While, in the decades that followed, many partisans came to the city in an effort to undermine the fragile coexistence, Nîmes's ruling elites did what they could to maintain it. This is not to say that the civic fathers of either faith believed in a modern definition of toleration. It is likely that neither side was happy about the situation, but the relative strengths of the two communities meant that both were forced to coexist.[15] The coexistence among the two faiths also helped to shape the forms poor relief and charitable health care took. Local needs, tempered by economic and religious conditions, had a strong impact on the history of Nîmes's hospitals.

The municipal hospital under a board divided by religion

From the Middle Ages, the focus for nîmois charity had been the municipal hospital. The Hôtel Dieu of Nîmes[16] traced its origins to the foundation, in 1313, of an institution to care for the sick poor of the city. Secularized and put under the governance of the city's four-man consulate, the hospital fell to Protestant control during the early sixteenth century.[17] In an attempt to undo Calvinist control, in 1549,

---

10   Cameron, 1991, pp. 258–61.

11   For example, de Sales, 1641, pp. 232.

12   Quéniart, 1985, p. 28.

13   For example, Colbert's opinion on the subject. Colbert, 1861–73, tom. II, p. 656.

14   The nature of the relationships between rich and poor in early modern European cities is best explored in Cavallo, 1995.

15   Hanlon, 1993, p. 7. Benedict, 2001, pp. 280–82.

16   The institution was known simply as the Hospital de Nîmes before 1661. It will be referred to as the Hôtel Dieu for the period before its official change of name in order to avoid confusion with the Protestant hospital founded in 1654.

17   Pugh, 1974, p. 350.

the fiercely Catholic Parlement of Toulouse imposed the hospital's first official constitution which, while confirming the consulate as the board of directors, decreed the administration to be under the authority of the Bishop of Nîmes.[18] However, the Protestant consulate ignored the ruling and met as sole directors of the Hôtel Dieu until the restoration of civil peace in 1629, excluding the bishop from his place on the board.[19]

Catholicism, the public practice of which had been suspended in the city as late as 1628 when the cathedral chapter had fled during the Huguenot rebellion, reasserted its interests following the Peace of Alès in 1629. At the crown's insistence, the membership of the city's consulate was divided equally in October 1631 between the two congregations, resulting in a return to lay Catholic representation on the hospital board.[20] The cathedral chapter returned and religious orders from other parts of the kingdom founded new houses in the city. The most important of these newcomers were the Jesuits, who had been active in the city as early as the 1590s, but built their college only after the peace was signed.[21] During the 1630s the regular orders acted in concert with the cathedral chapter in petitioning local, provincial and royal authorities for increased rights for Catholics. At the same time the strength of Catholicism in Nîmes grew as the Huguenots suffered from demographic challenges. The percentage of the Reformed population of the city compared with the Catholic decreased in the 1630s for two reasons: the devastating effects of the plague of 1629–30, and the influx throughout the decade of large numbers of Catholic migrants seeking employment in the silk trade.[22] The new arrivals increased the Catholic population to about one-third of the city's total. This growth in their population gave Catholics the excuse to insist on taking a part in the administration of charitable institutions to protect the concerns of their poor. Adding to their fears, although the population balance of the city shifted away from that of before 1629, Catholics still formed the minority and, consequently, were never wholly confident in their position in Nîmes since some workers abjured their faith in order to secure work with Protestant employers throughout the period before 1685.[23]

Buoyed by the defeat of militant Calvinism in 1629 and the subsequent rise in Catholic numbers, the early 1630s were a period of increased Catholic initiative in Nîmes led by the bishop, Anthyme-Denis Cohon, and the newly arrived religious orders.[24] Cohon was an activist strongly in favour of Tridentine reform. Following his arrival, the church petitioned the civic authorities to comply with existing canon law, much of which followed the Council of Trent in matters concerning the primacy of bishops in hospital administrations. Despite significant Protestant complaints, the bishop secured his place in the administration as a member of the board of

---

18 ADG HD A1, A3 & E1. It should be noted that the Toulouse Parlement acted against the terms of sixteenth-century crown edicts confirming the authority of local governments over urban hospitals.

19 ADG HD E3.

20 Sauzet, 1979, p. 275.

21 Ibid., pp. 131–9, 204.

22 Pugh, 1974, pp. 354–62.

23 Quéniart, 1985, p. 28.

24 See Sauzet, 1979.

directors in 1635.[25] As well as having a mixed directorate, the hospital derived its finances from both congregations. Financially, it relied on local sources of revenue: legacies; pensions; a customary tax on meat sold in the diocese; occasional door-to-door collections and, in emergencies, a tax on all citizens subject to paying the *taille*. Although the revenue was divided equally by a decision of the consulate in 1656 between the Catholic Hôtel Dieu and the new Protestant hospital, these sources remained the basis for the finances with only minor alterations throughout the seventeenth century.[26]

While the wards continued to be open to Protestants and Catholics alike, as Catholics gained places on the board of directors in the 1630s, the practice of Protestantism in the hospital came under threat. Catholics were successful in dismissing the Calvinist schoolmaster paid to instruct patients and in hiring a Catholic priest as the hospital chaplain.[27] This was done at the request of the bishop in order to bring the institution in line with his interpretation of French laws which viewed the religious functions of hospitals as his responsibility. This change could have been a flashpoint for civil unrest since the link between religion and healing was very strong; however, it proved to be the only serious grievance for Protestants following the rearrangement of the composition of the consulate. From the late 1630s until the early 1650s the main effects of this change on the poor were not very drastic, because Calvinist ministers and visitors nominated by the consistory, the governing body of the city's Protestant congregation, continued to visit the hospital at regular intervals.[28] For the most part, during the 1630s and 1640s, the terms of the Edict of Nantes were respected: Protestants were given unfettered access to treatment; there were regular visits by Calvinist ministers; and few attempts were made by the Catholic Church to secure conversions among the poor in the wards.

Despite the agitation of the early 1630s, in the period between 1635 and 1650 tensions over the control of the hospital decreased. Catholic gains in the early 1630s were not exploited during the 1640s to exclude the Protestant consuls from the hospital board. Although the bishop had been successful in securing a place among the hospital directors, there were no serious attempts to challenge the religious armistice following the peace of Alès. After gaining a seat on the board, Cohon diverted his energies toward other projects such as the reconstruction of the cathedral and the establishment in the city of various religious houses.[29] The Bishop of Nîmes during the 1640s, Hector Douvrier, attended few meetings of the board, which left wealthy laymen, represented by the consuls, to administer the hospital in the way they thought best for the interests of both faiths. In the early 1650s, however, there was a renewed vigour on the part of Catholic partisans. Beginning in 1653, the regular orders in Nîmes initiated a campaign to preach against Protestantism in an effort to win new converts.[30] The Protestant consistory feared that its poor would

25 ADG HD E3.

26 ADG HD E62 and Pugh, 1974, p. 351.

27 Pugh, 1974, p. 345.

28 AN TT 260/119.

29 Sauzet, 1979, pp. 276–94.

30 Ménard, 1755, tom. 6, pp. 108–109; AN TT 260/208; AN TT 431/6.

be targeted for conversion in the hospital since the sick in the wards could prove to be easy prey. At the same time, members of the city's religious orders ensured that Protestant visitors had difficulties in gaining access to those of their religion in the wards. After a letter of complaint had been sent to the crown by the Calvinist synod of Languedoc about Catholic contraventions of the Edict of Nantes in 1654, the Huguenot consuls established an independent Protestant hospital on their own authority.[31]

The Protestant hospital of Nîmes

The creation of Nîmes's Protestant hospital demonstrates the degree of independent action a local community could take during the seventeenth century. The decision for the Reformed consuls to withdraw from the administration of the Hôtel Dieu and found a hospital of their own came in a meeting of the consistory on 29 July 1653.[32] The consuls gave two reasons why they had the right to divide the funds of the hospital. Firstly, they argued that the division of the consulate between the city's two communities created a precedent for civic institutions, and the funds available to the Hôtel Dieu, being managed by the consuls, ought to be divided as well.[33] Secondly, they argued that the Huguenots were owed one-half of the municipal poor relief funds because of the terms of the Edict of Nantes which allowed free access to all hospitals of the kingdom by the poor of both faiths. The basis for creating a separate hospital stemmed from the belief that the activism of the Catholic clergy during the early 1650s prevented Protestants from being treated in the Hôtel Dieu free from harassment, as guaranteed by the Edict. The two Protestant consuls stated that:

> The king by his edicts and declarations has granted to the citizens of this city who make a profession of the reformed faith one-half of the hospital and its sources of income in order to assist the poor of the said reformed religion. Nevertheless for a certain period of time the entire hospital has been in the possession of the citizens of the Roman faith ... the poor of the reformed faith suffer from this situation.[34]

The consistory determined that the only course of action to resolve this situation was to take possession of half of the hospital's assets and to build a new institution for the care of the Protestant sick.[35] The consuls must have understood that their interpretation of the law was unlikely to hold up in any court held by Catholic judges. The foundation of new hospitals in the kingdom had, since 1579, required the

---

    31 Ménard, 1755, tom. 6, p. 108. and AN TT 259 and 260. Cf. Pugh, 1974, 363–4 where it is argued that Protestant loyalty during the Frondes was rewarded with royal permission to found the new hospital. The fact that the institution was closed because it was deemed to have been founded contrary to the law argues against this case.

    32 ADG/42/J/39.

    33 AN TT260/208.

    34 ADG/42/J/39.

    35 ADG/42/J/39. The Protestant hospital claimed one half of the income of the Hôtel Dieu in 1653, but these funds became available to it only in 1656.

sanction of both the local bishop and the crown.[36] While the government of Mazarin was, in theory, favourable to Huguenots thanks to their loyalty during the Frondes, no Catholic bishop would have agreed to the foundation of a Protestant hospital in his diocese.

The return of a known partisan of the Counter-Reformation as bishop, Anthyme-Denis Cohon, in 1655 served only to increase the tension felt by the Protestants.[37] After his first term as bishop (1633–44), he had been appointed to the bishopric of Dol, and was a supporter of Mazarin in Paris at the time of the Frondes, publishing tracts in favour of the cardinal. Cohon was reappointed at his own request to the see of Nîmes in 1655 by the cardinal,[38] and on his arrival, Calvinist merchants threatened to refuse to co-operate with Catholics in business and to withhold employment from all but Protestant workers.[39] The fear of civil unrest created an anti-Cohon faction among Catholics as well, disrupting the consular elections in that year.[40] A significant portion of the whole urban community disliked the disruption of the social peace of the city caused by the bishop's presence. The consuls, recognizing the need for both faiths to have a measure of control over such a charged issue as charity, limited the damage done to confessional coexistence by coming to an agreement against the bishop's wishes to divide officially the revenues of the Hôtel Dieu in 1656.[41]

During the middle decades of the century the two confessions were very interconnected in terms of social life. While the bishop and religious houses might have wished to confront and convert Protestants, lay Catholics preferred to keep the peace with their Huguenot neighbours, relatives, friends and business associates.[42] In addition, members of the Protestant elites accounted for a majority of the employers of the city. Should they have ceased to provide work for the large numbers of mostly Catholic migrant labourers, the system of Catholic poor relief in the city, dependant on fewer individuals for funding, would have been heavily burdened. Nor did the legal professionals who served on the board of the Hôtel Dieu wish the bishop and regular orders to put the social peace of the city in jeopardy and agreed to divide the revenue to ensure the survival of the two hospitals.[43]

Early in 1654, the consistory donated the money necessary to construct an entirely new building organized along similar lines as the Hôtel Dieu.[44] The new foundation was a small institution with space to hold from 50 to 100 patients. Despite the opportunity given by the need to construct an entirely new space for Protestant charity to flourish, the building was functional in design and simple in decoration. The wealthy merchants who sponsored the new hospital did not embark on a showpiece of baroque piety similar to that of the new Jesuit College or the renovated Hôtel Dieu of their Catholic neighbours because Calvinists believed that

36 Imbert, 1993, pp. 9–15.
37 Ménard, 1755, tom. 6, pp. 113–14.
38 Robert, 1895, pp. 115–59; Bergin, 1996, p. 598.
39 Ménard, 1755, tom. 6, pp. 123–6.
40 Ibid.
41 ADG HD E3.
42 An exception to this was the notary Etienne Borrelly, see Sauzet, 1998.
43 ADG HD E3 & ADG/30/J/82.
44 ADG/30/J/80.

charity was an obligation owed by all good Christians without resorting to personal aggrandisement. Additionally, because the legality of the hospital was in doubt (and it was certainly seen by the bishop as a source of irritation), the community had no desire to call attention to it as a rival to the Catholic Hôtel Dieu.

The hospital was administered by the two Protestant consuls with assistance given to them by members of the faith nominated by the consistory. The men who ran the institution came from the ranks of wealthy merchants or bourgeois of the city.[45] To assist the consuls in administering the day-to-day accounts of the institution, a receiver of funds was appointed by them. This post was always filled by men from a bourgeois or merchant background.[46] The consuls appointed men of these ranks because they were considered to be the most responsible, and because most were former consuls with experience in the Protestant hospital's affairs.[47]

The duties of the board were to pay for the visit to the hospital of a physician and surgeon, for food and medicine, and for the shelter and clothing of the patients. Medical care in the Protestant institution was limited because it had no access to a nursing order to act as amateur practitioners. The hospital governors provided such care by contracting Jean Chabrier, a local surgeon. He attended the patients in the hospital on a weekly basis, and seems to have been capable of performing some minor invasive operations, but his main task was to set the broken bones of injured workers.[48] A local physician was summoned by the board when his services were deemed necessary. Besides offering food, shelter and basic medical care to the sick, from its foundation the Protestant institution assumed the responsibility to care for orphans and abandoned children. It fulfilled this duty by hiring suitable rural women to house and feed these children. Because the care of abandoned and orphaned children was a great burden on the expenses of the hospital, the consuls developed a network of Protestant women in the countryside who regularly accepted the care of infants from the hospital for a period of up to two years. These rural wet nurses used their care of urban children as a means of augmenting their family incomes, each earning between three and four *livres* per year for their services.[49]

The daily staff of the Protestant establishment was smaller than that of similar Catholic hospitals. However, this did not reflect the regard that wealthy Huguenots had for charity. A single porter and his wife took care of all of the daily needs of the patients, including the feeding and clothing of patients, administering the medicines prescribed, and cleaning and heating the wards. Members of the Protestant community inspected the wards during regular visits organized by the consistory, monitoring the quality of care. These visits by members of the congregation echoed similar visitations by lay Catholics to their institutions. Those who donated to the poor, either through charitable bequests or by paying the poor taxes of both the city and consistory, did not wish to finance a building which would act, in effect, as a

---

45   ADG/30/J/80–87.

46   Ibid. It should be noted that Protestants who claimed bourgeois status in Nîmes were mostly retired merchants or their descendants living off investments.

47   Ibid.

48   ADG/30/J/81.

49   ADG/30/J/80 and 81.

warehouse for the ill and dying. These visits were an important part of the system of poor relief in the nîmois Calvinist community. It gave lay members, particularly women who would otherwise have no say in the operation of the hospital, a way to participate in charitable care of the poor. The consuls and consistory encouraged women to see the wards for themselves in the knowledge that their approval mattered in securing funds for the hospital from their families. The visits by members of the Protestant community were quite different from those made by their ministers for religious reasons. While women inspecting the hospital might pray with selected patients, their true importance lay in maintaining standards and improving the efficiency of the establishment. Women could be very effective in securing change. For example, following complaints made by visitors to the hospital about 'la mauvaise vie et conduite de l'hospitalier et sa femme' in January 1660, the couple were replaced.[50] Even after the hospital's closure the consistory continued to organize visits to Protestant patients in the Catholic hospital by its 'ladies of charity'.[51] These visitations became more important because greater numbers of the Protestant poor wound up at the Hôtel Dieu, which no longer had any Protestant representation on its board.

The history of the Protestant hospital's finances suggests that the community was committed to providing relief to its members who were ill. In 1654, the first year of operation, its finances were derived mostly from charitable sources. The consistory provided the greater portion of the income, granting 1,249 *livres* from its own charitable funds.[52] A further 400 *livres* came from a personal donation from the second consul, Jean Roux. Continuing a strategy which had been successful previously for the municipal hospital, the wives of the Protestant consuls assisted, raising 944 *livres* for the hospital by means of a door-to-door collection from Huguenot households. Without recourse to the revenues of the Catholic Hôtel Dieu, the Protestant hospital operated in its first year at a shortfall of 880 *livres*, which was made up by a second door-to-door collection of the Protestant community.[53] The permanent revenues were increased with an unofficial tax of 2,000 *livres* placed on Protestant households, which continued to be paid until 1657 when it was deemed no longer necessary due to the strong financial basis of the hospital.[54]

The shortfall in the revenues of the Protestant hospital in 1654, coupled with the financial difficulties faced by the Hôtel Dieu at the same time, led the city government to impose a direct tax on residents of both faiths to be shared equally by the two hospitals in 1656.[55] In 1661, this single imposition was continued permanently as a 4,000 *livres* per annum tax to be divided between them. In 1656, as has been mentioned above, the Protestant consuls increased the income of the

50 ADG/42/J/40 and 41.

51 ADG/42/J/42.

52 ADG/30/J/80–87.

53 Ibid.

54 ADG/30/J/82. The 2,000 *livres* imposition levied on the Protestant community was discontinued after 1656, a year in which the hospital showed a profit of 2,886 *livres*. The surplus came after the initial cost of founding the hospital had been fully paid.

55 Ibid. The initial value of this tax was 6,000 *livres* (subsequently reduced to 4,000 *livres* in 1661).

hospital by claiming and receiving one half of all the revenues from legacies and from the civic meat tax from the Catholic hospital which it had collected since the Middle Ages. The combination of direct and indirect taxes made up the majority of the hospital revenues, for example in 1660 when the hospital had a total income of 4,716 *livres*, of which 2,900 derived from these sources.[56] The Protestant institution owed its financial success to a good base of support among the community, and it continued to meet its expenses until it was closed in 1667.[57] Protestants were willing to pay what was necessary to keep it in operation both through taxation and the yearly collection. Because of these measures, the hospital, unlike many others in seventeenth-century France, fared well financially between 1656 and 1667, being solvent during its lifetime.[58]

Catholic reforms at the Hôtel Dieu

For Catholic nîmois the Protestant departure from the Hôtel Dieu's board in 1654 was seen as a new opportunity. The 1549 constitution of the hospital administration recognized that the four consuls of the city acted as governors, as had long been the tradition. According to these rules, the decisions taken by them were to be approved by the bishop and the Sénéchal, who were to head the board as the senior religious and judicial figures of the city. Once the Reformed consuls left, the remaining two Catholic consuls, acting as the hospital administration, soon recognized that there was a need for new members to assist them manage the hospital. A revised version of the official constitution was quickly adopted. The new hospital board became more visibly Catholic in orientation, moving its meetings to the newly built Catholic chapel of the hospital to emphasize the religious purpose of the institution.[59] From 1655 the directors consisted of the bishop (represented by his vicar), the juge-mage of the Présidial (or his deputy), the two Catholic consuls, and a number of intendants invited by the board to serve without fixed term from the ranks of the lawyers in the Présidial court and the Catholic bourgeois of the city.[60]

From the start of its existence as a strictly Catholic institution the directors committed themselves to making the Hôtel Dieu into a better functioning establishment, increasing its size by building a new ward to admit more poor and to alleviate overcrowding in the old building. To increase the medical services on offer, as well as to provide religious instruction for the sick, the administration entered into a contract with an order of serving nuns, the dames religieuses hospitalières de Saint-Joseph.[61] The contracting or nursing order was an important reform for the hospital. Besides offering spiritual solace to the poor, the nuns acted as amateur

---

56 ADG/30/J/84. 2,400 *livres* of the total income came from the direct tax and 500 *livres* from the indirect tax on meat. It should be noted that the total expenses of the Protestant hospital between 1654 and 1667 were never more that 3,500 *livres*.

57 ADG/30/J/84–88.

58 ADG/30/J/84–88.

59 ADG HD E3.

60 Ibid. and ADG HD E71.

61 Ménard, 1755, tom. 6, p. 173; ADG HD E22, E71 and H22.

practitioners: binding wounds, setting bones, prescribing and preparing remedies for the sick.[62] By 1661, the Huguenot departure had allowed the hospital to transform itself into an institution that reflected contemporaneous Catholic values about the religious virtue of charity and poor relief. From the 1654 departure of the Protestant consuls from the administration until long after the revocation of the Edict of Nantes in 1685, the hospital commonly presented itself as a showpiece of Catholic charity to entice the Protestants of the city to convert.[63] A redecoration scheme was begun and artwork commissioned to fill the wards. The board also altered the fabric of the hospital in order to demonstrate its charitable impulses. Much of this seems to have been the inspiration of Cohon, who was very influenced by the ideas of Catholic Reform theologians.[64] Financial concerns took second place to the desire to demonstrate the Catholic community's religious verve in the years after 1654. The board's building projects created a mounting debt during the 1660s, coming at a time when the institution had lost one-half of its earlier revenues in 1656 as a result of the creation of the Protestant hospital.[65]

After the foundation of the Protestant hospital, financial problems created the need for a new tax to support both hospitals, which was approved by the whole city consulate in 1656. The consulate imposed a levy of 4,000 *livres* applied to all of the residents of the city, and divided equally between the two institutions. The agreement of the Reformed consuls for this tax was secured in return for the division of the other revenues of the Hôtel Dieu and for tacit acceptance of the Protestant hospital's existence. Each confession wanted this new tax to secure a future for its hospital. The consuls decided among themselves that the fairest and least damaging solution was the division of all the municipal poor relief revenues between both institutions in 1656. The Hôtel Dieu earmarked the funds from the new levy to help purchase grain to feed the poor in the wards, which was constantly the greatest burden on its finances.[66] However, the division of revenues, coupled with the building plans of its directors, proved to be a long-term burden on the finances of the Hôtel Dieu. In 1656, for example, the loss of revenues forced the administration to borrow 10,000 *livres*, including a single loan worth 7,000 *livres* from the influential Catholic Fabre family. In 1659, the directors borrowed 4,734 *livres* from a Catholic lawyer, Louis Gaillard, and 1,000 *livres* from the city's Ursuline convent to pay for food for the poor.[67] The desire of the Hôtel Dieu's administration to emulate other Catholic hospitals in the kingdom by utilizing an order of nursing sisters to tend the sick, required it to contract large loans not only for the sisters' accommodation but also to feed them.[68] In order to cover the higher costs, the Hôtel Dieu borrowed a total of 15,000 *livres* from local notables and religious houses. Many of these debts were repaid as lifetime or perpetual pensions to the lenders. In the period from 1653 to 1668, the

---

62 Jones, 1989, pp. 162–205.
63 ADG HD E3.
64 Sauzet, 1979, pp. 239–40, and Robert, 1895, pp. 111–15.
65 ADG HD E22 and E71.
66 ADG HD E3.
67 ADG HD H22.
68 Ibid.

hospital's debt grew to over 45,000 *livres*.[69] Money owed to pay for the services of the sisters of Saint-Joseph continued to burden the Hôtel Dieu until the dames de la Visitation of Nîmes undertook the responsibility for the debt in 1676 in return for a substantial pension (which the hospital continued to pay until the Revolution).[70] The pattern of borrowing from local devout notables and religious houses of the city in favour of long-term or perpetual loans financed by hospital revenues continued through the period 1670–1715 and beyond.[71] Despite being high, the hospital's debt does not seem to have been particularly troublesome for the Catholic elites of Nîmes. Throughout the rest of reign of Louis XIV, the hospital regularly maintained a debt of around 24,000 *livres* which was repaid to lenders at an interest rate of four per cent.[72] That lenders continued to give money to the hospital, despite its indebtedness, even at points such as 1694 when repayments could be suspended for years, would suggest that they either regarded the institution as a secure risk in the long term because of its assured income through the municipal taxes it possessed, or that they considered these loans to be charitable donations on which repayments might be excused during troubled financial years in return for spiritual gain.

In the years of the Protestant hospital's existence, from 1654 to 1667, while points of contention arose between the two confessions, there were few open disputes over the assistance of the poor.[73] With the exception of some individuals, each side seems to have preferred to allow the other the freedom to take care of its own sick and unemployed. This peace did not mean that other tensions which lay under the surface disappeared. While the business and social relations between the Catholic and Protestant communities of Nîmes were interconnected and encouraged toleration on both sides, each side remained worried about losing members of its faith and sought to prevent abjurations.[74] The new opportunities to Catholicize the Hôtel Dieu after 1654 allowed lay Catholics to protect their poor and demonstrate the strength of their faith, but the lay elites were careful not to damage relationships with their Protestant neighbours.

Closing the Protestant hospital

The end of the Protestant hospital came in 1667, when it was closed by order of the Parlement of Toulouse. Wilma Pugh argues that it was the end of a significant period of confessional struggle and part of a general Catholic triumph in the city.[75] However, there had been no previous attempt on the part of the Catholic-controlled Présidial or the city consulate to shut it down. The reunification of the two hospitals was commanded on 22 February 1667 by the staunchly Catholic judges of the

---

69   Ibid.
70   Ibid.
71   Ibid.
72   ADG HD E22.
73   Sauzet, 1979, p. 311–24.
74   ADG/42/J/40.
75   Pugh, 1974, p. 365.

Parlement of Toulouse at the Grands Jours held at Nîmes.[76] The official reason given for the closure of the Protestant hospital was the illegality of its foundation on the sole authority of the Protestant consuls. They had not gained the approval of the crown and the bishop, both of which were required by law to found such an institution. Using a different interpretation of the terms under which the Protestants had claimed the right to open the institution, the Parlement decreed the hospital's existence contrary to the Edict of Nantes because it did not provide shelter for the poor of both faiths:

> Let the consuls of the city of Nîmes who make a profession of the religion which claims to be reformed be condemned to close down the new hospital which was established by them to assist only the poor of the Protestant faith ... the said new hospital will be united along with all of its goods and sources of revenue to the old hospital of this city. The entirety will be administered by the governors of the old hospital and that, in this manner, conforming to article XXII of the Edict of Nantes, the sick poor of the Protestant faith will be treated the same as those of the Catholic faith without being constrained or threatened because of the fact of their religion.[77]

The Parlement stressed that many of the *rentes* which the Protestant hospital used as revenue had been left to the Hôtel Dieu before the Reformation when it had been a Catholic establishment. This went to the heart of the belief of the kingdom's elites, especially the men of the judiciary, that the intentions of donors ought to have been respected, even after several centuries.[78]

Bishop Cohon was the principal figure who acted to close the Protestant hospital. He had already been vocal in his opposition to its presence in the city, citing it as an institution whose mere existence served to spread ignorance and heresy among the population.[79] The Grands Jours sessions of the Parlement of Toulouse in the city in 1667 had been his first chance to use a court of favourable judges to win a legal decision against the right of the Protestant consuls to manage the hospital.[80] Until then, neither the consulate nor the Présidial court had been willing to do so in the interests of maintaining harmony between the two faiths. Indeed the Catholic consuls in particular seem to have been tacitly supportive of the interests of their Calvinist neighbours for they had not made any attempt to have the hospital closed and had gone as far as making deals that ensured its survival. The bishop understood that the judges from Toulouse were hostile to the interests of the Protestant population of Nîmes. He argued that neither he nor the previous bishop had given the necessary approval either for the hospital's foundation or for its continued existence.[81]

---

76 Toulouse, located at the other end of the province of Languedoc, was the seat of the Parlement that had final authority over legal affairs in Nîmes. The Grands Jours were sessions of the Parlement of Toulouse held in other towns of its jurisdiction.

77 Le Blanc, 1869, pp. 234–6.

78 AN TT 260/119 and Gachon, 1899, pp. LIII–LV.

79 Debant, 1986, p. 65.

80 AN TT 260/119 and Gachon, 1899, pp. LIII–LV.

81 Ibid.

The Parlement ordered the closure of the hospital and the return of all properties and revenues which had originally been donated to the Hôtel Dieu. However, the Reformed consuls did not relinquish the enjoyment of the half of the imposition made for poor relief, nor their half of the meat tax. In the interest of civic harmony, the Catholic consuls preferred not to challenge the Protestant claim to these levies. The simple closure of the hospital was the most important object for the bishop so that the Hôtel Dieu would become the city's sole institution to care for the sick poor, and he believed it would gain considerable advantage in converting Protestants who entered the wards more often, even though the consistory began to house the sick of its faith in private homes.

After the hospital closed, with the toleration of the Catholic secular authorities, Protestants in Nîmes continued to manage their own poor relief, concentrating more and more on those forms designed to prevent abjurations. There was no effort to restore some Calvinist representation to the board of the Hôtel Dieu. The congregation chose instead to focus on dispensing aid outside of an institution in the years following 1667. While the consistory managed outdoor relief to widows and to the unemployed, the Reformed consuls continued to use the half-share in the civic poor taxes originally destined for the hospital to care for their sick poor. To prevent the sick from falling into the care of the nursing sisters at the Hôtel Dieu, they organized housing and medical visits for them in private homes. In theory, this was illegal, being contrary to laws intended to prevent the spread of communicable diseases, but it protected Protestants from being subject to conversion attempts. The Catholic consuls allowed this situation to continue until pressure from the crown forced them to put a stop to the practice in 1684.[82] In 1676, after the beginning of the crown's repressive legal campaign against the Huguenots, the charitable practices of the congregation as a whole came to focus on granting outdoor assistance in secret away from the prying eyes of the Catholic clergy. In the final years before 1685, as little attention as possible was called to acts of charity done by Protestants. The shift away from institutional care did bring about some benefit for the community. In general, it was less expensive to maintain the sick poor in either their own homes or in private residences than it had been to finance the hospital. While costs decreased, the number of people being assisted increased, leading to the levying of a direct tax on Protestants to provide for their poor. [83] The increase in the number of Protestants on poor relief seems to have been the result of two factors. Firstly, the economy of the city suffered a recession as the wool industry declined in the years after 1670, the effects of which were felt by both the Protestant and Catholic communities of the city. Secondly, the consistory was put under more pressure after 1679, as Catholic repression increased throughout the kingdom, to prevent its parishioners from converting by any means necessary.

In the early 1680s, following the exclusion of Protestants from the consulate, the consistory continued to offer most of its various forms of poor relief. By 1683, however, the payment of assistance to keep Protestant poor away from Catholic

---

82   Pugh, 1974, p. 365.
83   ADG/42/J/42.

sources of charity consumed most of the funds of the consistory.[84] The door-to-door collections for the congregation's poor continued until 1684, which shows that while the bishop and the city's clergy were opposed to Protestant poor relief, the Catholic magistrates were willing to co-operate, or at least turn a blind eye to the activities of their neighbours.[85] However, even the city consuls, who had not shown much interest in alienating their Huguenot neighbours by interfering with their system of poor relief, were drawn into the official repression in 1684 when they discussed removing sick Protestants from private homes and forcing them into the Hôtel Dieu.[86] By that point, however, decisions made in Versailles put an end to the precarious coexistence of the two faiths. The Revocation of the Edict of Nantes in 1685, lauded as it was by both Catholic clergy and laity alike, dramatically altered the nature of civic society in Nîmes.

Reforming poor relief after the Revocation

The foundation of an Hôpital Général intended to confine the deserving poor of Nîmes in a single place occurred in 1686. Before then, the idea of *enfermement*, popular in many other cities in the kingdom, had not wholly captured the imagination of the city fathers. There might be three reasons for this difference. Firstly, the religious divide in the city would have made the creation very difficult because hôpitaux généraux had a distinctive religious aspect to them. As such a hospital would necessitate revenues paid for by all citizens, it would have been difficult to secure compliance by wealthy Protestants for what would have been considered a Catholic establishment prior to 1685. No leaders of the Reformed community in the city would sanction the foundation of an institution whose aim, in part, would have been to teach Catholicism to the poor. Secondly, there does not seem to have been any individual or group to champion the benefits of confining the poor in the city before 1670. Thirdly, the large expense to pay for buildings seemed unnecessary in a city with an expanding industrial base during the 1660s. The city relied on its buoyant economy to absorb most of the able-bodied poor who arrived from other regions. The temporarily unemployed and those long-term poor, such as the infirm and elderly, were cared for in their own homes by the Hôtel Dieu or the Protestant consistory in the years before the Revocation of the Edict of Nantes. The social elites of the city were not willing to pay the costs involved with the policy of confinement and preferred their traditional system of poor relief.[87]

In the years after 1670, Nîmes faced the decline of its wool industry combined with general agricultural stagnation in the region. Increasingly the rural poor came to the city seeking opportunities that were not to be found due to the economic slump.

---

84 ADG/42/J/43. The amount of time spent on poor relief in the deliberations of the consistory of Nîmes following 1667, but particularly in the early 1680s, increased dramatically, representing the increased burden as elements of the Catholic Church increased their efforts to convert the poor before the final revocation of the Edict of Nantes in 1685.

85 Archives communales de Nîmes, TT8.

86 Ibid.

87 ADG HG A1.

While the situation created a need for new solutions to the problem of begging in the streets, little was done. During the 1670s the Catholic elites of Nîmes occasionally discussed the project to found a new hospital of confinement but rejected it on the grounds of its expense. The royal letters circulated to the bishops of the kingdom in 1670 and 1676, restating the need for each locality to take care of its own poor and giving authority to cities to found new hospitals from charitable sources, were ignored in Nîmes, unlike Montpellier where their reception gave the bishop the tool required to convince the city elites to reform the already established Maison de Charité into a larger confining institution. In Nîmes confinement was seen as an unnecessary solution for the problem of unemployment which the consuls were confident would diminish. In 1679, the consulate deliberated over the idea of confining 200 poor in a rented building, but no concrete action was taken. This inaction suggests both that the idea of *enfermement* was beginning to be accepted, but also that the elites were still unwilling to accept all of its inherent costs.

The crown was unwilling to grant any money to assist in the creation of new hospitals in the late 1670s; the letter sent to the bishops on the subject of hospitals in 1676 stated directly that it would not grant any central government funds, nor allow localities to raise any new taxes to begin such projects. The letter instructed the bishops to encourage local elites to raise the necessary funds through charitable donations rather than by taxes. The letter, written in the name of the king, amounted to an admission that the 1662 promise to allow localities to create new impositions in order to support confinement hospitals had been a miscalculation.[88]

The central government was particularly worried that charitable hospitals established in small provincial cities beyond the direct observation of its agents might, if supported by local taxes, compete with the crown for sources of revenue. The elites of Nîmes were aware of the central government's response to the plans of the nearby town of Mende to found its own Hôpital Général in late 1678. There, the consuls had created an imposition on wine sold in the town to raise the capital to build their hospital. Colbert, who otherwise believed in the economic benefits which hôpitaux généraux could provide for a locality, wrote an angry letter to the Intendant of Languedoc, Daguesseau, berating him for allowing the consuls to do this:

> His Majesty orders me to say to you in response that the hôpitaux généraux ought to be works of charity financed by the voluntary gifts of people and not by forced impositions … His Majesty has excluded, in all of the generalities of his kingdom subject to direct taxation, all local impositions on those which His Majesty is accustomed to tax according to the necessity of the state.[89]

Colbert admitted the difference between Languedoc, where there was no tradition of crown impositions, and the *pays d'élections*, but stressed his desire to have the same rule observed from fear that other towns in the kingdom might cite Mende as a precedent.[90]

88   ADG HG A1.
89   Depping, 1850, tom. I, p. 876.
90   Ibid.

The increased severity of the economic troubles facing Nîmes in the late 1670s and early 1680s gave impetus to the creation of a confinement hospital. The area around Nîmes suffered from a severe winter in 1679–80 which was followed by an economic crisis in what had become the primary industry of Nîmes, the manufacture of silk. The years from 1682–84 witnessed high unemployment among the 4,000 of the city population of 15,000 who were involved in the manufacture and trade in silk cloth.[91] The economic instability of the city in those years was compounded by the general agricultural and demographic crisis facing the Bas-Languedoc region as a whole in the years after 1665.[92] The economic crisis meant that the rural poor arriving in the city were not as easily assimilated, and the already existing poor relief systems were stretched to their limits by caring for the native unemployed. The Revocation of the Edict of Nantes in 1685 made matters in the city even worse because the network of poor relief maintained by the Protestant Church collapsed, leaving a number of poor families without financial support.

The idea to replace the defunct Protestant system of poor relief with an Hôpital Général was discussed by the city consuls in 1686 with the new Intendant of Languedoc, Nicolas de Lamoignon de Bâville.[93] Bâville was born in 1648, the son of Guillaume de Lamoignon the Premier Président of the Parlement of Paris and influential member of the administrations of both the Hôtel Dieu and Hôpital Général of Paris. Bâville had a family tradition about concern for poor relief and charity. His father had been the patron of a literary society held at the Hôtel Lamoignon attended, among others, by the Jesuit preacher Louis Bourdaloue and the Jansenist theologian Godefroi de Hermant, and, as a child, Bâville had been taught by the Jesuit René Rapin, a close friend of Bourdaloue, before attending the Jesuit Collège de Clermont.[94] He accompanied his older brother on his tour of England and the Dutch Republic in 1663 and made his own way to various Italian states in 1669. These journeys appear to have encouraged him to examine the examples of the systems of government and poor relief of other countries during his tenure as intendant. He believed that they demonstrated that welfare was by natural law a local issue:

> nothing is more natural in fact, nor is more approved than for each community to feed its own poor. The examples of England and Holland where this practice is in force lets us know that such a pious plan would not be impossible.[95]

Bâville's primary concern as Intendant of Languedoc was the health of the royal revenues in the province. The maintenance of order and the economic health of the province were important to ensure that the tax base could be kept as high as possible. While Nîmes was neither the largest city nor the most important socially, its economy was very important for the rest of the Bas-Languedoc. Bâville had problems to solve in the city: Firstly, he needed to secure a consensus in the city on a plan to reform poor relief to alleviate destitution and to ensure order. Secondly,

91 Pugh, 1974, p. 366.
92 Le Roy Ladurie, 1974, pp. 232–43.
93 ADG HG A1.
94 Poujol, 1992, pp. 15–24.
95 Lamoignon de Bâville, *Mémoires*, 1734, p. 74.

he faced the fact that the greater part of the city's population remained Protestant and would not take lightly the use of a general hospital to convert the Protestant poor. Although Bâville, as the Intendant of Languedoc, was the agent of the crown in the province, his participation in the foundation of the Hôpital Général of Nîmes owed more to his personal belief about the best method to solve both of the city's problems than to his duty to enforce the terms of the Edict of 1662. The administrative staff of the intendant of the province of Languedoc was far too small to exert control over every charitable institution while undertaking its main duty to observe the collection of royal finances. The officials under the authority of Bâville for his administration of the whole province of 24 dioceses with a total population of more than 1,500,000 (of whom at least 200,000 were Protestant) were himself, two secretaries, and six commis.[96] Given his role, and the small number of men for the task, the intendant was forced by necessity to trade favours with the very local elites who managed charitable institutions in their own interests in return for their services in administering the province. To accomplish his primary goal to keep the crown well financed, he needed to tread a fine line between the interests of the local elites and the needs of the central government.[97]

Bâville was given the position of intendant in 1685 to deal with the difficulties which arose in Languedoc following the Revocation of the Edict of Nantes. He recognized that the principal trouble facing Nîmes was the large number of newly converted Catholics. Contrary to the myth surrounding the intendant, he does not seem to have been personally in favour of the central government's policy of forced conversions. While to Paris he reported his attempts to comply with their wishes, he preferred to convert Protestants by demonstration of the truth of Catholicism rather than through the mostly ineffective dragonnades. Bâville sponsored a number of missions into the city and its hinterland during the late 1680s, including one headed by Louis Bourdaloue, in an effort to instruct new Catholics through preaching.[98] He understood that the best opportunity for conversion lay with the young. Older Protestants, and in particular the wealthy, ought to be allowed to worship in private in order to encourage them to remain in the city:

> This will always be the most important point in conserving the city of Nîmes and in helping and protecting the great merchants there. This is what has been done, happily, in the recent past. When the change of religion occurred in this city it brought about no ill effects for the city's commerce, despite the fact that all of the principal merchants and residents are Protestants. Trade has flowed there better than before, and if all of these merchants are still bad Catholics at least they have not ceased to be very good businessmen.[99]

The poor, particularly the young, could be taught to become good Catholics through example if poor relief in Nîmes was reformed.

The economic slump facing the silk industry of the city in the early years of the 1680s supported the creation of an Hôpital Général in the opinion of both the

---

96   Poujol, 1986, pp. 113–14.
97   See Beik, 1985, Kettering, 1986 and Mettam, 1988.
98   Poujol, 1992, pp. 87–8.
99   Quoted in Poujol, 1992, p. 121.

Catholic elites of Nîmes and Bâville. Both understood the need of an industrial city to keep the morale of workers high by providing support for those who were not able to care for themselves in times of trouble. The ending of Protestant outdoor relief in 1685 coupled with the city's economic recession increased tensions within civic society. Many families had no resources to fall back on in hard times. Bâville approved the Catholic elites' proposal that a hospital that combined the confinement of the young and old with no ties in the city with resources to provide outdoor relief to the unemployed was the best solution to the problem of poverty in the city. In August 1686, he replied to a letter from the Contrôleur-Général des Finances, which had suggested that public works be used to give the poor a means to subsist, stressing that in the case of Nîmes the threat of public disorder deserved support for the foundation of a new hospital:

> I have received the letter that you have given me the honour of writing me on the public works that the king wishes to be done in the provinces in order to give the poor the means to survive ... That of the canal [du Midi] will give a sufficient amount of work to the poor of the Haut Languedoc, and charitable funds will be employed in the Bas Languedoc, and principally in the Cévennes, in the city of Nîmes and in its environs where there is a shortage of grain and where it is vital to assist the newly converted and to sustain the artisans there. I am working on the foundation of an hôpital général in Nîmes which is absolutely necessary because all of the province's idlers retire there due to the fact that vagrants are locked up everywhere else. I hope that order will soon be very well established there so that those who are of the sort to be considered truly poor will be confined and the other artisans who have great need for assistance this year will also be helped in their own homes. It is very important to act to sustain this city both in order to preserve the manufactories which employ the population of the Cévennes and in order to establish the true faith firmly in the hearts of the newly converted there by all sorts of methods. It is very true that when they will perform their devotions well in Nîmes all the rest of the province will follow their example. It is vital to win over the people there by assisting them during the dearth which has come this year.[100]

Action was urged to prevent disorder and the city hoped that the central government would overcome its reluctance to allow the use of local taxes to fund new hospitals. The crown, however, did not act and Bâville assisted the civic elites of Nîmes to found the new hospital because it was the best method he knew to help reduce the visible signs of poverty in the city. In effect, the intendant acted on his own initiative to improve the conditions in his province of residence. This fact is further demonstrated because the Hôpital Général of Nîmes did not receive central government recognition until 1742 when its *lettres patentes* were granted.[101]

The city's most important citizens met with the intendant in order to solicit support for the plans for the hospital on 14 August 1686.[102] At this meeting, the urban elites claimed to be fulfilling the terms of the Edict of 1662, albeit 24 years after the fact, by establishing their own Hôpital Général, in order to lay claim to the local taxes

---

100 Boislisle, 1874, tom. I, p. 81.
101 ADG HG A1.
102 ADG HG E5.

previously possessed by the Protestant hospital.[103] Once the citizens had agreed on the creation of an Hôpital Général, they invited the Jesuit missionaries Chaurand and Guévarre, famous for their zeal in founding similar hospitals throughout the kingdom, to Nîmes. The two were brought in to assist in the operation of the institution and to help increase charitable support.[104] Chaurand and Guévarre continued to act as consultants for the administration for several years. For example, they returned to advise the board of directors during the financial crisis of the hospital in 1689.[105] The length of time the two spent in Nîmes was very unusual for them, as they had often spent only a few weeks in towns where they had assisted in the creation of such hospitals.[106] The two extended their stay in the region and returned to Nîmes several times in the years following the foundation in order to assist in the effort of the religious of the city to convert Protestants after the Revocation of the Edict of Nantes.

Outdoor relief and confinement in Nîmes

Initially the new institution replaced, as far as possible, the charity offered by the Protestant consistory before 1685. The official date for the opening of the Hôpital Général for the confinement of the able-bodied poor was 13 October 1686, when the directors used the buildings of the former Protestant hospital to house them. The new buildings of the hospital were not begun until 1690 as part of an enlargement and improvement scheme.[107] Even after the construction of the new buildings, the Hôpital Général of Nîmes took a different form from the Hôpital Général of Paris. The nîmois hospital was never intended to confine large numbers of the poor. Records of the poor confined in the hospital from 1686 to 1689 show that it originally held between 134 to 217 men, women and children during this early period.[108] After the new wards were opened in 1692, one of the syndics reported that the hospital regularly confined around 200 poor, mostly the young or the very old.[109] While the Hôpital Général was capable of caring for this number, the improvement of the city's economy after 1700 meant that the resident population of the hospital dropped to a low level. For example, it fell to only 53 in April 1701, when the number confined was 20 men (of whom only 4 were adults) and 33 women (of whom 19 were adults).[110] The capacity of the economy of Nîmes to absorb able-bodied new arrivals into the labour pool of the city kept the number of adults – most of whom were old, infirm or otherwise

---

103 Ibid.
104 ADG HG E5.
105 Ibid.
106 Paultre, 1906, pp. 236–7.
107 ADG HG B10.
108 ADG HG E3.
109 ADG HG E5.
110 ADG HG A1. It should be noted that this low number of poor in the Hôpital Général occurred at a time when the board of directors claimed that the royal edicts of 1699, commanding longer terms of confinement for the able-bodied poor, had dramatically increased the costs incurred by imprisoning a greater number of people.

disabled – very low.[111] The small number of those confined compared to those offered outdoor assistance away from where they would be subject to religious instruction would also suggest that the influence of Protestant employers continued after the Revocation. With the support of the intendant, the Catholic elites could have ended the practice of outdoor relief, but they did not. While many Catholics would have desired that religious training was a prerequisite for the poor receiving aid, the threat to order meant that there was no such obligation placed on the poor with ties in the city and temporarily unemployed workers.

The Hôpital Général spent a considerable amount of its resources on providing outdoor relief for the poor of the city. Between 19 and 21 August 1686, following the first meeting of the board, the directors of the Hôpital Général examined all of the poor of the city who came to claim relief in order to determine the viability and proper genre of aid. The administration selected who should be confined in the hospital, who should be granted relief in their own homes and who should be denied assistance.[112] The hospital gave relief in the form of a bread allowance and occasional cash payments to up to 600 people outside the wards, enabling workers to supplement their income when it was too little on which to subsist.[113] Besides this form of relief, the institution helped overburdened families by receiving one or more children in the hospital while allowing the rest of the family to remain at home. For example, in 1692 the hospital provided bread for Anthoinette Bourdel, aged 11, the crippled daughter of a worker in the city's silk industry. She had been accepted for care in the wards in 1687 aged 6 because her father had a second healthy daughter and had difficulty in providing for both. She was returned into the care of her father in 1692, but the hospital continued to provide a weekly bread allowance for her.[114]

Following financial problems during its first few years of operation, on 12 February 1691, new rules for acceptance of the poor were set. No poor with a contagious disease, those suffering from a mental disorder or women with a bad reputation would be confined.[115] The decision to exclude some types of poor was made along the lines of morality. Unlike the Hôpital Général of Paris, the nîmois hospital refused to confine syphilitics or ex-prostitutes because it was felt that they had brought their poverty on themselves.[116] Unlike Paris, where some categories of the able-bodied poor could be transferred to the Hôtel Dieu if they fell sick at the Hôpital Général, the Nîmes Hôtel Dieu refused to allow anyone confined in the Hôpital Général to be received. Instead, the sick of the Hôpital Général were put in a separate ward and treated by a surgeon paid for by the board of directors.[117]

The number of staff employed in the Hôpital Général throughout the period was very small. There were five nuns, one priest, one porter, one guard, and a physician or

---

111 ADG HG F1. The list of poor housed at the Hôpital Général during the period were either children or the elderly. Of the women confined, most were either single, widowed or abandoned wives.

112 ADG HG E5.

113 Ibid.

114 ADG HG F1.

115 ADG HG E5.

116 Ibid.

117 Ibid.

a surgeon of the city contracted to make occasional visits when there were sick poor in the wards.[118] This number of individuals was inadequate to the task of preventing any but the most infirm of those confined from escape, suggesting that the greater part of the hospital population remained in the wards of its own volition.

From the first meetings of the board, the hospital directors tried to cement a healthy relationship between the Hôpital Général and the industries of the city. The administration understood that in an industrial city like Nîmes, it would be necessary to choose manufactures to employ the poor that did not threaten to compete with existing labourers, and at the same time taught a skill which would be useful to the inmates once they left the hospital. On 22 September 1686 the board hosted a meeting with the city corps de marchands to determine what sorts of jobs the poor could do for them.[119] It quickly established the conditions for work at the Hôpital Général. The hospital became a resource to which the industries of the city could turn in search of inexpensive labour. A putting-out system was created where merchants could contract work with the hospital, providing materials and masters to train poor children in a skill. In return the city merchants would take their profits from the labour of the inmates. The poor performed the work unpaid for the first two months, then receiving a small sum for their labour.[120]

The poor were divided by age and sex while at work. The boys were put to toil at sorting raw materials while the girls divided silk for fabricants of the city. Adult men were given odd jobs both in the city and the hospital. Adult women were taught more complex textile jobs than the girls.[121] Besides being taught a skill, young boys and girls were regularly put into domestic service with respectable individuals of the city if no other work could be found for them. One of the girls of the women's ward, Isabeau Brousse, was selected to serve as domestic help in the house of one of the directors in April 1689.[122] Both the teaching of skills to the poor and the placement of children into service were part of the commitment of the board to tackle the problem of long-term poverty. As in other cities, the directors attempted to prevent the young from returning to seek relief again by providing them with a skill and with work.

At the same time as the hospital taught a skill to the poor, it performed what was considered by the Catholic elites of the city to be a vital religious function. The directors applauded the hospital for its care of: 'a great number of young children of both sexes, the majority of them new converts as well, who are being raised in the Catholic faith and in the fear of God'.[123] Conforming in part to the ideas which viewed such hospitals as instruments of educating children ignorant of the Catholic faith, it raised, taught and catechized the children of the poor at a time after the Revocation when such an institution was considered necessary by both the Catholic elites of the city and those of the kingdom at large.

---

118 ADG HG A1.
119 Ibid.
120 Ibid.
121 ADG HG B7.
122 ADG HG E5.
123 Ibid.

Governing the Nîmes Hôpital Général

The form of the board was established by an assembly of the city fathers on 17 August 1686.[124] The board of directors represented the new social order of Nîmes following the Revocation as Catholic judicial and legal elites and important members of the religious orders assumed the roles of civic leaders. At the top of the hospital board were those directors appointed by grace of their office: the bishop, the juge-mage of the Présidial court, the procureur du roi and the first consul. These men examined and approved the decisions taken by the rest of the board, but did not participate in an active sense in the governance of the hospital. Below this senior level of administration, there were the elected directors: three cathedral canons, three counsellors of the Présidial court, four 'gentilhommes' (landowners from the region around the city), three lawyers from the court, and six bourgeois of the city. All of these men were required to be good Catholics which would have excluded a significant portion of the wealthy of the city. These directors were elected for a term of two years, but there does not seem to have been a bar on one being re-elected if his service warranted. This lower level of the board selected from among its ranks: three syndics, the receiver of the finances of the hospital, the auditor, and the inspector of the manufactures. It was these officers who did the real administrative work, such as making decisions governing the daily life of the hospital, which were examined and approved by the board as a whole.[125]

The duties of the board were to hold a regular meeting of its members every Sunday, to depute a director to visit the hospital every day and to ensure that only those poor whom it had approved were granted relief at the Hôpital Général.[126] In order to deter the rural poor from flocking to the city, the administration set rules governing which sorts of poor would be eligible for aid. They published warnings that only those considered resident could seek assistance at the hospital, defining the poor as being resident if they had been an inhabitant of the city for three years, if they had arrived in Nîmes before 1686, and five years for those arriving afterward.[127] Although the established rules would have excluded the relief of many of the poor who came to the city in the famine years of 1694 and 1709, the board used its initiative in these circumstances to offer assistance to those it found worthy but otherwise ineligible.

In 1686, the first year of operation of the Hôpital Général, its finances were raised by a door-to-door collection in the city. This collection was advocated by every important citizen of Nîmes: the bishop, the intendant, the Lieutenant-Général of the Sénéchaussée, and the consuls. Many of these individuals made their approbation known with donations presented in public in order to encourage others to give.[128] The door-to-door collection remained an important source of income for the hospital

---

124 Ibid.

125 ADG HG B7.

126 Ibid.

127   Ibid.

128 ADG HG E4. Both Jacques Séguier, the bishop, and Bâville, the intendant, published the record of their gifts to the hospital. Séguier gave 1,000 of the 9,243 *livres* raised during 1686.

throughout the period. Subscriptions of this sort had already been customary in Nîmes, as both the Hôtel Dieu and the Protestant hospital had used them in the past.[129] In effect, the board of directors attempted to comply with the wish of the crown as stated in the letters to the bishops of 1670 and 1676 to exist off charity and not new taxes by levying what was a monthly voluntary tax on the city. The administration realized that the hospital could never be fully funded through charitable means alone, but its effort to conform to the desires of the government was something it was quick to emphasize.[130]

Besides the regular collection, the hospital received income from larger charitable bequests and donations. Those given to the Hôpital Général were mostly from Catholic judges, lawyers, bourgeois and, on occasion, nobles who had interests in the province.[131] Some of the bequests which provided the hospital with income were those seized from the consistory with the permission of the intendant after the Revocation, but the difficulty in proving which *rentes* had been left to the Protestant Church meant that only a few of these were actually gained by the Hôpital Général. For example, the hospital was able to claim the 50 *livres* per year *rente* donated to the Protestant poor by a M. Bastide in his will of 1677.[132] As was the case in other cities, most charitable donations were quite small and too irregular to rely on for revenue, and they were usually pooled in order to contract *rentes* on the income of the city.

The Catholic patrons of Hôpital Général of Nîmes profited from their involvement by publicly displaying their devotion and charity by accepting donations in return for saying mass in the hospital chapel for the benefit of the patron's soul. This sort of obligation was important to the hospital because it brought in many legacies from devout Catholics. Donors wanted the participation of the poor in the saying of prayers during memorial services because the traditional belief that their intercession for the soul of the benefactor was more valuable than that of others still prevailed. For example, in 1695 Jacques Colomb, a procureur in the Présidial court, left money to the hospital:

> with the charge that Messieurs the recteurs and administrators of the hospital will have said and celebrated in perpetuity a mass on the Thursday of each week, either in the church or in the chapel of the hospital, for the repose of his soul, that of Marion Guion his wife, that of the late Isabeau de Jurques his first wife, and those of his other relatives.[133]

Families of the city asserted their importance through founding services of this sort. The poor thanked not only those who donated the sums for the mass but also the members of the family still alive. For example, in 1704, Jules Paul Cohon dedicated masses for his own soul, that of his uncle Anthyme-Denis (the late bishop), and for his own brother. The foundation reinforced the link between the Cohon family and the charitable institutions of Nîmes decades after the death of Bishop Cohon.[134]

---

129 ADG HG E5.
130 Ibid.
131 ADG HG B8.
132 ADG HG B7.
133 ADG HG C1.
134 Ibid.

To the income derived from charitable sources, the Hôpital Général assumed the right to collect the share of the municipal taxes – the indirect tax on meat and the imposition for the poor – which the consistory had inherited from the Protestant hospital at the time of its closure in 1667. In order to levy these taxes, the board chose to accept the terms of the Edict of 1662 which had allowed the use of new local taxes to pay for poor relief while ignoring the central government's decision of 1670 to allow only charitable sources of revenue. Bâville must have given tacit approval to this situation, understanding the importance of the new hospital in a city divided along confessional lines following the Revocation. In March 1687, Bâville assisted the hospital by approving the seizure of the lands and revenues of Protestant fugitives, transferring them to the ownership of the hospital despite the fact that it was ineligible to receive them since it did not have royal *lettres patentes*.[135]

In 1687, the board of directors showed its inexperience by underestimating the costs of feeding both the poor in the wards and those who were relieved outside the hospital. In particular, it found difficulty raising capital to pay for the high price of grain in the summer of 1687. The directors deputed several of their members to ask the Archbishop of Narbonne, the Bishop of Nîmes and Bâville to intercede with the Provincial Estates to grant some revenue for the hospital.[136] The decision of the board to request the help of these figures demonstrates how social elites in French cities were willing to call upon senior figures of the church and central government to assist their interests. Acting in this way, the elites of the city traded deference to their superiors in return for assistance when it was needed.

By the summer of 1689, the hospital suffered more financial trouble due to a lack of funding and a low estimate made in 1686 of the costs of erecting new buildings and of daily operations. It attempted to reduce the deficit by undertaking a series of retrenchments of expenses. The directors ordered the *soeur oeconome* to monitor the costs of the daily care of the poor in the wards and to cut unnecessary expense whenever possible. They forbade the hospital from receiving any new inmates without the written permission of the board. They went as far as to sell the horse which the hospital owned for 22 *livres*.[137] More significantly, the board authorized the removal of many poor from the care of the institution, placing them into the care of relatives in the city or as domestic servants for wealthy individuals.[138] Many of those released were children who had been confined in the hospital in order to relieve financial pressures felt by overburdened families.[139]

On June 1689, an extraordinary meeting of the board of directors was held to determine methods of reducing both the problem of overcrowding in the hospital and the unexpected cost in caring for the poor. The hospital was able to raise 24,000 *livres* from the Provincial Estates to act as capital for a *rente*, the interest from which was used to pay for the construction of new wards. The greater problem faced by the hospital was the cost of grain and bread to feed the unexpectedly large number

---

135 ADG HG E5.
136 Ibid.
137 Ibid.
138 Ibid.
139 Ibid.

of people receiving aid. Both the intendant and the bishop urged the administration to ensure that no hospital money was wasted. Following this advice, the directors wrote new rules that stipulated that careful records be kept of all who were given assistance, and that in future the bread dole would only be carried out on Sundays and in public in order to prevent fraud.[140]

In 1689, the Governor of Languedoc granted both the Hôpital Général and the Hôtel Dieu the right to increase the amount each collected from the indirect tax on meat sold in Nîmes.[141] While the increased tax revenue helped the Hôtel Dieu to overcome a shortfall, it was unable to do much to reduce the deficit which the Hôpital Général suffered. The board of directors continued to discharge children either to their families or into domestic service from 1689 to 1700 in an effort to reduce its expenses. Between 1689 and 1692, the directors themselves lent money to the hospital, often with no prospect of being repaid, in order to reimburse the hospital's debts to grain merchants.[142]

On 24 August 1692, the administration asked Bâville to permit an increase in the amount of the meat tax it was allowed to collect. He raised the income from that source to 6,000 livres per year beginning in 1693.[143] At the same time as the directors asked for a greater indirect tax, they requested help with the expense of maintaining a network of outdoor relief. In 1692, the hospital was granted a fund of 6,000 livres annually for its care of the poor in their own homes by means of a new direct tax on the city. This tax was increased to 9,000 livres in 1694, presumably to assist with welfare to workers who could not afford bread during the famine.[144] The increased costs of dealing with the famine of 1694, however, outweighed any help which the new tax income could have provided for the hospital.

By 1698, the finances of the Hôpital Général were in a very poor state. The bishop and the rest of the administration, in separate pleas to the crown, asked for permission to hold a lottery.[145] Plans to organize the lottery had already begun among members of the board when the series of crown edicts, which were issued in February 1699, using the threat of imprisonment in hôpitaux généraux to frighten beggars back to rural parishes, gave the directors an excuse to plead the poverty of the hospital.[146] The hospital claimed that, although it was banishing the poor foreign to Nîmes, the increased costs of confining those native to the city for longer periods of time was placing it under undue financial pressure.[147] The crown agreed to the new lottery which began to provide income for the hospital in 1702.[148]

While the revenue from the lottery seems to have reduced the deficit between 1702 and 1708, the dramatic increase of costs created by the crisis of the winter of 1709 brought a need for a new and extraordinary source of income. The administration

140 Ibid.
141 Ménard, 1755, p. 311.
142 ADG HG E4.
143 ADG HG A1.
144 ADG HG E5.
145 Boislisle, 1874, t. II, p. 30.
146 ADG HG E35.
147 Ibid.
148 Ibid.

hosted a meeting of all the important figures in the city to secure agreement for a direct levy imposed for a single year on all citizens according to their ability to pay. The board claimed that the number of poor it maintained was greater than ever before:

> Monseigneur the Bishop of Nîmes has heard the complaints made by the directors of the hôpital général of this city concerning the extremity in which this hospital finds itself on account of the great expenditures that it has been obliged to make for the subsistence of the poor since the start of the grain shortage, both to about 300 individuals confined in the wards and to around 600 families that it assists outside its walls.[149]

The assembly formed a committee composed of the prévôt of the cathedral chapter, the juge-mage, the procureur du roi of the Présidial, the consuls and the syndics of the corps des marchands to assess the distribution of the tax burden. This committee decided that the tax would be in effect for a full year and that each individual's share would be paid in monthly instalments. The administration of the hospital bore the heaviest portion of the tax. The bishop agreed to pay 1,000 *livres* per month, while the cathedral chapter would pay 140 *livres*. The judges and lawyers of the Présidial together were assessed at 100 *livres* per month. The total of the tax was 2,503 *livres* received each month, paid by 370 individuals in the city.[150] This extraordinary level of taxation, paid for by the urban elites, demonstrated the commitment the wealthy of Nîmes had to the Hôpital Général.

Between the Peace of Alès in 1629 and the Revocation in 1685 coexistence between most lay Catholics and Protestants in Nîmes developed. Both sides sought to coexist, and in doing so civic order was maintained in the city. The tolerant attitude that the elites of each faith demonstrated toward the other should not be confused with a modern definition of toleration, however. Neither Protestants nor Catholics believed that their neighbours' religion had a right to exist. Each side believed that there was only one way to worship God: its own. Indeed, it was commonly accepted that it was impossible to compel religious uniformity without damaging civil society. Coexistence in Nîmes came about, not because of a new belief in freedom of worship, but because of the memories of the bloody civil wars of the sixteenth century. This seventeenth-century toleration that contained within it such distaste for the other side is clearly shown in the care each confession took in caring for its own poor. The Catholic and Protestant communities considered the survival of their charitable hospitals to be vital because the poor who wound up at the wrong one were considered likely to abjure their faith. Protestant and Catholic alike felt that the religious commitment to charity justified the heavy financial burdens of their respective institutions.

That their definition of coexistence had at its basis the fact that before 1685 neither side was strong enough to eliminate the other should not cloud the fact that,

---

149 ADG HG E53.

150 Ibid. The combination of the bishop, the chapter and the Présidial paid almost one-half of the tax. The remaining 1,263 *livres* of the monthly payment of the city was divided among the rest of the taxpayers. For example, the first consul, Roubiac, paid only 6 *livres* per month.

in order to preserve order in the locality, the lay elites of both denominations actively ignored royal and episcopal rulings. It is striking that this peace should extend as far as co-operation, at times bordering on collusion, in a religiously charged aspect of urban life such as poor relief. Those who held the office of Catholic consul demonstrated their desire to live alongside their Calvinist neighbours many times over the years from 1629 to 1685. The otherwise legally minded consuls took no action to prevent the foundation of the Protestant hospital in 1654 and they raised no complaint over the illegality of the new institution's existence in any court of law. In many ways the Catholic judges and lawyers who sat as consuls were willing to anger partisans among the clergy and population of their own faith as long as relations with the Protestant community remained peaceful. The Huguenots, for their part, went equally far to ensure the continuance of Calvinist charity in the city. The foundation and operation of an independent hospital was bound to enrage such a zealous proponent of Tridentine reform as Bishop Cohon, and came at a time when the best strategy for the community's welfare would have lain in not challenging the Catholic Church's authority over such matters.

The 'intolerant' nature of seventeenth-century tolerance most likely meant that the type of confessional coexistence present in Nîmes did not exist in areas of the kingdom where Calvinism had small and dwindling numbers after 1629. But in regions such as the Bas-Languedoc where the Huguenots remained the majority or a significant minority, such peace was likely the rule of interaction between the faiths before the Revocation. This sort of localized toleration, bred by close proximity, must have developed, not only in France, but in many other areas of early modern Europe after the Reformation.[151] Although local relations between confessions of similar strength gave rise to coexistence, the power of external forces often forced the issue in the opposite direction. The outward signs of joy displayed by Catholic nîmois at the announcement of the Revocation of the Edict of Nantes hid grave fears that the crown's unilateral decision to restore the Roman Church's spiritual monopoly would have serious repercussions for the social fabric of their city.

The reform of poor relief and the foundation of the Hôpital Général of Nîmes in 1686 attempted to allay fears of civic disorder. The civic taxes that had once supported the Hôtel Dieu and had then passed to Protestant forms of poor relief were used by the new institution. The hospital took on the name of an Hôpital Général in order to lay claim to those revenues and to the property of Protestant fugitives. It differed in form from other such hospitals in many other parts of the kingdom. The hospital functioned as a civic welfare institution to provide assistance to the able-bodied poor; however, it confined only a small number of poor (usually under 100) after the initial numbers of between 200 to 300 during the mid 1680s crisis. It looked after a far greater number of people outdoors, which the crown was opposed to in its Edict of 1662 and the subsequent letters of 1670 and 1676 endorsing the policy of *enfermement*.

Although the crown did not grant its endorsement to the hospital until the mid eighteenth century, it is important to note that Bâville, the intendant, assisted Nîmes's

---

151 See, for example, Po-Chia Hsia, 1984. A similar form of toleration that developed in many cities in the Netherlands is covered in Israel, 1995, pp. 637–76.

city fathers in their plans even though he knew that the new hospital would not be used as a place to confine and to convert the Protestant poor. He trod a fine line between his duties to ensure the success of the Revocation and to maintain order in his province. Nîmes was an important but still divided city: to confine all of the poor in an institution so identified with the Catholic Reform would have been dangerous to the social fabric – Bâville wanted conversions, but not at the cost of upsetting Protestant silk merchants. The city better suited a poor relief institution that offered a more adaptable form of relief than confinement – workers in Nîmes could use the Hôpital Général to supplement their income in times of economic downturns and to place burdensome children and the elderly in the wards. The role played by Bâville in assisting the city fathers to overcome their financial difficulties highlights the duty of the intendant during the reign of Louis XIV. He did not interfere with the form of poor relief delivered, even though the confinement of the poor was not as complete as those in Paris would have desired. As the chief royal agent in the province, he traded favours with local elites, securing loyalty to the crown on other issues such as war and foreign affairs in return for providing assistance with local difficulties.

Conclusions

By the late seventeenth century, the crown claimed that it was leading the fight against poverty throughout France. The medallions commissioned by Louis XIV to commemorate the great events of his reign included ones stating that the king had been responsible for the foundation of the Hôpital Général of Paris and the subsequent development of a system of confinement hospitals in the rest of the kingdom's cities and towns. A cartouche in the painted ceiling of the Hall of Mirrors in Versailles celebrated the Sun King's paternalist care of his people during the famine of 1662–63. Such declarations were made to raise the prestige of the crown; however, these assertions have subsequently overshadowed the fact that the reforms carried out to hospitals in many of the cities in France were led by local elites on their own initiative.

Many existing hospitals in seventeenth-century France grew in size and offered new services to the poor. New types of institution were built in many cities as ways to monitor the assistance granted to the able-bodied poor and to combat the perceived threat of vagrancy. While there was change in the nature of poor relief, continuity was maintained in terms of responsibility at both the national and local level. Local elites were the driving force behind this reform of urban social welfare in seventeenth-century France. In many cities, medieval forms of urban government, based on the power and social position of guilds and trade associations, no longer represented the true nature of civic power. During the early modern period urban elites, whose claim to rank lay in the possession of offices and wealth, formed patrician groups at the top of civic society which increasingly sought to emphasize their position in their communities. Ambitious families within these urban elites used their leadership as ways to prove their worthiness to rise further in social standing. Hospitals became important because, besides providing important services for the poor themselves, donating to and administering hospitals were important ways for the urban elites to fulfil religious obligations and to negotiate for social status and power. Poor relief was a point of contact between the upper and lower echelons of urban society. The elites offered services to the poor at local hospitals in return for deference from the lower orders.

The efforts of the urban elites of France during the seventeenth century deserve to be evaluated on their own terms and not as precursors to later developments. The examples of hospitals in Paris, Montpellier and Nîmes demonstrate that complex systems of poor relief, managed and financed by the urban elites, developed over the course of the century. Although late-eighteenth-century authors disapproved of the practices of many of these institutions, seventeenth-century elites were proud of their efforts to care for the destitute and rid the kingdom of criminal forms of poverty. Unlike today, social welfare reform did not mean retrenchment to the elites of seventeenth-century France. The histories of these hospitals illustrate that the wealthy of France gave much consideration to the problem they believed poverty posed to society, and as a consequence the forms of poor relief underwent reform during this period. A greater emphasis was placed on institutionalization of certain categories of the poor (the ill, the infirm, the aged and the very young) in order to combat the problem of beggars and vagabonds. The reforms made to French charitable institutions during the seventeenth century broadened the definition of the hospital. The concept of a hospital would now go further than a place that offered shelter to certain categories of the poor. The definition would include a place where the individual could be cured – whether, as in the case of the hôpitaux généraux, the poor were to be cured of their religious ignorance and innate idleness, or, as in the case of the hôtels dieu where the poor could be treated and their sicknesses cured.

The tradition that natural law dictated that each community was responsible for its own systems of poor relief was an orthodoxy rarely challenged during the period under study. Individual cities and towns provided the assistance each felt was needed. The fact that the cities under study possessed similar institutions, in particular the hôpitaux généraux, owed much to the spreading of the idea of confinement by the Compagnie du Saint-Sacrement and other like-minded individuals combined with similar economic and social factors affecting these regions of the kingdom. However, when the elites attempted to put theory into practice in cities such as Paris, Montpellier and Nîmes, they modified it to accommodate local religious, economic and social circumstances. Thus, there were differences between each hospital and the services offered according to the situation of the city in which it was located.

From the reign of Henri IV, the Catholic population of France revived its interest in matters of charity and poor relief. The theologians of the Catholic Reformation were very successful in equating the performance of good deeds with a commitment to a Christian life. Religion continued to be an important motivating factor for those individuals who took part in providing relief to the poor. Despite the debate which raged between Jesuits and Jansenists during the reign of Louis XIV over the proper motivations behind charitable endeavours, writers on both sides encouraged their audiences to be active in the care of the poor. Although with different aims in mind, a Jesuit such as Louis Bourdaloue and a Jansenist such as Pierre Nicole could agree that charity was an integral part of the Catholic faith. Religious motivations merged well with economic and social ones among most hospital directors and donors. Thus, the devout benefactors of hospitals toward the end of the seventeenth century quite easily mixed a desire to fulfil their religious obligations with paternalist concerns to care for their inferiors and the furtherance of their family's dynastic aspirations.

As complex poor relief systems developed in seventeenth-century French cities, the crown took credit while, in fact, sharing little of the responsibility for their successes and failures. The history of hospital reform provides an important insight into the workings of the absolute monarchy in France as it developed during the seventeenth century. The crown was most stable and effective (such as during Louis XIV's personal rule) when it worked with local elites, trading off support for the local elites' social position and local power in return for obedience in matters of the royal prerogative such as war and foreign affairs. J.B. Collins argues that the central government's primary domestic policy during the ancien régime was to maintain order. By supporting the efforts of towns and cities to reform poor relief and charitable health care systems through the granting of royal edicts (in the case of Paris) or by allowing localities freedom of action, the crown did so both among the lower orders and among the urban elites. The central government believed that it did not have a duty to take care of the poor of the whole realm. The king felt bound to care for his servants: the soldiers of his army and the tenants of the royal domain. However, his responsibility for them hardly differed from that of any noble to his tenants. The king acted, in the case of poor relief and charity, as the most senior noble of the kingdom. The government did not have the resources or the inclination to provide assistance to all of the poor of the country, leaving that duty to the local elites as tradition dictated.

It has been argued by many historians that the crown attempted to increase its jurisdiction into the area of social welfare during the reign of Louis XIV. However, it was to assist powerful elites like those of Paris that the central government issued laws such as the Edict of 1662. The crown already had a certain amount of authority over the area of poor relief, but this power had strict traditional limits. Men in the early modern period believed that each locality had a duty sanctioned by natural law to care for its citizens who became impoverished. The central government had the authority to intervene in local affairs when it considered that a community had not lived up to its responsibility. However, its ability to coerce co-operation from local elites was limited to issuing rebukes to wayward localities and the creation of punishments to dissuade the poor from moving about the kingdom. Although the Edict of 1662 authorized the creation of hôpitaux généraux, it was really a warning to localities that the crown was not prepared to allow towns near Paris to shirk their duty at the expense of the capital's elites.

Both the crown and local elites understood their relationship. Locals did not take royal edicts regarding poor relief as absolute commands, but as reminders of their traditional duties. Thus, Montpellier and Nîmes both ignored the terms of the Edict of 1662 because they believed that they were already doing enough to care for their own poor. In Montpellier, the bishop was instrumental in the transformation of the city's Maison de Charité into the larger Hôpital Général. However, he did not act as a royal agent, rather as an active proponent of Catholic Reform. His actions were only possible with the compliance and participation of those new elites of Montpellier's population who were not represented in the administration of the city's poor relief systems. In Nîmes, the urban elites were granted assistance by the intendant of the province in reforming poor relief after the Revocation, but his help should not be confused with leadership. The creation of the Hôpital Général of Nîmes was a response to severe economic and religious problems facing the city and the intendant's help was requested by the local elites in order to address the crisis.

Reforms were only successfully implemented in those towns and cities where local elites supported them. The transformation of poor relief and charitable medical institutions required sacrifices to be made on the part of the urban elites. The examples of these cities show that these systems of poor relief were founded, managed and financed by local elites and by local sources of revenue. This followed the central government's main policy which was to emphasize the tradition that each locality must care for its own (sanctioned both by previous edicts and by natural law). The crown had very little impact and never forced its policies on individual cities. It never compelled a town to create an hôpital général where it was not wanted, and, in fact, it actively discouraged the creation of such hospitals where it thought they might interfere with crown sources of revenue, as in the case of Mende. However, hospital revenues tended to rely more heavily on local taxation and less on charity for support by the end of the century despite the central government's wishes. This drift toward financing through taxation should be seen as part of the process of municipalization that began with the assumption of authority over hospital boards by local lay elites from the mid fifteenth century.

Local elites, in general, accepted their duty to provide assistance for the poor of their localities. In Paris, for example, the urban elites went to great lengths to secure finances for both the Hôtel Dieu and the Hôpital Général. In Languedoc, the elites of Montpellier and Nîmes undertook the difficult task of founding hospitals of confinement when local circumstances necessitated their creation. The elites of the kingdom provided what they considered to be necessary services for their poor. That their endeavours were largely unsuccessful in their stated aims to reform the poor themselves and to defeat vagrancy should not detract from the effort urban elites made. While begging and other visible signs of poverty continued to exist, the fact remains that more of the able-bodied poor were granted assistance than in previous centuries and the reform to the kingdom's hospitals for the sick poor made more medical care available to those who could not afford a period of sickness.

The reforms of the seventeenth century created institutions that would characterize the social welfare systems of French cities until the nineteenth century. Poor relief and charitable health care after the period under study would commonly be distributed through two sorts of urban hospitals: the hôtels dieu for the sick poor and the hôpitaux généraux for the able-bodied. During the seventeenth century, French elites discovered the social profits that could be made through the control and dispensing of welfare and, by the eighteenth century, the state would attempt to assist both the elites with their charitable programmes and the poor directly in an attempt to increase its own status.

Bibliography

Archival Sources:

Archives de l'Assistance Publique, Hôpitaux de Paris, fonds Hôpital Général.
Archives de l'Assistance Publique, Hôpitaux de Paris, fonds Hôtel Dieu.
Archives communales de Nîmes, série TT.
Archives départmentales des Côtes-d'Armor, séries B, G, H dépot.
Archives départmentales du Finistère, série 5H.
Archives départmentales du Gard, fonds Hôpital de Nîmes (Hôtel Dieu).
Archives départmentales du Gard, fonds Hôpital Général de Nîmes.
Archives départmentales du Gard, série J (Consistoire de Nîmes).
Archives départmentales de l'Hérault, fonds Hôpital Général de Montpellier.
Archives départmentales de l'Hérault, fonds Hôtel Dieu Saint-Eloi de Montpellier.
Archives départmentales de l'Ille-et-Vilaine, série C.
Archives départmentales du Morbihan, série 8Hs.
Archives nationales, séries K, TT. Fonds Marine, série B.

Printed Primary Sources:

Agrippa, H.C. (1630), *De l'incertitude, vanité, et abus des sciences*, Lyon: n.p.
Albert, C. d', duc de Luynes (1658), *Instruction pour apprendre à ceux qui ont des terres dont ils sont seigneurs*, Paris: n.p.
Allier, R. (1909), *Une société secrète au XVIIe siècle: la Compagnie du Très-Saint-Sacrement de l'Autel à Marseille*, Paris: H. Champion.
Allier, R. (1914), *La Compagnie du Très-Saint-Sacrement de l'Autel à Toulouse*, Paris: H. Champion.
Apologie des églises reformées du Languedoc, (1657), Montpellier: n.p.
Bloch, C. (1908), *Inventaire sommaire des volumes de la collection Joly de Fleury*, Paris: Daupeley-Gouverneur.
Bodin, J. (1576), *Les six livres de la Republique*, Paris: n.p.
Boislisle, A.M. de (1874–83), *Correspondance des contrôleurs généraux des finances avec les intendants des provinces*, 3 tom., Paris: Imprimerie Nationale.
Boislisle, A.M. de (1881), *Mémoire de la généralié de Paris,* Paris: Imprimerie Nationale.
Bonnefons, A. (1676), *Le devot chrestien charitable*, Paris: n.p.
Boulainvilliers, H. de (1727), *Mémoires presentés à Monseigneur le duc d'Orléans Régent de France*, 2 tom., Amsterdam: n.p.
Bourdaloue, L. (1900), *Oeuvres complètes de Bourdaloue de la Compagnie de Jésus*, 6 tom., Paris: Berche et Tralin.
Brièle, L. (1866–82), *Inventaire sommaire des archives hospitalières anterieurs à 1790*, 2 tom., Paris: Imprimerie Nationale.

Brièle, L. (1881), *Collection des documents pour servir à l'histoire des hôpitaux de Paris*, 4 tom., Paris: Imprimerie Nationale.

Brièle, L. (1888), *Supplément à l'inventaire sommaire des archives anterieures à 1790*, Paris: Imprimerie Nationale.

Code de l'Hôpital Général de Paris, (1786), Paris: n.p.

Colbert, J.B. (1861–73), *Lettres, instructions, et mémoires de Colbert*, ed. P. Clément, 7 tom., Paris: Imprimerie Nationale.

Délort, A. (1876), *Mémoires de ce qui s'est passé de plus remarquable dans Montpellier, 1622–1691*, Montpellier: n.p.

Depping, G.B. (1850–56), *Correspondance administrative sous le règne de Louis XIV*, 4 tom., Paris: Imprimerie Nationale.

Gachon, P. (1899), *Quelques préliminaires de le révocation de l'édit de Nantes en Languedoc (1661-1685)*, Toulouse: E. Privat.

Godeau, A. (1652), *Exhortation aux parisiens sur le secours des pauvres des provinces de Picardie et de Champagne*, Paris: n.p.

Guigue, G. (1922), *Les papiers des dévots de Lyon*, Lyon: Veuve Blot.

Hermant, G. de (1655), *Discours chrestien sur l'establissement du bureau des pauvres de Beauvais*, Paris: n.p.

L'Hospital General de Paris, (1676), Paris: n.p.

Isambert, F. (1821-33), *Recueil général des anciens lois françaises*, 29 tom., Paris: Belin-Leprieur.

La Bruyère, J. de (1981), *Les caractères*, Paris: Bordas.

Laffemas, B. de (1602), *Lettres et exemples de la feu royne mere comme elle faisoit travailler au manufactures, et fournissoit aux ouvriers de ses propres deniers*, Paris: n.p., reprinted in Cimber and Danjou (1836), *Archives curieuses de l'histoire de France*, tom. IX, Paris: Imprimerie Nationale, 1836.

Laffemas, I. de (1606), *L'histoire du commerce de France*, Paris: n.p.

La Fontaine, J. de (1898), *Fables*, Paris: Garnier frères.

Lamoignon de Bâville, N. de (1734), *Mémoires pour servir à l'histoire de Languedoc*, Amsterdam: n.p.

Le Blanc, P. (1869), *Journal de J. Baudouin sur les Grands-Jours de Languedoc (1666–1667)*, Paris: Dumoulin.

Le Maistre, A. (1651), *L'aumosne chrestienne ou la tradition touchant la charité envers les pauvres*, Paris: n.p.

Lister, M. (1967), *A Journey to Paris in the Year 1698*, ed. R.P. Stearns., Urbana IL: University of Indiana Press.

Loix municipales et économiques de Languedoc, (1780-88) 7 tom., Montpellier: n.p.

Médailles sur les principaux évenements du regne de Louis le Grand, (1702), Paris: n.p.

Montchrétien, A. de (1889), Traicté de l'oeconomie politique, Paris: E. Plon.

Moreil, F. (1985), L'intendance de Languedoc à la fin du XVIIe siècle, Paris: Louis-Jean.

Pascal, B. (1964), *Oeuvres complètes*, ed. J. Mesnard, 3 tom., Paris: Desclée.

Pascal, B. (1965), *Les provinciales*, ed. L. Cognet, Paris: Garnier frères.

Poujol, R. (1982), *La naissance de l'Hôpital Général de Paris d'après des documents inédits*, Paris: PUF.

Rabutin-Chantal, M. de, marquise de Sévigné (1953-57), *Lettres*, ed. Gérard-Gailly, 3 tom., Paris: Gallimard.

Racine, J. (1952), *Oeuvres complètes*, ed. R. Picard, Paris: Gallimard.

Sales, F. de (1641), *Introduction à la vie dévote*, Paris: n.p.

Salignac de La Mothe-Fénelon, F. de (1920), *Écrits et lettres politiques*, ed. C. Urbain, Paris: Bossard.

Tenon, J. (1788), *Mémoires sur les hôpitaux de Paris,* **Paris: n.p.**

Thiers, J.B. (1676), *L'avocat des pauvres*, Paris: n.p.

Secondary Sources:

Aigrefeuille, C. d' (1876-83), *Histoire de la ville de Montpellier*, Montpellier: n.p.

Allier, R. (1902), *La cabale des dévots*, Paris: A. Colin.

Barry, J. and Jones, C. eds (1991), *Medicine and Charity before the Welfare State*, London and New York: Routledge.

Baumel, J. (1976), *Montpellier au cours des XVIe et XVIIe siècles*, Montpellier: Causse.

Beik, W. (1985), *Absolutism and Society in Seventeenth-Century France*, Cambridge: CUP.

Bélin, F. (1875), *La société Française au XVIIe siècle d'après les sermons de Bourdaloue*, Paris: Hachette.

Benedict, P. ed. (1989), *Cities and Social Change in Early Modern France*, London: Routledge.

Benedict, P. (1991), *The Huguenot Population of France, 1600-1685,* Philadelphia: American Philosophical Society.

Benedict, P. (2001), *The Faith and Fortunes of France's Huguenots, 1600-1685,* Aldershot: Ashgate.

Béral, P. (1899), *Histoire de l'hôpital de la Charité de Montpellier (1646-1682)*, Montpellier: n.p.

Berger, P. (1978), 'Rural Charity in Late-Seventeenth Century France: The Pontchartrain Case', *French Historical Studies*, **10** (1978), 393-415.

Bergin, J. (1996), *The Making of the French Episcopate, 1589-1661,* London: Yale.

Bernard, L. (1970), *The Emerging City: Paris in the Age of Louis XIV*, Durham NC: Duke University Press.

Briggs, R. (1977), *Early Modern France, 1559-1715*, Oxford: OUP.

Brockliss, L. and Jones, C. (1997), *The Medical World of Early Modern France*, Oxford: OUP.

Broomhall, S. (2004), *Women's Medical Work in Early Modern France*, Manchester: Manchester University Press.

Cameron, E. (1991), *The European Reformation*, Oxford: OUP

Cavallo, S. (1995), *Charity and Power in Early Modern Italy,* Cambridge: CUP.

Chalumeau, R. (1971), 'L'assistance aux pauvres malades aux XVIIe siècle', *Dix-Septième siècle*, **90**, 75-86.

Châtellier, L. (1989), *The Europe of the Devout*, trans. J. Birrell, Cambridge: CUP.

Châtellier, L. (1997), *The Religion of the Poor*, trans. B. Pearce, Cambridge: CUP.

Chaunu, P. (1978), *La mort à Paris (XVI–XVII–XVIIIe siècles)*, Paris: Fayard.

Chill, E. (1962), 'Religion and Mendicity in Seventeenth-Century France', *International Review of Social History*, 7, 400-24.

Cholvy, G. ed. (1984), *Histoire de Montpellier*, Toulouse: Privat.

Cole, C.W. (1931), *French Mercantilist Doctrines Before Colbert*, New York: R.R. Smith.

Collins, J. (1995), *The State in Early Modern France*, Cambridge: CUP.

Corvisier, A. (1983), *Louvois*, Paris: Fayard.

Coyèque, E., (1889-91), *L'Hôtel Dieu de Paris au Moyen Age*, 2 tom., n.p.

Debant, R. (1986), 'Une Œuvre Catholique d'assistance et de conversion des pauvres au cours du dernier tiers du XVIIe siècle: la Maison de la Providence de Nîmes' in *La Révocation de l'Édit de Nantes dans les Cévennes et le bas-Languedoc*, Nîmes: Lacour.

Debus, A. (1991), *The French Paracelsians: The Chemical Challenge to Medical and Scientific Tradition in Early Modern France*, Cambridge: CUP.

Delumeau, J. (1971), *Le Catholicisme entre Luther et Voltaire*, Paris: PUF.

Dent, J. (1973), *Crisis in Finance*, Newton Abbot: David and Charles.

Depauw, J. (1999), *Spiritualité et pauvreté à Paris au XVIIe siècle*, Paris: PUF.

Dessert, D. (1987), *Fouquet*, Paris: Fayard.

Desgranges, H. (1952), *Hospitaliers d'autrefois: l'Hôpital Général de Paris 1656-1790*, Paris: Hachette.

Déthan, G. (1990), *Nouvelle histoire de Paris: Paris au temps de Louis XIV*, Paris: Hachette.

Dewald, J. (1993), *Aristocratic Experience and the Origins of Modern Culture in France, 1550-1715*, Princeton NJ: Princeton University Press.

Dissard, F. (1938), *La réforme des hôpitaux et maladreries au XVIIe siècle*, Paris: Éditions internationales.

Durand, Y. (1985), *Le Diocèse de Nantes,* Paris: Beauchesne.

Dulieu, L. (1953), *Essai historique sur l'Hôtel Dieu Saint-Eloi de Montpellier, 1183-1950*, Montpellier: Déhan.

Elmore, R. (1975), *The Origins of the Hôpital Général of Paris,* unpublished doctoral thesis, Ann Arbor MI: University Microfilms Edn.

Fairchilds, C. (1976), *Poverty and Charity in Aix-en-Provence, 1640-1789,* Baltimore MD: Johns Hopkins University Press.

Fosseyeux, M. (1912), *L'Hôtel Dieu de Paris au XVIIe et au XVIIIe siècles*, Paris: Berger-Levrault.

Foucault, M. (1961), *Folie et déraison: Histoire de la folie à l'âge classique*, Paris: Plon.

Foucault, M. (1973), *The Birth of the Clinic*, London: Tavistock.

Frangos, J. (1997), *From housing the poor to healing the sick: the changing institution of Paris hospitals under the old regime and revolution*, London: Associated University Presses.

Garrisson, J. (1985), *L'Edit de Nantes et sa révocation: Histoire d'une intolérance*, Paris: Editions du Seuil.

Gelfand, T. (1980), *Professionalizing Modern Medicine, Surgeons and Medical Science in the Eighteenth Century*, Westport CN: Greenwood Press.

Geremek, B. (1987), *The Margins of Society in Late Medieval Paris*, trans. J. Birrell, Cambridge: CUP.

Granshaw, L. and Porter, R. eds (1989), *The Hospital in History*, London and New York: Routledge.

Greenbaum, L.S. (1978-79), 'Nurses and doctors in conflict: piety and medicine in the Paris Hôtel-Dieu on the eve of the French Revolution', *Clio Medica*, **13**, 247-68.

Grell, O., Cunningham, A. and Arrizabalaga, J. (1999), *Health Care and Poor Relief in Counter-Reformation Europe*, London and New York: Routledge.

Gutton, J.P. (1965), 'À l'aube du XVIIe siècle: idées nouvelles sur les pauvres', *Cahier d'Histoire*, **10**, 87-97.

Gutton, J.P. (1970), *Société et les pauvres: L'exemple de la généralité de Lyon, 1534-1789*, Paris: les Belles Lettres.

Gutton, J.P. (1973), *L'état et la mendicité dans la première moitié du XVIIIe siècle*, Roanne: Centre d'études foréziennes.

Hamscher, A.N. (1976), *The Parlement of Paris After the Fronde: 1653-1673*, Pittsburgh PA: University of Pittsburgh Press.

Hanlon, G. (1993), *Confession and Community in Seventeenth-Century France: Catholic and Protestant Coexistence in Aquitaine*, Philadelphia PA: University of Pennsylvania Press.

Harouel, J. ed. (1989), *Histoire du droit sociale*, Paris: PUF.

Hickey, D. (1992), 'Closing Down Local Hospitals in Seventeenth-Century France', *Histoire Sociale/Social History*, **25**, 9-34.

Hickey, D. (1997), *Local Hospitals in Ancien Régime France: Rationalization, Resistance, Renewal, 1530-1789*, Montréal and Kingston: McGill-Queen's University Press.

Hoffman, P. (1984), *Church and Community in the Diocese of Lyon, 1500-1789*, London: Yale.

Holt, M. (2005), *The French wars of religion, 1562-1629*, Cambridge: CUP.

Les hôpitaux disparus, (1912), Paris: n.p.

Hufton, O. (1974), *The Poor of Eighteenth-Century France, 1750-1789*, Oxford: OUP.

Imbert, J. (1993), *Le droit hospitalier de l'ancien régime*, Paris: PUF.

Imbert, J. (1996), *Les hôpitaux en France*, Paris: PUF.

Israel, J. (1995), *The Dutch Republic, Its Rise, Greatness, and Fall, 1477-1806*, Oxford: OUP.

James, E.D. (1972), *Pierre Nicole, Jansenist and Humanist*, The Hague: Martinus Nijhoff.

Jeorger, M. (1977), 'La structure hospitalière de la France sous l'ancien régime', *Annales ESC*, **32**, 1025-51.

Jones, C. (1982), *Charity and Bienfaisance*, Cambridge: CUP.

Jones, C. (1989), *The Charitable Imperative*, London and New York: Routledge.

Jones, C. (1999), 'Perspectives on Poor Relief, Health Care and the Counter-Reformation in France' in Grell, O., Cunningham, A. and Arrizabalaga, J., *Health*

Care and Poor Relief in Counter-Reformation Europe, London and New York: Routledge.

Joret, C. (1889), 'Le Père Guévarre et les bureaux de charité au XVIIe siècle', *Annales du Midi,* **3,** 340-93.

Jutte, R. (1994), *Poverty and Deviance in Early Modern Europe,* Cambridge: CUP.

Kettering, S. (1986), *Patrons, Brokers and Clients in Seventeenth-Century France,* Oxford: OUP.

Kleinman, R. (1962), *Saint François de Sales and the Protestants,* Geneva: Ambilly-Annemasse.

Knecht, R. (1996), *The French wars of religion, 1559-1598,* London: Longman.

Labrousse, E. (1985), *Une Foi, une loi, un roi? La Révocation de l'Édit de Nantes,* Paris: Payot.

Lallemand, L. (1909-12), *Histoire de la charité,* 5 tom., Paris: A. Picard et fils.

Lebrun, F. (1980), *Histoire des Catholiques en France,* Toulouse: Privat.

Le Grand, L. (1898), 'La Désolation des églises, monastères et hôpitaux en France vers le milieu du XVeme siècle', *Revue des questions historiques,* pp. 180-88.

Le Roy Ladurie, E. (1974), *The Peasants of Languedoc,* trans. J. Day, Chicago IL: University of Chicago Press.

Ligou, D. (1968), *Le Protestantisme en France, 1598-1715,* Paris: Sedes.

Martin, C. (2000), *Les Compagnies de la propagation de la foi (1632-1683),* Geneva: Droz.

Ménard, L. (1755), *Histoire civile, ecclésiastique et littéraire de la ville de Nîmes,* 7 tom., Paris: n.p.

Mettam, R.C. (1988), *Power and Faction in Louis XIV's France,* Oxford: Blackwell.

Norberg, K. (1985), *Rich and Poor in Grenoble, 1600-1814,* Berkeley CA: University of California Press.

Paultre, C. (1906), *De la répression de la mendicité et du vagabondage en France sous l'ancien régime,* Paris: L. Larose et L. Tenin.

Po-Chia Hsia, R. (1984), *Society and Religion in Münster, 1535-1618,* New Haven CT, Yale.

Poujol, R. (1986), 'Le system du gouvernement de l'intendant Basville,' in n.a. *La Révocation de l'édit de Nantes dans les Cévennes et le bas-Languedoc,* Nîmes: Lacour.

Poujol, R. (1992), *Basville, roi solitaire du Languedoc,* Montpellier: Presses du Languedoc.

Pugh, W. (1974), 'Social Welfare and the Edict of Nantes', *French Historical Studies,* **8,** 349-77.

Pugh, W. (1980), 'Catholics, Protestants, and Testamentary Charity in Seventeenth-Century Lyon and Nîmes', *French Historical Studies,* **14,** 479-540.

Pujo, B. (2003), *Vincent de Paul,* trans. G. Champe, Notre Dame IN: University of Notre Dame Press.

Pullan, B. (1994), *Poverty and Charity: Europe, Italy, Venice, 1400-1700,* Aldershot: Variorum.

Quéniart, J. (1985), *La Révocation de l'Édit de Nantes,* Paris: Desclée de Brower.

Risse, G. (1986), *Hospital Life in Enlightenment Scotland: Care and Teaching at the Royal Infirmary of Edinburgh,* Cambridge: CUP.

Risse, G. (1999), Mending *Bodies, Saving Souls. A History of Hospitals,* Oxford: OUP.

Robbins, K. (1995), 'Municipal Justice, Urban Police and the Tactics of Counter Reformation in La Rochelle', *French History,* **9**, pp. 273-93.

Robert, C. (1895), 'Anthyme-Denis Cohon, evêque et compte de Dol; son rôle pendant la Fronde', *Bulletin et mémoires de la Société Archéologique du département d'Ille-et-Vilaine,* **XXIV**, 111-66.

Rothkrug, L. (1965), *Opposition to Louis XIV,* Princeton NJ: Princeton University Press.

Sauzet, R. (1979), *Contre-réforme et réforme catholique en bas-Languedoc; le diocèse de Nîmes au XVIIe siècle,* Lille: University de Lille III.

Sauzet, R. (1998), *Le Notaire et son roi, Etienne Borrelly (1633-1718), un Nîmois sous Louis XIV,* Paris: Plon.

Serres, P. (1878), *Histoire de la Cour des Comptes, Aides et Finances de Montpellier,* Montpellier: F. Seguin.

Shelley, H. (1958), 'Cutting for the Stone', *Journal of the History of Medicine,* **13**, 50-67.

Shennan, J.H. (1968), *The Parlement of Paris,* London: Eyre & Spottiswoode.

Tallon, A. (1990), *La Compagnie de Saint-Sacrement 1629-1667,* Paris: les Éditions du Cerf.

Taveneaux, R. (1980), *Le Catholicisme dans la France classique 1610-1715,* 2 tom., Paris: Société d'éd. d'enseignement supérieur.

Vess, D. (1974), *Medical revolution in France, 1789-1796,* Gainsville FL: University Presses of Florida.

Vigarello, G. (1999), *Histoire des pratiques de santé,* Paris: Seuil.

Walter, J. and Schofield, R. (1989), *Famine, Disease and the Social Order in Early Modern Society,* Cambridge: CUP.

Wolff, P. ed. (1969), *Documents de l'histoire du Languedoc,* Toulouse: n.p.

Index

For Product Safety Concerns and Information please contact our
EU representative GPSR@taylorandfrancis.com, Taylor & Francis
Verlag GmbH, Kaufingerstr. 24, 80331 München, Germany